OXFORD WELLS SHAKESPEARE LECTURES

Circumstantial Shakespeare

Circumstantial Shakespeare

LORNA HUTSON

OXFORD
UNIVERSITY PRESS

OXFORD
UNIVERSITY PRESS

Great Clarendon Street, Oxford, OX2 6DP,
United Kingdom

Oxford University Press is a department of the University of Oxford.
It furthers the University's objective of excellence in research, scholarship,
and education by publishing worldwide. Oxford is a registered trade mark of
Oxford University Press in the UK and in certain other countries

Published in the United States of America by Oxford University Press
198 Madison Avenue, New York, NY 10016, United States of America

British Library Cataloguing in Publication Data
Data available

Library of Congress Control Number: 2015937098

ISBN 978–0–19–965710–0

Printed and bound by
Clays Ltd, St Ives plc

For Linda

Acknowledgements

This short book has incurred a long list of debts. Andrew McNeillie first invited me to give the Oxford Wells Shakespeare Lectures and Jacqueline Baker followed up the invitation with characteristic warmth and encouragement. The generous hospitality of the Oxford English Faculty, Oxford University Press, and St Catharine's College enabled me to enjoy many conversations over the two-week period of the lectures' delivery in October 2012. Special thanks are due to Bart Van Es, whose thoughtfulness both as the host of my visit and as the host of the lectures made the experience of delivering them less daunting and much more of a pleasure. It was an honour for me to be delivering a lecture series named for Stanley Wells: many years ago Stanley was one of my DPhil examiners.

I gave talks from the series at a number of other Universities. I would like to thank Joanne Wilkes and Sophie Tomlinson at the University of Auckland, where I was 2012 Alice Griffin Shakespeare Fellow; Elaine Hadley at the University of Chicago; Kristine Johanson at the University of Amsterdam; Subha Mukherji at Cambridge; and Richard Wilson at Kingston University. Thanks, too, to all the audiences at these different venues who patiently listened and asked thought-provoking questions. At St Andrews the Centre for Mediaeval and Early Modern Law and Literature has been an immensely stimulating forum—thanks to Andy Murphy, my support-ive Head of School, and to CMEMLL's co-director, John Hudson. In 2013 postgraduates Rachel Holmes and Toria Johnson humoured me with a CMEMLL conference that included 'circumstances' in its title, thereby allowing the topic yet another airing.

A number of people have been kind enough to read and comment on the lectures as they were gradually transformed into the chapters of the book. From the first vague ideas and disorganized drafts, Victoria Kahn and Bradin Cormack encouraged me to believe I actually had an argument. St Andrews colleagues with whom I discussed the ideas, Alex Davis and Neil Rhodes, helped sustain me in this belief. Mary Nyquist read the lecture drafts and astutely pointed out many places where the arguments needed tightening up. At a later stage, just when I seemed unable to break through a conceptual impasse, Linda Hardy made a crucial reading suggestion, pointing me towards narratology. The enthusiasm of Robert Crawford and Natalie Davis was a huge boost, making me feel that I was on to something.

I owe particular thanks to four people who read the entire book manuscript in its latter stages. John Kerrigan ploughed through both lecture and book drafts and to his comments, as well as to his work on binding language, I happily acknowledge myself bound and indebted. Though I delivered and titled the *Circumstantial Shakespeare* lectures before I knew about Quentin Skinner's *Forensic Shakespeare*, I have benefited from Quentin's generosity in sharing his typescript with me, learning a great deal from his erudition in matters rhetorical, as well as from his exemplary graciousness. To Colin Burrow I offer grateful thanks for going through the whole typescript with pencilled marginal comments. In response to Colin's urging I rethought claims for Shakespeare's exceptionality and wrote a bit more about other dramatists' uses of the topics of circumstance. My extensive debt to Kathy Eden's foundational work is recorded in footnotes; at a late stage, she also read the typescript and made wise criticisms. At Oxford University Press, I'd like to thank Rachel Platt, my editor, and Edwin Pritchard, my copy-editor, each exemplary in their roles.

Nearer home, I'd like to thank Ben Seal and Kirsty Whiten without whose practical kindness and compassion and creative inspiration I would never have been able to balance full-time teaching and writing the book with looking after the dog. My own family, the Hutsons, and my late partner's, the Sprents, have been a mainstay, as have many friends, Charlotte Dormandy, Jocelyn Stoddard, and Maggie Lloyd among them. My daughter Ellie has coped admirably in a sorrowful time, for which I am grateful. Last and most, however, Linda Hardy has traded hemispheres to share life with me, for which no words could ever adequately express my gratitude.

Contents

Introduction

I.1. *Causa Tempus Locus*: Motive, Time, and Place

My title—'*Circumstantial Shakespeare*'—may seem, perhaps, to suggest a Shakespeare who is cautious or circumspect. Or it might seem to imply a dramatist whose plays are full of inessentials, of those fussy details implied in phrases like Antonio's chiding Bassanio for winding about his love 'with circumstance' (1.1.163), or Hamlet's urging his companions to shake hands and part 'without more circumstance at all' (1.5.819), or Iago's complaint that Othello used 'a bumbast Circumstance' to avoid promoting him (1.1.17).[1] The prefix 'circum' means, in Latin, 'round about', and 'stance' comes from *stare*, 'to stand', so circumstances seem necessarily to stand round about or mark out a place for something more important, *more central*, and so more essential or substantial. Young Clifford thus opposes 'essence' to 'circumstance' in Shakespeare's *2 Henry VI*, when he exclaims that any soldier who loves himself, 'Hath not essentially, but *by circumstance* | The name of Valour' (5.2.3261–2, my italics). In the account that follows in these chapters, however, I want to reverse this way of thinking. It is in part, I will propose, Shakespeare's revolutionary dramaturgical deployment of 'circumstances' that has enabled us, for hundreds of years, to imagine and argue about his 'characters' as though they existed autonomously, centrally, and essentially, independent of the composition of the plays.

Circumstantial Shakespeare is based on four lectures delivered in Oxford in October 2012. In these lectures, which form the four chapters of this book, I identify 'circumstances' in a specific, technical sense as the rhetorical topics or 'places' from which many different kinds of argument of proof were drawn. As such the word 'circumstances' was not limited to the sense it subsequently acquired, in the eighteenth century, of the irreducible material particulars that might either, in legal cases, constitute a more objective proof than testimony ('circumstantial evidence'), or, in the development of national statistics, form the basis of a mathematical understanding of chance.[2] Rather, the associations of the sixteenth- and seventeenth-century understanding of 'circumstances' (known as 'peristasis' in Greek) were rhetorical, dialectical, and poetic. The word was powerfully associated with narrative, with the forensic invention of so-called artificial or technical proof (*probationes artificiales*), and with descriptions so vivid that they conjure up visual and auditory illusion (*enargeia*) and evoke strong emotions.[3] Narratives could not be composed, nor descriptions written, in sixteenth- and seventeenth-century school exercises, without the children being instructed to 'set downe all the circumstances to expresse the nature and manner of it'.[4]

This means that whereas we habitually think of 'circumstances' as the objective material particulars or calculable variables specific to an individual or situation, Renaissance writers thought of them primarily as topical aids to the composition of persuasive arguments in the interests of narrative intelligibility and poetic power. Along with 'accidents' (the more common term in dialectic, and as the term associated with arguments of 'person' rather than 'thing'), 'circumstances' were an indispensable category of Renaissance rhetorical and dialectical invention. Both Cicero and Quintilian identified 'accidents' of person and 'circumstances' of the thing (*res*) as the key *loci*—that is, 'topics' or 'places'—from which to find *argumenta*, or arguments, of proof; indeed they were known as *loci argumentorum*, places of argument (see Cicero, *Topica*, §8; Quintilian, *Inst.*, 5.10.20–2).[5] For Renaissance writers, 'accidents' and 'circumstances' offer, of all the topics, 'the clearest artistic principles for constructing arguments'.[6]

At their simplest, 'circumstances' were the topics that made any human action intelligible and able to be narrated and enquired into: '*causa tempus locus occasio instrumentum modus et cetera*', as Quintilian lists them, 'motive, time, place, opportunity, means, method and the like' (*Inst.*, 5.10.23). The most popular compositional textbook for schoolboys of Shakespeare's generation—Erasmus' *De copia*—included, in the notes to its section on 'circumstances', a handy little verse which gave a similar list of topics in the form of questions:

> *Quis quoties occasio ubi cur quomodo quando.*
> *Casus et instrumentum cuiusque,* περιστασις *esto.*[7]
>
> (Who, how often, occasion, where, why, how, when,
> chance and instrument, and whose; let this be *peristasis*)

Though not all topics are everywhere relevant, it is easy to see that arguments of Motive, Time, and Place—Quintilian's *causa tempus locus*, or (in question form) *cur, quando*, and *ubi* (why, when, and where) would be more or less indispensable to most forms of composition involving human action. Writing of drama, Philip Sidney referred to the 'circumstances' of 'place and time' as 'the two necessary companions of all corporal actions'.[8] But because circumstances were not objective facts, but merely topics of probability, they are often represented as plausibly misleading or fictional. Thus, Shakespeare's Polonius is pompously sure of having discovered 'the very *cause* of *Hamlets* Lunacie' by means of 'Circumstances'; Ophelia, he says, has told him of Hamlet's solicitings 'as they fell out by *Time*, by *Meanes, and Place*' (2.2.1073; 1180; 1153). At the end of *Twelfth Night* the mysterious but attractive Cesario claims to Orsino that he can prove, by means of circumstances of place, time, and chance (or fortune), that he is, in fact, a woman. He begs his lover not to embrace him 'till each circumstance | Of *place, time, fortune*, do co-here and iumpe | That I am Viola' (5.1.1417–19). And it was, of course, this 'coherence' and 'jumping' (that is, coinciding or agreeing) of circumstances—that contributed to their (deceptive) probability or truth-likeness.

In Act 5, scene 2 of *The Winter's Tale* such circumstantial coherence is, with the dry scepticism of hyperbole, likened to oath-bound eyewitness testimony. In this scene the highly unlikely news that a Bohemian shepherd girl has turned out to be the King's long lost daughter is said to be 'in strong suspition'. But a gentleman declares that it is 'Most true, if ever Truth were pregnant by Circumstance. That which you heare, you'le sweare you see, there is such vnitie in the proofes' (5.2.3039–42). 'Pregnant' in an evidential context means 'clear' or 'obvious', so truth being 'pregnant by Circumstance' means truth becoming clear by the coherence of time, place, means, and so forth.

But when the gentleman predicts that his listeners will go on oath that they have witnessed events with their own eyes ('That which you *heare*, you'le *sweare* you *see*'), he invokes what is, in effect, a theory of rhetorical *trompe l'œil* known, variously, as *enargeia* or *evidentia*. According to this theory, a narrative or description might be made so evocative, so powerfully affecting as to seem to appear before the eyes. The illusion produced by circumstantial coherence is more vividly convincing than mere truth.

Why should we care about the musty old rhetorical and dialectical traditions that peddled this doctrine of 'circumstances'? What does any of it matter, if Shakespeare's language of circumstance is perfectly intelligible to us in spite of historical changes in the meaning of the word? It matters, I will argue, because recovering the full emotional and imaginative resonance of the old sense of the word will help us rethink two fundamental and very misleading assumptions that underlie the criticism and reception of Shakespeare both within and beyond the academy. These assumptions—which have been going strong since the eighteenth century and which show no sign of weakening with age—are, first, the idea that Shakespeare's plays transcend, with a brilliant insouciance, the neoclassical rules of unified Time and Place and, second, the idea that his 'characters' are imaginatively autonomous—that they, in turn, transcend and *don't need* the fussy mechanics of 'plot' and 'argument'. Indeed, these two assumptions—that of Shakespeare's extraordinary insight into human nature, and that of his relative indifference to the details of temporality, locality, and motivation that define plot and argument—are mutually reinforcing, mutually dependent, and each as wrong as the other.

The critical and popular common opinion about Shakespeare is, in short, that he put character first, before plot, ignoring compositional 'rules' that would constrain the freedom of his characters to achieve their marvellous 'selfhood'. *Circumstantial Shakespeare* aims to reverse this way of thinking. The following chapters will challenge the governing antithesis between a continental neoclassicism (understood as the straitjacketing of drama by the unities of Time and Place) and a native English dramaturgy based purely in the 'freedom' of collaborative theatrical practice. They will argue, rather, for the common ground between continental neoclassical theory and English dramatic practice in the concern each shows with the rhetorical and dialectical techniques by which a complex sequence of events is persuasively invented and *communicated*, both within the fiction (between the *dramatis personae*) and to the audience or spectators.

Both sixteenth-century neoclassical theorists and practising English dramatists recognized that more was involved, in the dramatization of such complex sequences of connected events, than the immediate, deictic 'here and now' of what might be shown and enacted on a stage. Techniques were required for representing all that is not showable—past or distant occurrences, implied motives, habitual actions—the whole inferred or virtual 'world' which apparently subtends the performance we watch, but which, as we know, is actually an effect of our trying to make sense of it. These techniques were closely identified with the rhetorical and dialectical invention of *arguments of proof* and they took very varied forms. Their pervasive integration into the theatrical practice of the late sixteenth century was not fortuitous, nor can it be denied that they contributed to the enormous dramaturgical changes that critics have recently tended to attribute almost exclusively to changes in the relations and working practices of dramatists and acting companies.

I.2. Neoclassical 'Reported Action' and the *Fabula/Sjuzhet* Distinction

Critics tend to identify neoclassical dramatic theory with one principle alone—that of the unities of time, place, and action—and they consequently assume that Shakespeare's rejection of this principle is a rejection of all the thinking and techniques that, deriving from the humanist study of Latin rhetoric and drama, we should term 'neoclassical'. A very distinguished medievalist, whose views may be taken as representative, sees humanist rhetorical composition in terms of 'rules and restrictions' and characterizes Shakespeare's dramaturgy as progressively distancing himself from these:

> Shakespeare seems to have started his career with the ambition of establishing himself as a poet and playwright in the approved neo-Classical mode, matching the achievements of the ancients . . . His writing, however, evolved away from the humanist, *with all its rules and restrictions*, and *towards the greater freedoms offered by the medieval*: towards making the theatre a world in miniature.[9]

It might be objected, of course, that neoclassical theorists and play-wrights did not embrace rules and restrictions for their own sake; they were concerned with working out a solution to an imaginative problem, that of representing a fictional 'world' of complex causality and sequence as a single, coherent, and moving narrative.[10] One solution to this problem was that of representing events leading up to the moment of the action, as well as events taking place at some distance, through a *nuntius*, a messenger, or reporter. In Shakespeare criticism, just as it has become commonplace to take the 'rules' of unified time and place as a metonymy for dramatic neoclassicism in general, so it has been commonplace to polarize classical and neoclassical reliance on 'reported' action and Shakespeare's preference for a drama of 'enactment'. Here is the previously cited critic again, taken as representative of this line of thinking:

> the key feature of a play was that it *acted its action*. Classical drama was above all a rhetorical construct, with almost all its action, and especially violent action, converted into spoken report.[11]

All this sounds very persuasive. We should, however, pause before we pour such disdain on the 'rhetorical construct' of classical drama and on the 'spoken report' of the classical and neoclassical *nuntius*. For Shakespeare's dramaturgy makes extraordinarily varied and inventive use of *nuntius*-figures—that is, of persons who offer reports of past histories or offstage actions—as part of the process of implying a larger imagined world beyond the *deixis* or 'show-ing' of staged performance. This process is so familiar to us from Shakespeare that we take it for granted; we need, then, to estrange it a little in order to analyse it.

For this purpose it will be useful to recall and adapt the analyt-ical distinctions of structuralist narratology, particularly the distinc-tion between 'story', '*histoire*', or '*fabula*' ('a sequence of actions and events conceived of as independent of their manifestation in dis-course') and 'discourse', '*récit*', or '*sjuzhet*' ('the discursive presenta-tion in narrative of those events').[12] We need to try and think about how the dramatic *récit* or *sjuzhet*—the presentation of events through stage action and dialogue—relates to the sense we have of their nar-rative coherence—the *histoire* or *fabula*. For, in spite of the well-known Aristotelian distinction between the diegetic nature of narrative (epic poetry) and the mimetic nature of tragic drama, it is evident that certain forms of drama, as Charles Whitworth has observed, need more than the direct mimesis of enactment or of what can be shown onstage. 'When we speak of theatre and its action', says Whitworth,

> we usually have in mind what occurs onstage, before the eyes and in the hearing of the spectators-auditors. We deal of course with a verbal text that is spoken by actors, but also with movement, gesture, business, and we also take into account all the visual and aural dimensions of the *mise en scène*: set design, costume, music, special effects and lighting. We distinguish drama-in-performance from pure narrative, as the earliest critics did: *mimesis* or direct imitation, was in Aristotle's terms distinct from *diegesis* . . . Mimesis has its limits, so does an audience's patience. The here-and-now of the stage is not sufficient in itself: there are also before, after, during and elsewhere . . . a playwright is obliged to indicate the implied world offstage and relevant action that is imagined to occur in it to spectators who cannot be shown it. What is the dramatic status of events that are said to occur elsewhere than onstage during the course of the action? Can they be said to 'happen' in the play? Do they belong to its *histoire*?[13]

Whitworth's remark, 'mimesis has its limits, so does an audience's patience', might seem to recall Ludovico Castelvetro's much-ridiculed argument that the playhouse audience would grow restive and incredulous if the play's imagined action exceeded that of a day. Yet Whitworth in the twentieth century and Castelvetro in the sixteenth are, in fact, both observing something we all now take for granted, namely, that certain kinds of dramatized stories require the techniques of reporting action from what we might call the 'unscene'—from extramimetic, *imagined or conjectured* locations and temporalities—in order to endow the human actions they stage with the richness of narrative significance and interiorized causality.[14]

As a way of explaining how spectators interpret reported and merely implied elements of theatrical action and use them to construct a more or less coherent imaginative world (which he labels 'W_D'), Kier Elam adapts the *sjuzhet/fabula* of structuralist narrative theory. Elam points out that, in the case of a play like *Macbeth*, the *sjuzhet* (the dramatic unfolding of events by way of dialogue and enactment onstage) is extremely discontinuous, and relies on a heterogeneous, non-linear representation—some events, such as the witches' forecasts and the

Macbeth–Macduff encounter—are portrayed mimetically, others, such as Macbeth's defeat of MacDonald and the Thane of Cawdor and his killing of Duncan are inferred from report. Thus, as Elam concludes,

> the world $W_{Macbeth}$ [the imagined dramatic world of *Macbeth*] constructed by the spectator as *fabula* or story will be quite a different matter from the *sjuz[h]et* . . . of *Macbeth* itself. In the former, the predictions of the witches, the murder of Duncan, the death of Lady Macbeth, the encounter between Macbeth and Macduff, etc., occur on the same level and form a logical and chronological chain. In the latter, these happenings are strongly differentiated in the mode of their representation. Some (the witches' forecasts and the Macbeth–Macduff encounter) are shown directly, the others are reported *a posteriori*.[15]

The *fabula*, in structuralist narratology, is said to be the sequence of events ('what really happened') anterior to and independent of their manifestation in discourse, but this sequence must be inferred by the reader from a *sjuzhet*, a narrative discourse, which may be marked by gaps, discontinuities, and analepses. Analogously, the *fabula* in theatre is the spectator's or reader's imaginative inference or *projection* of a coherent order of events onto a discontinuous and heterogeneous series of techniques for conveying both immediacy and its significance in relation to pasts, futures, and elsewheres. 'It is clear', Elam writes, 'that the *fabula*, being an abstraction from the *sjuz[h]et* . . . as such, is a *paraphrase* of a pseudo-narrative kind, made, for example, by a spectator or critic in recounting the "story" of the drama.'[16]

Elam sees this recounting of the 'story' of the drama as, essentially, an exercise in following the logic of plot, but it is clear from his own remarks that in attempting to interpret and make sequential sense of discontinuous representations, the spectator or reader of a Shakespeare play will, in fact, hypothesize interior states, such as emotions and intentions, as a part of this imagining of causes and connections. For example, in attending to the series of distinct actions that form Act 1 of *Macbeth*—'the collaborative interaction between the witches (fixing an appointment), the (reported) heroic deeds of Macbeth in battle, the (reported) acts of treachery by the Thane of Cawdor, the witches' predictions to Macbeth and Banquo'—the spectator will begin to imagine the relationships of dependence, ambition, and mistrust that so richly inform the significance of the (reported) assassination of Duncan in Act 2. As Elam writes, the projection of a *fabula* is

> usually the prime object of the spectator's hypothesizing in witnessing the representation: he anticipates events, attempts to 'bridge' incidents whose connection is not immediately clear and generally endeavours to infer the overall frame of action from the bits of information he is fed.[17]

In response, then, to Charles Whitworth's question—'What is the dramatic status of events that are said to occur elsewhere than onstage during the course of the action? Can they be said to "happen" in the play? Do they belong to its *histoire*?'—the answer (acknowledging '*histoire*' to be the same as '*fabula*') must surely be yes. And Whitworth, like Elam, gives sophisticated Shakespearean examples—the examples, in *Julius Caesar*, of, first Brutus' and Cassius' hearing of noises offstage which Casca later interprets for them with feigned circumstantial incompetence ('I can as well be hanged as tell the *manner* of it'); and then the example, in Act 5, scene 3 of the same play, in which Pindarus mistakenly interprets what he 'sees' offstage to be the defeat of Titinius—a mistake which results in the suicide of Cassius.[18]

If we take the simple step of acknowledging that reported action is indispensable to the projection of the *fabula* or *histoire*—that is, the imagined dramatic 'world' of which we are, ostensibly, shown only a part—then we need to concede that the neoclassical device of the *nuntius*' report, and, as we shall see, of other techniques of extramimetic representation and rhetorical argumentation, do indeed become a part of English dramatic practice by the 1590s. However, it is equally clear that these devices had no place even in the most skilful and admirable examples of English and Scottish allegorical morality drama. John Skelton's *Magnificence* (1533?) and John Bale's *King Johan* (1538), both generically sophisticated plays, offer little 'in terms of techniques of conveying offstage action and extramimetic locations' not because of being dramaturgically defective, but 'simply because that kind of implied action and location did not figure largely in [their] dramaturgy'.[19]

Once we understand that extramimetic or 'reported' offstage action is indispensable to the possibility of projecting or inferring a whole fictional world it becomes possible to see the so-called rules and restrictions of neoclassical theory and practice as essentially concerned with enabling imaginative inference; that is, with encouraging audiences and readers to conjecture or imagine what cannot be staged. Such extramimetic elements as mute characters and 'acoustic scenery' (that is, *ekphrases* or descriptions of locations, whether off or onstage) likewise bear witness to the creativity of neoclassical experimentation. The earliest neoclassical comedies are marked by a playful consciousness of the way restrictions on what can be seen on stage relate to the audience's reliance on inference. In the very first of these, Ariosto's *La cassaria* ('The Coffer', 1508), the eponymous coffer itself figures, in its crucially *invisible* but apparently richly filled interior, such a playful consciousness. The play involves a plot of entrapment in which an amorous young man called Erofilo will (unbeknownst to his father) pay over his father's coffer replete with precious textiles to a pimp (Lucrano) in exchange for a beautiful courtesan. The pimp is thereafter to be accused, by a detailed circumstantial narrative, of having stolen the coffer from Erofilo's father. Though the scheme goes awry and several new circumstantial narratives have to be quickly improvised, the play jokes throughout on the implied parallel between these thickly multiplying fabrications designed to persuade Erofilo's father and Lucrano of various unlikely scenarios of theft and deception, and the circumstantially detailed, but equally imaginary 'Mytilene' of the play, furnished with beautiful courtesans and rich domestic interiors, taverns, and brothels never witnessed by us (since the fixed-locale stage cannot show an interior scene, and since the maiden to be married rarely appears in Roman comedy).[20] In the closing words of the play, the wily servant, Fulcio, proposes that he and the girl join his master at the 'Moor's Inn' (*casa del Moro*) tavern for a drink and then turns to address the audience in a joking demystification of the imaginative hold of this 'unscene' world of the play:

> You in the audience may as well go home, for the girl whom I'm going to take doesn't want to be seen coming out; and, as the procurer has to flee, it would not be proper for there to be too many witnesses. And give us a sign of your enjoyment.
>
> (*Brigata, tornatevene a casa, che questa fanciulla ch'io vo a tôrre, non vuole esser veduta uscire, e dovendo anco el ruffiano fuggirsene, non è a proposito che si sieno tanti testimonii. E fate segno d'allegrezza.*)[21]

Charles Whitworth's work makes it clear that it was through neoclassical experimentation that English dramatic practice first began to encourage an audience to infer the play's *fabula* or *histoire* by means of imagining offstage times and spaces. He notes that while Bale's *King Johan* includes no reporting, no offstage action, nor any narrative of past events, the neoclassical comedy *Gammer Gurton's Needle* (*c.*1550–60) 'conveys somewhat more a sense of places and goings-on beyond the stage world than many of its predecessors'.[22] In *Gammer Gurton*, of course, neoclassical restrictions of location make it impossible, as in *La cassaria*, to stage an interior scene. This has imaginatively generative possibilities: in one scene, the mischief-maker, Diccon, knocks on the door of the alewife, Dame Chat, in order to tell her a (false) and highly circumstantial tale of how her neighbour, Gammer Gurton, suspects of her being a chicken-thief. Dame Chat is, of course, 'within' her house (that is, offstage) and from her doorway she issues an invitation into this imagined space: 'What Diccon? Come near, ye be no stranger. | We be fast set at trump, man, hard by the fire; | Thou shalt set on the king if thou come a little nigher.'[23] It's important to register not only that this delightfully precise evocation of the imaginary interior is an unthinkable effect in morality-style dramaturgy, but that its function here is to imply *psychological causation*, to make the spectator imagine not only the alehouse hearth, but the interior, or heart, of the alewife herself. As Diccon, of course, can't go inside, Dame Chat comes 'outside' (appears onstage) and calls to a mute or merely textual character—her maid, Doll—to take her place in the card game:

DAME CHAT
Come hither, Doll! Doll, sit down and play this game,
And as thou sawest me do, see thou do even the same.
There is five trumps beside the queen, the hindmost thou shalt find her.
Take heed of Sim Glover's wife—she hath an eye behind her! (2.2.27–30)

Here we see how neoclassical 'rules' of temporal and spatial unity generate a psychology by encouraging us to project a *fabula*, to infer connections and causes from the 'unscene' to explain the action we see. From Dame Chat's instructions to Doll we infer that Dame Chat is always ready to believe that others are eying her suspiciously and this inference prepares us for Chat's credulous response to Diccon's report that Gammer has accused her of stealing a cockerel, roasting it for breakfast, and even getting Doll to bury the carcass 'a foot deep in the dung' (2.2.66).

Projecting the *fabula*, then, includes projecting psychological, as well as logical, causality in order to make sense of what is seen on stage. This kind of projection only became possible in English drama with the advent of neoclassical experimentation. To put it bluntly, while projections of the *fabulae* of Shakespeare plays abound, it is impossible to project the *fabula* of a morality play, because its *fabula* is indistinct from its *sjuzhet*. No matter how magnificent an example of its genre—and plays such as Skelton's *Magnificence* and David Lyndsay's *Ane Satire of the Thrie Estatis* are masterpieces, finely exploiting the double-voicedness of actor and *dramatis persona*—the allegorical morality play produces no sustained imagined dramatic world anterior to, beyond, and explanatory of the mimetic representations that we see.[24]

The history of Shakespeare's reception from the eighteenth century onward is testament to the plays' capacity to encourage spectators and readers alike to project a peculiarly powerful sense of their *fabulae*. Charles and Mary Lamb's *Tales from Shakespeare* (1807), William Hazlitt's *Characters of Shakespeare's Plays* (1817), and, indeed, almost the whole of Shakespeare criticism is necessarily founded on this capacity. While we don't like to think that we prize coherence—we like to discover disruption, discontinuity, ambiguity, and subversion in our readings of Shakespeare's plays—these discoveries acquire the richness of their significance for us precisely because of the plays' historic power to generate psychologically coherent, if competing, *fabulae* for different generations of deeply influential readers, from Samuel Taylor Coleridge to Sigmund Freud.

Scandalized discoveries that the *fabulae* have no objective coherence—in the case of Othello's 'double-time', for example—only serve to emphasize the sceptical artistry with which the dramatic *sjuzhet* has been composed to give the impression that they do. This extraordinary impression we have of each play generating its own temporally, spatially, and psychologically coherent world—coherent enough to survive, as in *The Winter's Tale*, its own ostentatious destruction—is not an effect of embracing 'the greater freedoms offered by the medieval', but an effect, rather, of embracing the opportunities offered by the resources of the rhetorical and dialectical invention of circumstances—resources towards which classical and neoclassical practice and theory helped point the way.

I.3. Inferring the *Fabula* in Shakespeare Criticism

It is impossible to overemphasize the extent to which the criticism and performative interpretation of Shakespeare—and, by extension, the entire body of work, of whatever critical stripe, devoted to the study of 'early modern theatre'—takes for granted our capacity to infer a coherent *fabula*, or imagined world, from a theatrical *mise-en-scène* or *sjuzhet*. Critics of all kinds, from liberal humanist to poststructuralist, from text-based to performance-based, tend to offer readings which assume the validity of inferring both a coherent fictional 'outer' world—including the existence of times and places other than those that are staged—as well as the fictional 'inner' world of *dramatis personae* construed as characters into whose motives it makes sense to enquire. When Stephen Greenblatt, for example, read in *Othello* the effects on the early modern psyche of such discursive regimes as Counter-Reformation confessional practices and the Protestant marriage manual, his interpretation involved inferring, from Iago's metaphors and strategies, a 'psychic structure' or inner world:

> It is at the level of this dark, sexual revulsion that Iago has access to Othello, access assured, as we should expect, by the fact that beneath his cynical modernity and professed self-love, Iago reproduces in himself the same psychic structure. He is as intensely preoccupied with adultery, while his anxiety about his own sexuality may be gauged from the fact that he conceives his very invention, as the images of engendering suggest, as a kind of demonic semen that will bring forth monsters.[25]

Inferring a dramatic character's *inner* preoccupations with adultery leads Greenblatt (not unreasonably) to infer at the same time an expansive *outer* world—the before, during, and after that the play does not in fact show. Othello, approaching the marriage bed on which Desdemona has laid her wedding sheets, 'comes close', says Greenblatt, 'to revealing his tormenting identification of marital sexuality—*limited perhaps to the night he took Desdemona's virginity*—and adultery'.[26] Suspended between the terms of Othello's imagined identifications of marital sexuality and adultery, Greenblatt's tentative speculation about the limits of Othello's sexual experience with his wife here conjures a pathos-laden extramimetic scene.[27]

What I am remarking here is not surprising, but absolutely to be expected. This is how literary criticism of Shakespeare has tended to proceed, changes of emphasis with respect to critical movements notwithstanding. For example: Greenblatt emphatically does not make claims for the 'universality' of the psychic structures he infers, as an older liberal humanist criticism would have. Nevertheless, he still *infers them* as the vivid traces of a past culture.

Why do we so rarely analyse or scrutinize the grounds of this inferential procedure? Such analyses as have been undertaken are those which, in the names of various critical movements—Leavisite rigour, structuralist reduction, poststructuralist cultural materialism—have questioned ascriptions of a limitless autonomy and plenitude to 'character'.[28] The analytical challenge, in other words, has been to liberal humanism's assumption that 'character exceeds the formal means of its representation'.[29] Yet, as we see from Greenblatt's critical procedure, the inferring of the *fabula* does not necessarily entail a liberal humanist universalizing of the autonomous, lifelike 'character'. What it does entail, however, is the *simultaneous* inference of psychic structure and narrative circumstance (here the circumstance of *Time*—speculation on the question, '*when* would Othello have been able to consummate his marriage with Desdemona?') from the formal aspects of dramatic speeches—in this case, the form taken by Othello's contemplation of his wife's murder.

Greenblatt cites Othello's chilling prediction: 'Thy Bed, lust-stain'd, shall with Lusts blood bee spotted' (5.1.3123). These words make murder's bloodstains a punitive repetition of the stains of lust but, in so doing, weirdly identify the latter with hymeneal blood, proof of virginity. Something like a crazy, pseudo-dialectic definition of the signs of 'lust' lies latent in Othello's figure of speech ('lust stains; blood also stains; therefore, bloodstains *are* signs of lust'). This prompts thoughts about the psychology that lies behind such an argument and, hence, an imagining of how the narrative circumstances hyperbolize the psychology by suggesting how recently the speaker—Othello—must have read bloodstains as blissful signs of wedded chastity.

I have dwelt at perhaps unwarranted length on Greenblatt's analysis as a rich example of how criticism of Shakespeare is grounded in the inference of a *fabula* (implying both psychological and external causation) in order to emphasize two points. First, that such inferential processes are not limited to liberal humanist notions of 'character' and second that our imagining of extramimetic elements as part of the play's *fabula*—the times, places, and events that are merely implicit—takes the form of what, in the sixteenth century, would be thought of as the topical invention of arguments from players' speeches. In this and the following sections, I will develop each of these points. First, I'll outline why neither historically sceptical accounts of the rise of 'character criticism' in the eighteenth and nineteenth centuries nor the current defence of a character-centred criticism based on performance studies pre-empt the subject of this book's enquiry. Second, in the last sections of this Introduction, I will show how both sixteenth-century neoclassical theory and English dramatic practice are concerned to enable audiences to infer psychology and imagine dramatic time and space by inventing topical and, indeed, *circumstantial* arguments.

The interrogation of character criticism has been most illuminating in its account of the place of Shakespeare in the eighteenth- and nineteenth-century valorization of the cultivation, through literature, of the moral self. Deirdre Lynch, building on a seminal essay by Ian Hunter, offers an illuminating account of the emergence, in the late eighteenth and nineteenth century, of 'character appreciation' as a specific reading practice responding to the democratization of the book market. The capacity to excavate deeper meanings, 'to appreciate a character as an "old friend," to activate moral norms common to oneself and the character', became, in the late eighteenth century, a 'means of probing one's receptiveness to literature' and so constituting a discriminating moral self.[30] More or less invented by Maurice Morgann in his 1777 essay on Falstaff, this new practice of 'character appreciation', Lynch argues, itself '*produces* the depth that needs explicating, and with it the textual effects that signal the psychological real'.[31]

Ian Hunter and Deirdre Lynch have offered extremely persuasive accounts of eighteenth- and nineteenth-century changes in the moral and affective function of reading, which encouraged the practice of inferring psychological depth from the textual medium of Shakespeare's plays. Their accounts cannot, however, explain why Shakespeare's sixteenth-century compositional habits should enable and encourage such inferences in the late eighteenth century. Why is it that, when the English vernacular tradition of theatrical mimesis enabled little or no inference of an imagined world beyond the immediate *mise-en-scène*, we find such inferential practices constitutive of our response to Shakespeare's dramatic writing? If the eighteenth-century Hamlet could acquire inner regions of selfhood and the eighteenth-century Falstaff a convenient house in town, what aspects of Shakespeare's text encouraged readers to infer such circumstantial acquisitions?[32]

A very recent body of Shakespeare criticism has declared itself in favour of returning to the analytical category of 'character' as central to Shakespeare's dramatic writing, but this body of criticism ignores the materialist analysis of nineteenth-century reading and seeks the answer to the formal power of 'character' in the history of collaborative theatrical practices—in company structure, in a loose-leaf, part-based conception of the playtext, and in the contingencies and ruptures of embodied rehearsal and performance.[33] Clearly, theatrical practices both derive from and modify the effect of inferences drawn from the text. For example, as Tiffany Stern and Simon Palfrey observe, the practice of distributing the play in separate 'parts' for different actors requires the actor to pay particular attention to the information encoded in his 'cue'. 'When an actor is anxiously trying to pick up his character from particulars of nuance and address', they write, 'the cues will give direction for just such matters; the acting direction held in the cue thus often doubles as a pithy characterisation.'[34] As this example shows, however, performance merely *interprets* from hints written into the text—though Palfrey and Stern stress the fragmentation and openness of Shakespeare's text to the actor's modification and interpretative choice, this openness to contingency cannot in itself be said to produce the imaginative hints it exploits.[35]

So, while studies of collaborative theatrical practice—including company structure, repertory, rehearsal, and performance—have transformed and enriched Shakespeare studies in recent years, they have not been able to tell us why early modern English dramatists, and Shakespeare in particular, began to *write* in a way that invites actors, audiences, and readers to project, from the slightest textual hints, the *fabula* of the play as an extramimetic world expanding both inwardly (into 'character') and outwardly, into the 'unscene' of imagined places and times.[36]

I.4. 'This Accident is not unlike my dreame': Arguments and Episodes

One of the problems with separating English 'theatrical practice' from the rhetorical and dialectical bases of humanist literary composition is the tendency, remarked earlier, to misrecognize diegetic and rhetorical elements of dramatic writing as 'untheatrical'. So, as we saw, 'classical drama' is said to be 'a rhetorical construct' which converts action into 'spoken report'. Related to this has been the tendency to assume that Shakespeare's innovations in 'characterization' must come from theatrical practice (for example, from working closely with company members known to him) rather than from innovations in compositional techniques deriving from habits of rhetorical argumentation. Bart Van Es intriguingly sees the diegetic 'building blocks of Seneca's drama' (entrance monologue, stichomythia) dominating Shakespeare's earlier, more 'literary' drama, 'at the expense of gradual characterisation', which, he proposes, Shakespeare only achieves once he is a shareholder in a theatrical company.[37] While some aspects of what Van Es calls Shakespeare's 'gradual characterisation' (complex onstage interaction; appellative and phatic speech) do indeed seem ascribable to his writing for a single company, we should guard against the conclusion that the 'Senecan' aspects of earlier drama are somehow textually prefabricated 'building blocks' which are therefore inimical to processes of 'characterization'.

It is important to recognize that early modern English dramatists' most enduring achievement—that of the coherently imaginable dramatic *fabula*—would have been unthinkable without the classical and humanist or neoclassical conception of reading and writing (including the reading and imitation of Seneca) as a process of the rhetorical and dialectical *invention of arguments*. Rudolph Agricola's revolutionary humanist dialectic, *De inventione dialectica*, incorporated the topics of accident and circumstance (in chapters on *connexa*, *adiuncta*, and *contingentia*—'relations', 'adjuncts', and 'contingents') into a more comprehensive classification of 'topics' or strategies of argument, including genus, species, similarities, differences, etc.[38] In doing so he followed Cicero's incorporation of the 'circumstances' of *De inventione* into the more comprehensive strategies of the *Topica*; Quintilian had done the same, importing the 'circumstances' along with Cicero's *Topica* wholesale into his chapter on the place of 'argument' as key to 'artificial proof' (Quintilian, *Inst.*, 5.10). It is important to stress that Agricola's topical analyses influenced the reading and composition of literary texts; in a popular edition of the literary textbook, Erasmus' *De copia*, the notes to 'circumstances' glossed them in relation to the 'topic from associated accidents' proposed by 'our dialecticians' and mentioned that 'Rodolphus' (Agricola) 'calls circumstances attachments of the thing' ('*Rodolphus circunstantias vocat applicita rebus*').[39]

Van Es draws on John Fitch's introduction to his new Loeb translation of Seneca to show how early Elizabethan 'literary' drama (Kyd, Marlowe, early Shakespeare) is indebted to its rhetorical architecture, its 'building blocks'.[40] But the dialectical and rhetorical habits of reading as the 'invention' of arguments can perhaps alert us to ways in which Seneca's techniques might be integrated into and compatible with the writing Van Es takes as exhibiting features of 'gradual characterisation'. The apparently impersonal *sententiae* and epigrams of Senecan dialogue can invite dialectical invention as a way of appreciating characters' motives and emotions. Rudolph Agricola offers an example of reading as dialectical invention from Seneca's *Hercules furens*. Hercules is in the underworld, and Thebes has meanwhile been taken over by the usurper Lycus. Amphitryon, Hercules' human father, and Hercules' wife Megara, are being threatened and intimidated by Lycus, who mocks their desperate hope that Hercules will return and save them. The exchange is taut with Lycus' manipulation of the family's anxious uncertainty over Hercules' absence; it turns on the question of whether or not Hercules is a god.

> AMPHITRYON: There is always a great cost to being born a god.
> LYCUS: Whoever you see wretched, you know he is mortal.
> AMPHITRYON: Whoever you see resolute, you cannot call wretched.
>
> (AMPHITRYON: *Semperque magno constitit nasci deum.*
> LYCUS: *Quemcumque miserum videris hominem scias.*
> AMPHITRYON: *Quemcumque fortem videris, miserum neges.*)[41]

Analysing this example dialectically, Agricola shows how Lycus tries to deny Hercules' godhead by making *miseria*, 'wretchedness', the middle term uniting two arguments, one invented from the topic of '*difference*' ('*e diversis deo ducitur*'), that is, 'a difference between gods and men is that men can be wretched', and one taken from the topic of 'accident' or 'adjacents' ('*ab adiacentibus Herculis*'), that is, that 'wretchedness' is an *accident* or *circumstance* of Hercules.[42] If Hercules can be wretched, Hercules is a man, not a god, and will never return from the underworld. Amphitryon counters Lycus by denying that the circumstance of wretchedness applied to Hercules, because Hercules is strong and resolute, therefore he *is* a god. Attending to the close texture of the argument, by 'inventing' the tensely witty power play of the arguments, we become aware that there is nothing prefabricated about Senecan drama. John Fitch has compared decoding the epigrammatic pointedness of Seneca's dialogue to reading dialogue in Jane Austen; the challenge is 'to appreciate both the verbal brilliance and the reality of emotion, motive and situation which it expresses or masks'.[43] Rudolph Agricola likewise notes that in inventing the argument of Lycus' epigram, the reader infers his manipulative 'intention' (*intentio*) to deny Hercules' deity.

While there may seem a wide gulf between Agricola's exercise in dialectical invention and Greenblatt's interpretation of Othello, the principles of reading are in fact similar. 'Thy Bed lust-stain'd, shall with Lusts blood bee spotted' (5.1.3123) is as pointed and epigrammatic as anything in Seneca. Greenblatt's analysis of Othello's 'psychic structure' (Othello's 'tormented identification') and of its particular history (Othello's limited experience of marital sex) are all inferred from the twisted invention that so brilliantly emerges from any analysis of this locution. Othello's murderous prediction contains a compressed and specious dialectical argument from 'similarities'—the stains of lust are like the bloodstains that prove married chastity—and it is the appreciation of the argument here that permits the inference of Othello's *causa*, his motive and the feelings that prompt it. Questions of whether or not English dramatists followed neoclassical 'rules' about the dramatic unities or about the strict separation of comedy and tragedy pale into insignificance next to the achievements made possible by the humanist and neoclassical emphasis on rhetorical and dialectical invention. This emphasis produced a dramatic language replete with arguments perpetually inviting the inference of *causae*—that is, motives, intentions, or purposes—and, from the inference of motives and intentions, the further inference, using the topics of circumstance, of unseen times and places.

How might arguments have been imagined as forming part of the diegetic means by which psychological causation and a coherent 'outer world' are inferred from speeches in the play? Lodovico Castelvetro, who is famous to Shakespeareans as the formulator of the notoriously restrictive dramatic unities, was himself an admirer and follower, in his criticism, of Agricola's *De inventione dialectica*.[44] Though Castelvetro is generally disparaged by anglophone critics for conceiving an audience so wanting in imagination as to require that fictional duration equal performance time, we may read his concerns with verisimilitude more sympathetically.[45] Recognizing that mimesis and audience patience have their limits, Castelvetro thinks hard about how complex incidental particularity and a plurality of times and locations may be represented in the theatre. By way of a gloss on Aristotle's term 'episode', and countering that term's connotations of casual sequence, he produces a fourfold taxonomy of theatrical diegesis. The first sense of 'episode' signifies events anterior to or postdating the dramatic action; the second sense 'incidents that occur at the time of the action and are part of it, but take place at some distance'; the third sense 'applies to the things invented by the poet to particularize a plot known only in summary form'; and the fourth is the quantitative part of a tragedy falling between two choral songs. This last is actually always identified, says Castelvetro, with one or other of the first three definitions, since in these parts of the tragedy the poet both particularizes the story and acquaints the audience with things that are temporally and spatially distant. The apparently restricted action of the unified play is thus replete with temporal and spatial alterity and incidental particularity.[46]

Having thus defined the 'episode' as the means by which the dramatist brings before the audience's imaginations distant times and places and dense 'particulars', Castelvetro goes on to produce a further taxonomy of how these 'episodes' are introduced into the play: (1) *ex proposito* (by way of argument), (2) *ex accidenti* (as things happen); (3) *per miracolo* (miraculously). He defines all 'particularized events' as being introduced '*ex proposito*', or as part of the texture of the play's argument; events which take place before the play began are likely thus to be '*ex proposito*', or part of a history which results 'in a web of incidents (*testura delle cose*) so related that they have a probable or necessary dependence on one another'.[47] But incidents taking place at some distance may be said to be introduced *ex accidenti* when they are related by messengers. Finally, incidents may be said to be introduced miraculously when they are made known by apparitions of the dead, or by dreams, visions, prophecies, oracles, or the like.[48]

Castelvetro's taxonomy is tied at every point to uses of the term 'episode' in Aristotle's *Poetics*, reworking Aristotle to exclude the pejorative sense of 'episode' as mere digression.[49] The result is a theory of how a mimesis restricted to the here-and-now is able, through a kind of infrastructure of varied forms of diegesis, to offer the illusion of a coherent fictive world encompassing anteriority, exteriority, and psychology (through dreams and by way of argument). Castelvetro's emphasis is thus not on thinking merely about how to 'represent' or 'stage' human action, but on the argumentative and narrative strategies, the modes of proof, and the levels of credibility that distinguish the ways human beings come to 'know' what they know. And although it is commonly assumed that Castelvetro's theories are irrelevant to English dramatists, it is quite striking to think of how well his classification of types of 'episode' fits the diversified extramimetic techniques used, for example, by Shakespeare to inaugurate the action of *Othello*. In the opening of *Othello*, the exchange between Roderigo and Iago introduces, *ex proposito*, or by way of argument, the rivalry between Roderigo and Othello and Iago's discontent in the latter's service. Roderigo's then making known to Brabantio the circumstances of his daughter's elopement might be construed as a narration *ex accidenti*—as a near-simultaneous event vividly and credibly reported by witnesses as having taken place elsewhere. Indeed, Brabantio himself nominates it as an 'accident', completing Castelvetro's scheme by declaring he finds it credible because he already knows it *ex miracolo*, by way of a vision: 'This Accident is not unlike my dreame', he says, 'Belief of it oppresses me already' (1.1.155–6).

I.5. 'Many Days and Many Places, Inartificially Imagined'

I am not proposing that Shakespeare knew Lodovico Castelvetro's *Poetica d'Aristotele* (though it is worth noting that Lodovico's nephew, Giacomo Castelvetro, was working and living in London in the early 1580s and was reported, by one of his later English students in Cambridge, to have been '*erede de la scienza del suo zio (unico lume d'Italia)*' ('the heir of the knowledge of his uncle, unique light of Italy').[50] What I am proposing, however, is that instead of thinking about neoclassical 'rules and restrictions' as irrelevant to Shakespeare's dramatic 'freedom', we think of what sixteenth-century neoclassicism and sixteenth-century English dramaturgy share by way of a concern with using the rhetorical and dialectical invention of arguments to enable the audience's imaginative inference of times, spaces, and psychological recesses beyond the capacity of the stage's power to show.

I will conclude with Philip Sidney, no less notorious than Castelvetro for mistakenly backing the dramatic unities over the temporal and spatial freedoms embraced by the English stage.[51] It is Sidney who seems so uncompromisingly to have privileged diegesis over stage mimesis, distinguishing, in a much-quoted passage, between 'reporting' and 'representing':

> How, then, shall we set forth a story, which containeth both many places and many times? . . . many things may be told which cannot be showed, if they know the difference betwixt reporting and representing. As, for example, I may speak (though I am here) of Peru, and in speech digress from that to the description of Calicut; but in action I cannot represent it without Pacolet's horse. And so was the manner the ancients took, by some *nuntius* to recount things done in former time or other place.[52]

Here Sidney seems to offer a classic definition of the neoclassical conversion of dramatic enactment into the messenger's 'spoken report', with none of the nuance of Castelvetro's differentiation between the modes of making known. Sidney's comments on English vernacular drama of the 1560s and 1570s nevertheless make use of a terminology that is illuminating. Sidney is aggrieved by the artlessness of English stage productions, but he distinguishes tellingly between the temporal and spatial transgressions of Thomas Norton and Thomas

Sackville's *Gorboduc* (1561) and those of other vernacular romances of the 1570s. *Gorboduc*, he says, for all it climbs 'to the height of Seneca's style', is very

> *defectious in the circumstances* . . . For it is faulty both in place and time, the two necessary companions of all corporal actions. For where the stage should always represent but one place, and the uttermost time pre-supposed in it should be, both by Aristotle's precept and by common reason, but one day, there is both *many days and many places, inartificially imagined.*[53]

Gorboduc in Sidney's account both transcends the generality of English comedies and tragedies and, at the same time, exemplifies their defects, being 'faulty both in place and time'.[54] Yet its fault is said to be a defect in 'the circumstances' and in the 'inartificial imag-ining' of the many days and places represented. These are technical criticisms, using a vocabulary derived from rhetorical and dialectical theories of how to invent arguments and proofs to bring a story or description vividly before the eyes ('circumstances' being topics of argument and therefore 'artificial proofs'). Although Sidney employs this vocabulary to indict *Gorboduc* for failing to make time and place artificially 'probable', he might have used it in precisely the oppo-site way, for, as we shall see, it is through arguments on the circum-stances of time and place that *Gorboduc*'s warring brothers, Ferrex and Porrex, find their suspicions of one another 'probable' enough to motivate a war.

Before we turn to *Gorboduc*, however, it is worth recalling Sidney's strictures against the general run of 1570s stage plays:

> But if it be so in *Gorboduc*, how much more in all the rest? where you shall have Asia of the one side, and Afric of the other, and so many other under-kingdoms, that the player, when he cometh in, must ever begin with telling where is, or else the tale will not be conceived. Now ye shall have three ladies walk to gather flowers and then we must believe the stage to be a garden. By and by we hear news of a ship-wreck in the same place, and then we are to blame if we accept it not for a rock. Upon the back of that comes out a hideous monster with fire and smoke, and then the miserable beholders are bound to take it for a cave. While in the meantime, two armies fly in, represented with four swords and bucklers, and then what hard heart will not receive it for a pitched field?[55]

Striking, here, is Sidney's reason for laughing at the romances that held the stage in the previous decade. The suspension of sceptical, critical judgement—what we've called, since Coleridge, the 'suspension of disbelief'—is not, as it is so often imagined to be, the issue. It's not that people are unable to suspend their disbelief—Sidney explicitly says that no one is so *unreceptive* (his word) as not to be able to accept the stage for a sea-shore, monster's den, or a battlefield with the help of a few props, costumes, and sound-effects. But belief is a critical and active thing, it needs material to work on. Agricola defined dialectic as that which is 'concerned with speaking convincingly (*probabiliter*) and *probabile* will mean whatever can be said as suitably as possible for creating belief' (*quam aptissime ad fidem dicetur*).[56] It's not that we need to *suspend belief*, then, but that our judgement of probability needs to be engaged, even for marvellous things. We don't want to be *told*, at every turn, where the action now is and how many days have passed—we want to infer and imagine. Sidney is implicitly criticizing these romantic adventure plays for not bringing *circumstantial arguments* of Time and Place before 'the imaginative and judging power' either of the *dramatis personae* or of the audience. No one is being asked to 'invent' the arguments for themselves and so to imagine times and places and motives.

Sidney seems to be referring to plays such as the delightful *Sir Clyomon and Sir Clamydes* (*c*.1577), a perambulatory romance in which the players are obliged, as they enter, to 'ever begin with telling where' they—and the scene—presently are. The action opens with Sir Clamydes 'Bringing my Barke to *Denmarke* here', as he tells us.[57] We witness him vowing to slay a dragon in Swabia in order to marry Juliana, who is, in the absence of her brother Clyomon, heir to the throne of Denmark. 'To *Suauia* soile', he says, 'I swiftly will prepare my foot-steps right' (94). The next scene opens with Sir Clyomon who immediately lets us know that 'being here in *Suauia* | And neare vnto the Court', he plans to deprive Sir Clamydes of his knighthood (156–7). This unsurprisingly occasions a quarrel between the knights, and they vow to fight in fifteen days' time in the presence of King Alexander in Macedonia. But Sir Clamydes, imagining that fifteen days gives him ample leisure to make it to the forest of Sir Brian Sans Foy, slay the dragon, and be back with time to spare for the combat, is unfortunately captured by the evil Sir Brian, sent into an enchanted sleep, and imprisoned in Sans Foy's castle for ten of his precious days. The next scene opens with the stage direction, '*Here let them make a noyse as though they were Marriners*'. The seasick Sir Clyomon comes on stage with a 'Marriner' and asks how far his ship is from Macedonia, only to be told that it has, in fact, just anchored at an island 'More then twentie dayes sayling, and if the weather were faire' from that destination (731). More delays and digressions accumulate, as Sir Clyomon frets over his vow and is nursed to health by a princess called Neronis. She is subsequently kidnapped by the King of Norway and forced to disguise herself as Clyomon's page (in which disguise, Imogen-like, she later mistakes Norway's corpse for that of her lover). What is evident, however, is that for all the play's humour and ingenuity, and for all its thematic interest in the ironies of misfortune and miscommunication (the Vice, *Subtle Shift*, masquerades as 'Knowledge' and a figure called 'Rumour' brings news), it has no resources to help audiences 'conceive' or 'invent' the spatio-temporal complexity of the action *ex proposito*, or by way of argument. Soliloquies are used to bridge the gaps between staged times and places, many of these beginning with 'general declarations of woe before the character tells what has happened to him' and where he or she now is.[58] No use of argument invites us to imagine time and place as circumstances in which the characters find themselves and to which they respond emotionally. This is why there needs to be, at almost every scene's opening and closing, an explicit announcement both of where the action presently is, and where the agent—knight or page or evil enchanter—plans to go next.

By contrast, *Gorboduc* represents an extraordinary advance in the conceivability of movements of time and place and it does so because of the way in which it conveys action through scenes of deliberative argument about what is *probable* which turn more and more on the fostering of mistaken conjectures about another's *causa*, or motive. The play opens with a scene in Gorboduc's Queen, Videna, shares with her elder son, Ferrex, her aggrieved conjecture that he'll be deprived of his inheritance by Gorboduc's 'causeless, unkindly' plans to divide the kingdom, and give an equal share to Ferrex's younger brother, Porrex. The second scene is entirely devoted to Gorboduc's taking advice on this plan from his counsellors. He gives arguments in favour of his two-part plan, to abdicate and to divide his kingdom between his sons, that '[m]ay so be taught and trained' to govern while he still lives.[59]

The replies of his counsellors are schematically divided three ways, with the first counsellor, Arostus, offering proofs in favour of both the abdication and the division and the second, Philander, approving the division, but opposing the idea of yielding governance by abdication. The third, Eubulus, opposes both parts of the plan. Among his arguments against the division, he emphasizes the sons' likely reactions. Ferrex, 'whom kind and custom give a rightful hope . . . | Shall think that he doth suffer greater wrong', he suggests (1.2.285–7), while Porrex, having been so elevated 'in state', will start to take his new eminence for granted and 'perhaps in courage be upraised also' (1.2.289–90). These emotional responses, he points out, will almost certainly precipitate violence, for flattering courtiers will soon see their way to encouraging, on the one hand, King Ferrex's feelings of having been injured and, on the other, King Porrex's newly acquired sense of self-importance. Finally, Eubulus pleads, keep your sons 'near unto your presence still'—do not, by any means 'plant' them 'in further parts', where 'Traitorous corrupters of their pliant youth | Shall have, unspied, a much more free access' (1.2.313, 316–17).

No such deliberative arguments enabled the audience to begin to 'conceive', in *Clyomon and Clamydes*, the location of the subsequent scenes or the sense of time elapsed between them—this is why the knights need to keep totting up, for the information of the audience, the numbers of days they have been wandering, or have been asleep or immobilized by seasickness. In *Gorboduc*, however, Act 1's scene of deliberation enables the audience to grasp immediately, as the second act begins to unfold, that the courtier busy aggravating Ferrex's sense of grievance and persuading him to prepare against Porrex's likely invasion is precisely the type of 'traitorous corrupter of pliant youth' of which Eubulus had spoken. We therefore easily 'conceive' the tale—we know that this scene, in which Ferrex is moved by the courtier called Hermon to make secret preparations for war against his brother—must be taking place in the southern part of Britain, in Ferrex's kingdom, and that the time must be some months after the execution of Gorboduc's plan to abdicate and divide the kingdom so that 'Humber shall part the marches of the realms' (1.2.345). When the second scene of Act 2 opens with Porrex's exclamation, 'And is it thus? And doth he so prepare | Against his brother as his mortal foe?' (2.2.1–2), we are already fully on board, as it were, immediately ready to fill in and infer the events that must have passed. Porrex must be addressing a courtier (Tyndar) who just come from Ferrex's court, with news of the 'great preparèd store | Of horse, of armour, and of weapon there' (2.2.6–7). Nor is this conceiving of the time and location of the action merely a matter of anticipation (once again, that is, we immediately know that the location of this scene must be Porrex's northern realm, and that the time elapsed has allowed Ferrex's mobilization of troops and arms). It is, much more importantly, a matter of the *psychologizing* of dramatic action and its time and space. That is to say that the dramatists have understood that what matters in a dramatic narrative may not be action itself, but the way in which the action (whether enacted or reported) is construed by other *dramatis personae*. In the case of *Gorboduc*, Porrex's readiness to infer and imagine Ferrex's 'cause' from Tyndar's vivid account of the warmongering atmosphere of his court leads to his self-persuasion that it would be dangerous to seek to know directly what Ferrex has in mind. The spatial and temporal distance between the brothers—their having been 'planted in further parts'—is thus, as Eubulus feared, what leads them to produce and act on *fantasies* of one another's 'cause', or motive, seeking each to anticipate the other's imagined aggression by ever more murderous pre-emptions. Tyndar uses *enargeia* to persuade Porrex to imagine a pervasive national hostility in Ferrex's kingdom, based on a legitimate sense of grievance:

> Lo, secret quarrels run about his court
> To bring the name of you, my lord, in hate.
> Each man almost can now debate the cause
> And ask the reason of so great a wrong,
> Why he, so noble and so wise a prince,
> Is, as unworthy, reft his heritage . . .
> The wiser sort hold down their griefful heads;
> Each man withdraws from talk and company
> Of those that have been known to favour you. (2.2.10–20)

Tyndar's report to Porrex skilfully evoked the tension of a change of political mood by suggesting, in image of the 'wiser sort' lowering 'their griefful heads', all the associations that go with that downcast gesture—premonitions of sorrow, for example, as well as the dread of courting suspicion by meeting the glances of others. This vividly imagined scenario then provides in itself the proof Porrex needs to refuse Philander's soberer counsel that Porrex should, before making any warlike preparations of his own, merely 'Send to your brother to demand the cause' (2.2.30). Philander observes—as indeed is the case—that Ferrex himself may be preparing for a defensive war on the basis of merely imagined fears of invasion. Porrex's refusal to make any direct enquiry into Ferrex's cause, however, has an air of even greater prudence, building as it does on the fantasy of already knowing that 'cause', or that 'intention' by way of Tyndar's vivid description:

> If danger were for one to tarry there
> Think ye it safety to return again?
> In mischiefs, such as Ferrex now intends,
> The wonted courteous laws to messengers
> Are not observed, which in just war they use. (2.2.40–4)

Strictly speaking, of course, the inference (based on an invention of the dialectical topic of 'difference'—just war/mischievous invasion) is overhasty. Hermon did not persuade Ferrex to muster men to invade Porrex, but to anticipate Porrex's likely invasion, 'You will not be the first that shall invade', Hermon had said in the previous scene, 'Assemble yet your force for your defense' (2.1.159–60). Yet the argument about the safety of sending messengers, based as it is on the vivid, circumstantial reality of Tyndar's description, has a compelling plausibility. What is almost schematically evident, then, is that, in a recursive fashion, the imagined distance of time and space between the brothers is deployed to motivate their receptiveness to highly coloured conjectures about one another's predisposition to violence, which, in turn, produce further imagined reasons to act upon these hostile fantasies rather than dispel them by an attempt to reach one another's minds and 'causes' directly. Even Time becomes subject to this imaginative process, as Porrex finds in the circumstantial topic of Time, an argument for haste, an argument against the 'delay' that might be involved in following Philander's peaceable advice and sending to his father before deciding to prepare for war:

> Or shall I to the King my father, send?
> Yea, and send now, while such a mother lives
> That loves my brother, and that hateth me?

Shall I *give leisure by my fond delays,*
To Ferrex to oppress me all unware?
I will not; but I will invade his realm. (2.2.49–54)

It would not be too much to say that *Gorboduc* is the first tragedy in English to produce *imagined and imaginative time and space*; indeed, in *Gorboduc* it is imagined time and space—in Porrex's conviction that to send for his father would turn time into the 'leisure' Ferrex requires to execute his intended invasion—that brings about tragedy. As Tyndar's report of the military preparations and heightening of political tension at Ferrex's court grips Porrex's imagination, Porrex indignantly conjures a vision of peaceful consultation with his father as the opportunity, or 'leisure' that would allow his brother to murder him. This prolepsis collapses the future and we feel time implode as Act 3 opens with Gorboduc's and Eubulus' receiving the news of successive instalments of the inevitable acceleration in violence, until a Nuntius finally enters to announce that Porrex 'with sudden force' has invaded Ferrex's land and slain his brother (3.1.160). Far from being 'defectious in the circumstances', Sackville and Norton's tragedy might be read as the first to exploit the tragic potential concealed in the vividness of the 'circumstances' as arguments of Time and Place.

Notes

1. Shakespeare quotations are taken from *The Norton Facsimile: The First Folio of Shakespeare*, ed. Charlton Hinman, second edition with an introduction by Peter W. M. Blayney (New York: W. W. Norton, 1996), giving act and scene, followed by through-line numbers. Although I quote, throughout these chapters, from the First Folio and early quartos, I refer to Shakespeare's *dramatis personae* by their modernized names in order to prevent confusion: thus 'Proteus' instead of 'Protheus', 'Lance' instead of 'Launce'.
2. For a more detailed account of these developments, see Chapter 2.
3. See Quintilian, *Institutio oratoria (The Orator's Education)*, ed. and tr. Donald A. Russell, 5 vols (Cambridge, Mass.: Harvard University Press, 2001) 5.10; 5.10.20–53; 5.10.104. On the Aristotelian origins of the 'circumstances' see Michael C. Sloan, 'Aristotle's *Nicomachean Ethics* as the Original Locus for the Septem Circumstantiae', *Classical Philology*, 105:3 (2010) 236–51; on 'artificial proof', see Kathy Eden, *Poetic and Legal Fiction in the Aristotelian Tradition* (Princeton: Princeton University Press, 1986); on 'circumstances' in relation to emotion, see P. H. Schrijvers, 'Invention, imagination et théorie des émotions chez Cicéron et Quintilien', in J. den

Boeft and A. H. M. Kessels (eds), *Actus: Studies in Honour of H. L. W. Nelson* (Utrecht: Instituut voor Klassieke Talen, 1982); in relation to *enargeia*, see Ruth Webb, *Ekphrasis, Imagination and Persuasion in Ancient Rhetorical Theory and Practice* (Farnham: Ashgate, 2009) 87–94. For further discussion, see Chapter 2.

4. John Brinsley, *Ludus literarius: or, The Grammar Schoole* (London, 1612) 180.

5. Cicero, *Topica*, ed. and tr. Tobias Reinhardt (Oxford: Oxford University Press, 2003) §8, 'Therefore we may define a Place as the location of an argument, and an argument as a reasoning that lends belief to a doubtful issue' (*Itaque licet definire locum esse argumenti sedem, argumentum autem rationem quae rei dubiae faciat fidem*). On Cicero's inclusion of the 'circumstantial' topics of person and thing in the more comprehensive *Topica*, see Marc Cogan, 'Rodolphus Agricola and the Semantic Revolutions of the History of Invention', *Rhetorica*, 2:2 (1984) 163–94, 168–9.

6. Michael C. Leff, 'The Topics of Argumentative Invention in Latin Rhetorical Theory from Cicero to Boethius', *Rhetorica*, 1:1 (1983) 23–44, 25.

7. *D. Erasmi Roterodami de duplici copia verborum ac rerum commentarii duo* (London: Henry Middleton, 1573) fol. 134ᵛ. The text is from the commentary of Johannes Weltkirchius. Johannes Weltkirchius (also called Velcurio, Velcurius, Feldkirchus) was born Johannes Bernhardi, younger brother of Bartholomeus Bernhardi, at Feldkirch. I thank Matthijs Wibier for his help with translating Weltkirchius' commentary.

8. Philip Sidney, *An Apology for Poetry (or The Defence of Poesy)*, ed. Geoffrey Shepherd, rev. R. W. Maslen (Manchester: Manchester University Press, 2002) 110, lines 34–6.

9. Helen Cooper, *Shakespeare and the Medieval World* (London: Methuen, 2010) 3 (my italics).

10. A similar argument has been eloquently made by Peter Womack, 'The trouble with putting it that way is that it makes dramatic classicism appear merely as that which says no to the open stage, limiting its freedoms, cramping its mobility, impoverishing its imaginative richness. It is as if the medieval tradition consisted of nothing but spontaneous practices, and Renaissance humanism of nothing but codified regulations. This is a comfortable English myth and . . . it is not true . . . The makers of the unitary stage, in other words, were Terence, Plautus, Machiavelli, Ariosto, Aretino: and they made it not by prohibiting something but by *producing* something,' 'The Comical Scene: Perspective and Civility on the Renaissance Stage', *Representations*, 101 (Winter 2008) 37–8; see also Bernard Weinberg, *A History of Literary Criticism in the Italian Renaissance*, 2 vols (Chicago: University of Chicago Press, 1961), which gives evidence throughout of the neoclassicists' concern with achieving verisimilitude and coherence in order to move and persuade audiences.

11. Cooper, *Shakespeare and the Medieval World*, 48.

12. Jonathan Culler, 'Story and Discourse in the Analysis of Narrative', in *The Pursuit of Signs: Semiotics, Literature, Deconstruction* (London: Routledge and Kegan Paul, 1981) 169–87.

13. Charles Whitworth, 'Reporting Offstage Events in Early Tudor Drama', in André Lascombes (ed.), *Tudor Theatre: 'Let There be Covenants'* (Berne: Peter Lang, 1977) 45–66, 45–6.

14. I borrow the term 'unscene' from Marjorie Garber, ' "The Rest is Silence": Ineffability and the "Unscene" in Shakespeare's Plays', in Peter S. Hawkins and Anne Howland Schotter (eds), *Ineffability: Naming the Unnameable from Dante to Beckett* (New York: AMS Press, 1984) 35–50. See also William Gruber, *Offstage Space, Narrative and the Theatre of the Imagination* (New York: Palgrave Macmillan, 2010) and Richard Meek, *Narrating the Visual in Shakespeare* (Aldershot: Ashgate, 2009).

15. Keir Elam, *The Semiotics of Theatre and Drama* (London: Routledge, 1994) 120.

16. Elam, *Semiotics of Theatre*, 120.

17. Elam, *Semiotics of Theatre*, 123, 120.

18. Whitworth, 'Reporting Offstage Events', 47.

19. Whitworth, 'Reporting Offstage Events', 56–9, 58.

20. L. Hutson, ' "Che indizio, che prova . . .?" Ariosto's Legal Conjectures and the English Renaissance Stage', *Renaissance Drama*, 36/37 (2010) 179–205; on 'fixed locale' staging, see Alan H. Nelson, 'The Universities: Early Staging in Cambridge', in John D. Cox and David Scott Kastan (eds), *A New History of English Drama* (New York: Columbia University Press, 1997).

21. *The Comedies of Ariosto translated and edited by Edmond Beame and Leonard G. Sbrocchi* (Chicago: University of Chicago Press, 1975) 46; *Tutte le opere di Ludovico Ariosto* a cura di Cesare Segre (Mondadori, 1974) iv. 64.

22. Whitworth, 'Reporting Offstage Events', 59.

23. *Gammer Gurton's Needle*, ed. Charles Whitworth (London: A & C Black, 1997) 2.2.22–4. Further references to this edition will appear in the text by act, scene, and line number.

24. We do, of course, get glimpses of an offstage world; a complex and brilliant example of this occurs in Lyndsay's *Satyre of the Thrie Estatis* (1552) when Diligence asks the Pauper to show 'al the circumstances' that have brought him to misery and forced him to seek legal remedy in St Andrews. The Pauper's narrative of the ruin of his family by the local vicar's predatory claims of mortuary dues is indeed vividly circumstantial. It does not, however, contribute to a coherent fictional 'world of the play'; rather, as the Pauper seems to come out of the audience, interrupting the allegory, the speech powerfully exploits the *locus/platea* distinction, bringing the play world into politically explosive contact with the world of the audience in 1550s Fife. See David Lyndsay, *Ane Satyre of the Thrie Estatis*, ed. Roderick Lyall (Edinburgh: Canongate Classics, 1989) 71–2.

25. Stephen Greenblatt, *Renaissance Self-Fashioning from More to Shakespeare* (Chicago: University of Chicago Press, 1980) 251.

26. Greenblatt, *Self-Fashioning*, 251.

27. Greenblatt's inference is contested by Graham Bradshaw, *Misrepresentations: Shakespeare and the Materialists* (Ithaca, NY: Cornell University Press, 1993) 198.

28. Notable examples of such analyses include L. C. Knights, 'How Many Children had Lady Macbeth? An Essay in the Theory and Practice of Shakespeare Criticism', *Explorations* (New York: George W. Stewart, 1947) 15–54; Catherine Belsey, *The Subject of Tragedy: Identity and Difference in Renaissance Drama* (London: Methuen, 1985); Alan Sinfield, 'When Is a Character Not a Character? Desdemona, Olivia, Lady Macbeth and Subjectivity', in *Faultlines: Cultural Materialism and the Politics of Dissident Reading* (Oxford: Clarendon Press, 1992) 52–79.

29. Deirdre Lynch, *The Economy of Character: Novels, Market Culture and the Business of Inner Meaning* (Chicago: University of Chicago Press, 1998) 11.

30. Lynch, *Economy of Character*, 141. Lynch makes clear her indebtedness to Ian Hunter's powerful 'Reading Character', *Southern Review*, 16:2 (1983) 226–43.

31. Lynch, *Economy of Character*, 135.

32. Lynch, *Economy of Character*, 137: 'The now-urgent pursuit of character's essential meaning opened up new depths in texts. In the last quarter of the eighteenth century, Hamlet thus acquired inner regions of selfhood. In a related development, he also acquired a youth . . . Falstaff acquired a house in the country and a house in town.'

33. Paul Yachnin and Jessica Slights (eds), *Shakespeare and Character: Theory, History, Performance and Theatrical Persons* (New York: Palgrave Macmillan, 2009); see especially the introduction, 1–18. See also Laurie Maguire, who notes that Shakespearean characters themselves try to read one another's 'character' and argues that 'Character is important in editorial decisions' but then asserts: 'Shakespeare doesn't write characters. Shakespeare writes *roles*; it is actors who create characters,' 'Audience–Actor Boundaries in *Othello*', *Proceedings of the British Academy*, 181 (2011) 123–42; 128–9, 131–3. It would seem, if actors create characters, that 'character' could not be important in editorial decisions, which must be about 'roles'. See also Tiffany Stern and Simon Palfrey, *Shakespeare in Parts* (Oxford: Oxford University Press, 2007).

34. Stern and Palfrey, *Shakespeare in Parts*, 97.

35. Stern and Palfrey suggest that the fragmentation of the playtext into parts enables an appreciation of how contingency and actorly choice contribute to the richness of 'character': 'Rather than of plays as finished books, we might better conceive of them as loose-leaf sheets, commissioned or swapped or shuffled with facile aplomb'; 'Shakespeare was far less suspicious of actors than, say, Jonson seems to have been; he gave his players crucial freedoms, moments of actorly choice, often no doubt terrifying moments, that inevitably coincide with moments of decision for character.' *Shakespeare in Parts*, 78; 7. Patrick Tucker's *Secrets*

of *Acting Shakespeare: The Original Approach* (London: Routledge, 2002) shows actors how the language of any specific scene encodes all the information they need to infer and therefore perform effectively and spontaneously. Both books bear witness to the rich inferential potential of Shakespeare's texts.

36. For more on collaborative composition, see Chapter 3, section 3.5.

37. Bart Van Es, *Shakespeare in Company* (Oxford: Oxford University Press, 2013) 66.

38. See Cogan, 'Rodolphus Agricola and the Semantic Revolutions of the History of Invention' 168–9; Peter Mack, *Renaissance Argument: Valla and Agricola in the Traditions of Rhetoric and Dialectic* (Leiden: Brill, 1993) 165–6; Rodolphus Agricola, *De inventione dialecticae lucubrationes* (facsimile of the Edition Cologne, 1539) (Nieuwkoop: B. de Graaf, 1968) 103–17; 174; Quintilian, *Inst.*, 5.10.20–53; 5.10.54–97.

39. Erasmus, *De copia* (1573) fol. 134ʳ; on Agricola's interest in literature, see Peter Mack, 'Rudolph Agricola's Reading of Literature', *Journal of the Warburg and Courtauld Institutes*, 48 (1985) 23–41.

40. Van Es, *Shakespeare in Company*, 65–6; Seneca, *Tragedies*, ed. and tr. John G. Fitch, 2 vols (Cambridge, Mass.: Harvard, 2002) i. 1–30.

41. Seneca, *Hercules furens*, tr. John G. Fitch, i. 86–7, lines 462–4. I have made Fitch's translation a bit more literal.

42. Agricola, *De inventione dialecticae*, 359; see Mack, *Renaissance Argument*, 228.

43. Fitch, 'Introduction', Seneca, *Tragedies*, i. 4.

44. On Castelvetro's reading of Rudolph Agricola and uses of Agricola's methods of 'dialectical reading', see the important work by Claudia Rossignoli on Castelvetro's criticism of Dante, ' "Dar materia di ragionamento": strategie interpretative della *Sposizione*', in *Lodovico Castelvetro: Filologia e acesi*, ed. Roberto Giliucci (Rome: Bulzoni Editore, 2007) 91–113. Rossignoli writes that Castelvetro's commentary on Dante, 'clearly reveals a wholehearted adherence to the paradigm of humanist dialectic in its continuous use of a rather technical logical terminology' ('*rivela chiaramente un'adesione senza riserve al paradigma della dialettica umanistica nell'uso continua di una terminologia logica puttosto tecnica*'), 104. She shows how Castelvetro uses Agricola's topical circumstantial categories to analyse the tercet opening canto 3 of the *Inferno*, which gives the inscription on the door leading to the realm of the damned, 107. See also 'Castelvetro on Dante: Tradition, Innovation and Mockery in the *Sposizione*', in Paola Nasti and Claudia Rossignoli (eds), *Intepreting Dante: Essays on the Tradition of Dante Commentary* (Notre Dame, Ind.: University of Notre Dame Press, 2013) 359–88.

45. For a thoroughly disparaging reading of Castelvetro, see the otherwise excellent article by David Riggs, 'The Artificial Day and the Infinite Universe', *Journal of Medieval and Renaissance Studies*, 5 (1975) 155–85.

46. Lodovico Castelvetro, *Poetica d'Aristotele vulgarizzata e sposta*, ed. Werner Romani, 2 vols (Rome: Laterza, 1978) i. 342–4; Andrew

Bongiorno, *Castelvetro on the Art of Poetry* (an abridged translation) (New York: Binghampton, 1984) 62–3.

47. Castelvetro, *Poetica d'Aristotele*, i.344, '*Per la via* ex proposito *sono tirate nelle favola le cose particolari trovata dal poeta, o ancora le cose avenute prima dell'azzione, o pure avenute nel tempo dell'azzione ma in luogo lontano da quello dove si rapprensenta l'azzione . . . E domando questa via* ex proposito *avendo rispetto alla testura delle cose, che sono per quelle cosi congiunte insieme che l'una dipende dall'altra second verisimilitudine o necessità*' ('All particularized events invented by the poet may be said to be introduced into the plot *ex proposito*, as may all accounts of events that took place before the beginning of the action, or simultaneously with it but in a different place when the speaker makes them known as he ostensibly tells of other matters or for an end other than the mere telling . . . I call this method *ex proposito* because it results in a web of incidents (*testura delle cose*) so related that they have a probable or necessary dependence on one another', tr. Bongiorno, *Castelvetro on the Art of Poetry*, 63).

48. Castelvetro, *Poetica d'Aristotele*, 344: '*Per la via* accidenti *vengono nella favola le cose passate or lontane, quando s'introducono messi o altre persone a posta per recare simili novella . . . La via per miracolo contiene l'apparizioni de' morti, I sogni, le visioni, le profezie, i riposi divini, e simili cose*' ('Past occurrences and those that take place at a distance from the scene of the action may be said to be introduced *ex accidenti* when they are related by messengers or other persons who come upon the stage for the express purpose of relating them . . . Incidents may be said to be introduced miraculously when they are made known by apparitions of the dead, or by dreams, visions, prophecies, oracles or the like', tr. Bongiorno, *Castelvetro on the Art of Poetry*, 63).

49. Castelvetro's first definition of 'episode' (actions taking place at another time) corresponds to Aristotle, *Poetics*, 23.49a 35–7, on Homer selecting one action, but including others as 'episodes'; the second definition (actions taking place elsewhere) is Aristotle, 11.52a 23–9, on the man coming to Oedipus to reveal his parentage and effecting '*peripetea*'; the third, on filling out the particulars of an action known in summary form, is Aristotle, *Poetics*, 17.55a 34–55b 23, on working out plot detail. Castelvetro's fourth definition corresponds to Aristotle, *Poetics*, 11.52b 20–1, but further defines this sense in relation to all the previous definitions, excluding from it Aristotle's pejorative sense of 'episodic' as 'pointlessly digressive', *Poetics*, 9.51b 33–5.

50. Katherine Butler, 'Giacomo Castelvetro, 1546–1616', *Italian Studies*, 5 (1950) 1–36, 5; 8. Castelvetro tutored Sir Roger North's son John, and knew and 'probably read Italian with' Sir Philip Sidney, Sir Christopher Hatton, and Sir Francis Walsingham. Around 1580, he was living in Tower Ward, near or with Sir Horatio Pallavicino. On Giacomo Castelvetro's work for the printer John Wolfe, see R. J. Roberts, 'New Light on the Career of Giacomo Castelvetro', *Bodleian Library Record*, 13:5 (1990) 365–9.

51. Lodovico Castelvetro is frequently referred to in the endnotes to Sidney's *Apology for Poesy*, but the connection between their theories is not close. If Sidney was, as has been said, 'the first to introduce English readers to the literary theories set forth by Ludovico Castelvetro', observes Katherine Butler, 'one can only say that it was by opposing the Italian's main principles without ever naming him', 'Giacomo Castelvetro', 8.

52. Sidney, *Apology*, 111, lines 19–28. On 'Pacolet's horse', see Cyrus Mulready, '"Asia of the One Side, and Afric of the Other"': Sidney's Unities and the Staging of Romance', in *Staging Early Modern Romance: Prose Fiction, Dramatic Romance and Shakespeare* (New York: Routledge, 2009) 47–71.

53. Sidney, *Apology*, 110, lines 32–4, my italics.

54. For an analysis of Sidney's version of the 'unities' doctrine, involving the grafting of 'crisis plot' on to the 'artificial day', see Riggs, 'Artificial Day', 167–71.

55. Sidney, *Apology*, 110–11, ll. 41–3, 1–8.

56. Mack, *Renaissance Argument*, 170.

57. *Sir Clyomon and Sir Clamydes* (printed 1599), ed. W. W. Greg (Malone Society Reprints, 1913) line 9. Further references to this edition will be made by line number in the text.

58. Robert Y. Turner, 'Pathos and the "Gorboduc" Tradition', *Huntington Library Quarterly*, 25 (1962) 97–120, 113.

59. Thomas Sackville and Thomas Norton, *Gorboduc, or Ferrex and Porrex, Drama of the English Renaissance*, i: *The Tudor Period*, ed. Russell A. Fraser and Norman Rabkin (Upper Saddle River, NJ: Prentice Hall, 1976) 1.215. Further references to this edition are by act, scene, and line number in the text.

1

'*Quando?*' (When?) in *Romeo and Juliet*

Tempus ita quaeritur: quid anni, qua hora,—noctu an interdiu—et qua die, qua noctis hora factum esse dicatur, et cur eiusmodi temporibus (Time is inquired into as follows: In what season of the year, in what part of the day—whether at night or in the daytime—at what hour of the day or night, is the alleged act to have been committed, and why at such a time?, *Ad Herennium*, 2.4.7)

1.1. Shakespeare in Parts/Shakespeare is Pants?

In 1756, Dr Johnson published a small pamphlet entitled 'Proposals for Printing, by Subscription, the Dramatic Works of William Shakespeare'. Assembling justifications for such a bold undertaking, Johnson cited various 'causes of obscurity' in Shakespeare, one of which was the unfortunate 'exactness with which Shakespeare followed his authors':

> Instead of dilating his thoughts into generalities, and expressing incidents with poetical latitude, he often *combines circumstances unnecessary to his main design, only because he happened to find them together.* Such passages can be illustrated only by him who has read the same story in the very same book which Shakespeare consulted.[1]

Johnson was careful, of course, both here and in his more famous 1765 Preface, to explain that the unnecessary circumstantiality of Shakespeare's plots, though a defect in itself, could not detract from Shakespeare's greatness. In his plots Shakespeare insouciantly followed the popular taste of the age, neglecting the unities of time and place, but 'his chief skill was in human actions, passions and habits'. The irregular variety of incident in the stories he followed so artlessly thus actually permitted him the freedom to diversify his 'characters'.

This disposition of the age concurred so happily with the imagination of Shakespeare that he had no desire to reform it, and indeed to this he was indebted for that licentious variety . . . his chief skill was in human actions, passions and habits; he was therefore delighted with such tales as afforded numerous incidents and exhibited many characters, in many changes of situation. These characters are so copiously diversified, and some of them so justly pursued, that his works may be considered as a map of life, a faithful miniature of human transactions, and he that has read Shakespeare with attention, will perhaps find little new in the crouded world.[2]

It is a very familiar argument: Shakespeare's plots are *second-hand*; he did not make them up, nor care much about how they hung together: he flouted the 'rules' of temporal and spatial probability. His true interest and genius was in the depiction of human nature; disregard for plot is thus the condition that enables his characters' autonomy and truth-to-life, or, as we would now say, their 'selfhood'. This argument, articulated two and half centuries ago by Dr Johnson, still has wide currency and prevails as general common sense about Shakespeare's working practice and about what we value most in his plays. In March 2013 a reader of the *Guardian* newspaper online made this comment in response to the latest media eruption of the authorship debate:

Shakespeare's plots are uniformly pants . . . needlessly convoluted, most of them rehashes. If you're not along for . . . the startling insights into every aspect of existence, there's little to admire.[3]

What is most striking about this casual online comment is not the distance of its style from that of Samuel Johnson's, but the similarity, stylistic differences aside, of the general shape of the thought. For over three and a half centuries it has seemed true to say that Shakespeare's insights into human experience transcend *and don't need* his plays' shapeless, derivative plots. Student essays frequently open with declarations that Shakespeare's 'characters' are his greatest legacy, surpassing his merely borrowed plots. A recent book on *Shakespeare and Character* makes the argument somewhat more authoritatively:

Aristotle places plot ahead of character . . . Shakespeare tends to overturn the Aristotelian ranking of plot and character by reworking the traditional narrative types such as revenge tragedy, romantic

courtship, struggle for mastery between husband and wife, or the story
of growth-into-adulthood so that character displaces plot as the center
of interest in ways that determine the kinds of elements we find in the
plays and how those elements are organized . . . we are far more interested, say, in how the action of revenge seems to Hamlet than we are in
working out the revenge plot.[4]

Here, though plots are not said to be second-hand, they are transh-
istorical generic structures ('traditional narrative types') which stand
apart, as structures, from the 'character' whose sensibility and perception they serve to reveal: 'we are more interested in how the action of
revenge seems to Hamlet than we are in working out the revenge plot'.

To set out to contest a view that Shakespeare's 'characters' are the
beneficiaries of a carelessness about plot might seem an utterly super-
fluous undertaking at this stage in the history of Shakespeare criticism,
as if the materialist, deconstructive, and Lacanian critiques of 'character' had never taken place.[5] Indeed, the superfluity of the gesture
might seem to be compounded by the fact that the most vital work in
Shakespeare criticism over the last twenty years has been driven by
a desire to demolish the edifice of the very eighteenth-century editorial tradition to which Dr Johnson's observations belong.[6] Recent
decades have seen a thorough dismantling and discrediting of the tradition which produced the idea of Shakespeare as solitary genius, the
singular Author whose poetic Intention needed to be recovered and
restored to integrity from the mass of printers' and players' errors
and transgressions of transmission. Yet, oddly enough, 'character' has
emerged from this deconstruction virtually unscathed.

In a comprehensive critique of the complicity of modern anglophone Shakespeare criticism with these Enlightenment assumptions,
Margreta de Grazia and Peter Stallybrass identified four categories
'basic to the dominant post-Enlightenment treatment of Shakespeare'
which needed to be rethought. These were: the 'single *work*', the 'discrete *word*', the 'autonomous *author*', and 'the unified *character*'.[7] De
Grazia and Stallybrass showed how, in modern editions, the 'work' of
Shakespeare was an impossible unity created by ideologically driven
conjectures of authorial intention. The orthographic and semantic
plasticity of the Shakespearean 'word' was, in such editions, subject to anachronistic lexical and grammatical standardization. The
author 'Shakespeare' was an idealized construct, insulated from the

collaborative materiality of textual and theatrical production and separated from processes that enabled him to be a writer and subsequently ensured the transmission of his texts to us. Shakespearean 'character' was likewise revealed to be an eighteenth-century construction: sixteenth- and seventeenth-century playtexts had featured variable speech-prefixes which eighteenth-century editors had insisted on replacing with the consistent nomenclature of the play's 'characters'.[8] With these editors, too, began the practice of prefacing each play with a list of 'characters', enabling the latter to seem to pre-exist the play itself, and to take on a life of their own.

Since the publication of De Grazia's and Stallybrass's article in 1993—which synthesizes and acknowledges much ground-breaking work in the field, most notably that of Randall McLeod—the tenets of the Shakespearean text's materiality and dis-integrity have become an orthodoxy. Scholarly editions of Shakespeare no longer castigate the errors of pirated editions and memorial reconstructions, but embrace the fluidity and plurality of the play's varying texts. Criticism emphasizes the text's multiform instability and offers nuanced analyses of the material determinants of the processes of theatrical production—of repertory, rehearsal, casting, doubling, part-based memorialization, and of collaborative plotting. Of all De Grazia's and Stallybrass's post-Enlightenment categories, only 'character' has remained remarkably 'unified', resisting deconstruction. This is not in itself surprising, since the new emphasis on the materiality of theatrical production is also an emphasis on performance and on the body of the actor, which lends a somatic continuity and coherence to the mutable speech-prefixes that designate 'character' on the page. Both surprising and intriguing, however, are the terms on which Shakespearean character has achieved its new lease of critical life. These terms uncannily reproduce some of the structuring antitheses of eighteenth-century Shakespeare criticism. Once again the vitality of Shakespearean 'character' is ascribed to working practices that emphasize the contingency of plot composition and are defined against any humanistic or neoclassical interest in achieving temporal and spatial probability over the course of a whole fiction.

'Character' has, according to a recent essay collection, 'made a comeback' after '[h]aving all but disappeared from Shakespeare criticism as an analytic category in the second half of the twentieth

century'.[9] What has enabled this 'comeback' is, essentially, the disso-
lution of the illusion of the unity and completeness of the authorial
'work' and a corresponding new emphasis on the collaborative process and contingency involved in performance. This explains Laurie
Maguire's otherwise rather surprising declaration that 'Shakespeare
writes *roles*; it is actors who create characters.'[10] That 'character'
might, historically, have been the product of specific eighteenth- and
nineteenth-century reading practices becomes irrelevant—'much
character criticism is based on the novel, and the novel has no inter-
mediary', Maguire writes—what matter to the new character criticism
are inscribed traces of embodiment and performance, or what Robert
Weimann calls 'the actor-character'.[11] The concept of the whole play
as a discrete, finished product—once a staple of an author-centred
Shakespeare criticism—has given way to the concept of the play as a
provisional patchwork of assorted elements. Plays were, writes Tiffany
Stern, 'written patchily from the start', professionally 'plotted' and
then parcelled out to different writers; we may look for conceptual
integrity within scenes, Stern argues, but not across a whole play.[12]

The provisional and incomplete nature of the playtext—'loose-leaf
sheets, commissioned or swapped or shuffled with facile aplomb'—
along with the practice of distributing the different 'parts' as separate
documents for the actors to memorize in solitude—allows for a new
kind of analysis of Shakespearean character. No longer the imaginative product of 'Shakespeare the Author' working away in solitude,
'character' is now analysed as the effect of embodied and collaborative processes of actor-memorization and response to cues.[13] That
something as imaginatively generative as 'character' can emerge from
the 'jazz-like peril and contingency of performance' becomes itself
a marker of a truly 'Shakespearean' (for which read, 'collaborative')
effect. Shakespeare was less suspicious of actors than, say, Jonson;
moreover he wrote for a specific group of actors whom he knew well,
so that mutual knowledge and trust 'allowed for, and perhaps created,
the boundary-bending energy of his plays'.[14] And Shakespeare, as a
sharer in the Lord Chamberlain's Men, was in the unique position
of composing plays for actors he knew very well indeed. Bart Van
Es's innovative analysis of the relation of Shakespeare as a 'company'
man thus finds—once again—that one effect of collaborative work for

a given set of actors is the achievement of the 'psychological depth' that is the mark of 'character':

> [T]he development of Shakespeare's techniques of characterisation in the mid- to late 1590s is a consequence of his new position as owner and controller of the dramatic life of his plays. Shakespeare could now plan an entire play by thinking about the capacities of his actors—making contrasts between them a building block in the constructions of scenes . . . After 1594, when Shakespeare composed, he occasionally used actors' names instead of the names of characters and such slips reveal a new kind of creative process quite different from the humanist models that he had imbibed at school. Control over casting enabled the creation of psychological depth.[15]

This stimulating new body of work on Shakespeare's 'actor-characters' has indeed taken 'our minds off the solitary genius immanent in the text and removed from the means of mechanical and theatrical reproduction'.[16] But it has also deterred us from enquiring into the textual means by which Shakespeare's characters have seemed, to generations of audiences, readers, and critics, to live a life beyond the stage and page. 'Character' itself—understood in the sense of the inner life implied by words like 'development' and 'depth', as well as the inferred extramimetic continuity of a named role in an offstage 'elsewhere' between scenes ('You *Capulet* shall go along with me | And *Mountague* come you this afternoon')—is, more than anything else, an effect of a play's capacity to ask audience or readers to infer a coherent *fabula* from its *sjuzhet*. 'Character' implies the extramimetic life, extending imaginatively before, during, after, and elsewhere, that results from audiences' and readers' ability to imagine both inward causes (emotions, motives) and an outward expansiveness of time and space, all merely from the arguments of speakers onstage. In *Gorboduc*, such extramimetic effects of inward life and of outward temporal and spatial expansiveness were discernibly generated by Porrex's arguments against sending to know the reasons for his brother's rumoured military preparations. These are not effects that can be ascribed to theatrical collaboration or to working with known actors (though they are not, obviously, incompatible with such practices). In Shakespeare's plays, moreover, we see them advanced to such a degree that we take them for granted instead of recognizing them as an achievement.

To be able to talk about these extramimetic effects, we need to be able to conceive of compositional practices that extend beyond the integrity of the scene and the inscription of performance techniques within it. We need to be able to think of Shakespeare and of other dramatists as learning from the neoclassical reliance on diegetic techniques—such as Castelvetro's 'episodes'—to find ways of including the representation of offstage times and spaces, the representation of the 'unscene'. We also need to be able to think of Shakespeare and other dramatists reading chronicle histories and *novelle* with a mind to transforming their temporally and spatially expansive narratives into probable or provable *arguments* on the circumstantial topics of time and place. It is these arguments that enable audiences and readers to infer the exterior circumstances of time and place, as well as the inner circumstantial topic of *causa* or motive/purpose. Arguments enable audiences imaginatively to 'conceive' the play's temporality and shifts of location as believable and probable because they infer them in relation to the subjectivities—the motives and desires—of *dramatis personae*.

We need, in other words, to overcome our attachment to the eighteenth-century identification of 'probability' with a strict adherence to the neoclassical unities, for it is this identification that remains implicit, even in the most recent deconstructive work on eighteenth-century editing practices. In spite of Dr Johnson's assumption that Shakespeare's plays merely followed the plots of novels and romances written for minds 'not accustomed to balance probabilities' and in spite of Coleridge's theory that our receptivity to Shakespeare's plays depends on the 'slumber of our sense of probability' and the 'willing suspension of disbelief', the fact is that Shakespeare's plays do strive for temporal and spatial probability.[17] Our failure to recognize has partly to do with the semantic revolution that attended what Ian Hacking has called 'the emergence of probability' at the end of the seventeenth century, which transformed the older rhetorical meaning of probability into the mathematical likelihood of relative frequency.[18] The rhetorical and dialectical senses of arguing *probabiliter*—that is, making subject matter available to the mind's apprehension by 'proving' it through various topics—had vanished long before Coleridge or even Johnson. In this semantic revolution, all the vocabulary stayed the same—eighteenth-century literary criticism still speaks of 'probability', 'circumstances', and 'causes'—but the meanings ascribed to these terms have been subtly transformed.

Our failure to recognize the innovative ways in which Shakespeare's plays strive to make times and places imaginatively 'probable' also has to do with our insistence, even in the wake of the deconstruction of eighteenth-century editing practices, on seeing the available choices open to a dramatist in terms of a stark antithesis between an 'artificial order' demanding unified time and space, and a 'natural order' defined by permissiveness and latitude.[19] In 1947 T. W. Baldwin massively overstated the case for Shakespeare's dependence on Terentian five-act structure and was thoroughly refuted, in 1960, by Henry Snuggs, who, after an extensive survey, concluded that Shakespeare's plays eschewed the 'artificial order' of the Terentian crisis plot and stuck closely to their novelistic sources, beginning *ab ovo* and freely ranging in time and place, following the circumstances of the original.[20] Once again, then, in the mid-twentieth century, the antithesis between a regulated and unified neoclassical probability and a permissive and spontaneous 'realism' of time and space was reinstated. If Shakespeare did not go in for the full set of spatio-temporal regulations laid down by neoclassical theory, the wisdom goes, he must have merely followed the order of plots as he found them. As Nicholas Rowe put it, as early as 1709: 'His tales were seldom invented, but rather taken either from the true history, or novels and romances: and he commonly made use of them *in that order, with those incidents, and that extent of time in which he found them in the authors from whom he borrowed them*' (my italics).[21] Or, as we might put it nowadays, needlessly convoluted, most of them rehashes, Shakespeare's plots are uniformly pants.

1.2. 'It was the Nightingale, and not the Larke'

To sum up, then, Shakespearean 'character' has, since the eighteenth century, been assumed to be a creative effect of writing from the life, without any concern for neoclassical rules of dramatic probability. Against this, I propose to argue that if we consider time, place, and *causa* (motive or purpose) as three of the most important rhetorical topics of circumstance, we can begin to see that it is Shakespeare's innovative concern with the probable invention of arguments on these topics that has enabled generations of readers to infer from them the subjective experience and psychological depth to which we have given the name of 'character'. To demonstrate this, I will turn to the two early quartos of *Romeo and Juliet* (1597 and 1599), but first I would like to return briefly to the deconstruction of eighteenth-century editing practices.

In a mischievously funny and revealing essay on 'Editing and the Invention of Dramatick Character', Randall McLeod quotes Alexander Pope's hyperbolic claim that 'every single character in *Shakespear* is as much an Individual as those in Life itself', a claim which extended itself so far as to hazard that, 'had all the Speeches been printed without the very names of the Persons, I believe one might have apply'd them with certainty to every speaker'.[22] (It hardly needs to be said that Pope's commendation of Shakespeare's characters accompanied the observation that Shakespeare's plots merely '*follow'd the thread of any Novel as they found it*'.[23]) In insisting on character individuality, McLeod comments, 'Pope is quite offtrack.'

> However unified the interpretation of a Shakespearean role can be made to seem in performance or in modern editions, the very names of the Persons in the earliest Shakespeare texts very frequently vary.[24]

Not only do speech-prefixes vary—in the second quarto of *Romeo and Juliet*, for example, Lady Capulet's role is designated variously by '*Wife*', '*Old La.*' and '*Mo.*' in the course of a single scene—but, as McLeod shows, whole speeches are sometimes duplicated in ways which would pose a challenge to the individualization of 'characters' by their words alone.[25] McLeod selects one such crux from Q2 of *Romeo and Juliet*, the transition between Romeo's leave-taking of Juliet at her balcony, and the first entrance of Friar Laurence '*alone with a basket*', enacting the gathering of herbs at dawn. At this point in the text, Q2 duplicates a speech on the advent of daybreak:

> *Ro.* Would I were sleepe and peace so sweet to rest
>   The grey eyde morne smiles on the frowning night,
>   Checkring the Easterne Clouds with streaks of light,
>   And darknesse fleckted like a drunkard reeles,
>   From forth daies pathway, made by *Tytans* wheeles.
>   Hence will I to my ghostly Friers close cell,
>   His helpe to craue, and my dear hap to tell.
>
> *Exit.*

Enter Frier alone with a basket.

> *Fri.* The grey-eyed morne smiles on the frowning night,
> Checking the Easterne clowdes with streaks of light:
> And fleckled darknesse like a drunkard reeles,
> From forth daies path, and *Titans* burning wheeles:
> Now ere the sun aduance his burning eie,
>
>   (sig. D4ᵛ)

Evidently, as McLeod observes, the fact that this speech might be assigned indifferently to an old friar or a young lover shows that there is nothing in the strange simile of daybreak as a drunkard narrowly missing a road accident that is inherently 'redolent of the *personal* character' of either character. The speech is dramatically functional: it tells the time.

Yet to say this is not quite the same as to say that the strong sense we have of the subjectivities of the *dramatis personae* in Shakespeare's *Romeo and Juliet*—which is what we label 'character'—is entirely an effect of the editing practices of the eighteenth century. The play shows quite an extraordinarily innovative interest in what we might call the invention of arguments of Time through activating time-related topic questions such as 'when?' or 'how long?' or 'how old?' These scenes and dialogues organized around debating these topic questions serve as a way of both unifying the action and expanding representation into the past and the future. Diegetic representations of nostalgically remembered pasts or impatiently desired futures invite us to infer various psychological states that we then ascribe to the play's 'characters'. As G. Thomas Tanselle noted fifty years ago, scenes repeatedly feature conversations which ask questions about time, whether the question concerns disputing the signs of dawn (insisting that the lark's song is that of the nightingale, or that the morning's grey is the moon's reflected light) or how many minutes it will be till the nurse arrives, how many years it has been since someone last danced, how old a certain relative might be.[26]

This structuring of scenes and transitions between scenes around questions of time is by no means routine in non-neoclassical plays composed in the early 1590s. For example, in *The Lamentable and True Tragedie of M. Arden of Feversham in Kent* (1592) (a play in which Shakespeare is thought by some to have had a hand), the opening scene suffers precisely from a lack of 'invention' around the topics of time and place, so that the stream of encounters at and near the Arden household feels a little too predictable. As soon as Master Arden has left Alice to go down to the quayside to unload goods, we have the entrances of the go-between innkeeper; Michael, Alice's man; Mosby, her lover; and, finally, the painter whom Mosby met the previous night who has agreed to help them murder Arden.[27] At the end of this steady flow of entrances, Master Arden returns for his breakfast: 'In good time, see where my husband comes,' comments Alice. Yet the times and distances feel somewhat transparently functional, the entrances and encounters seem a bit pat. Alice no sooner thinks of Mosby, than Mosby is 'come to towne' and shortly after follows the stage direction, 'Here enters Mosbie'; Mosby tells Alice, 'I happend on a Painter yes-ternight'; in fewer than fifteen lines Alice and he are at the painter's house: 'This is the painter's house Ile call him foorth'.[28] The text does not invent arguments to imply any relationship between the purposes, desires, and fears of the *dramatis personae* and the times and spaces of the action. I am not talking here about the text indicating (for exam-ple) enough time to get out of the house and down the street; all that can be done by interpretation and performance. Nor am I talking about what used to be called (and perhaps still is) a 'time scheme'. Rather, I am concerned with the way in which indications of time and place may or may not be textually formulated to imply motive, desire, or anxieties—to be enmeshed in human purposes and plans. In the *Tragedie of M. Arden of Feversham* such implications are absent.

By contrast, in the second scene of *An Excellent conceited Tragedie of Romeo and Iuliet*, published five years later in 1597, the text shows how the audience becomes immediately involved in a hypothetical future—the future as desired by a father and a young suitor—by way of their negotiation over questions of time and age, and of the readi-ness or not of a young girl (Juliet) for courtship and marriage. We quickly grasp that the older speaker—Capulet—thinks his daughter too young to marry, and that he has repeatedly said so, as he responds to the young Paris's suit, 'What should I say more than I said before?' He then gives us his daughter's age in a curiously negative form, a negative or imperfect perfect tense—'Shee hath not yet attainde to fourteene yeares'.[29] The second quarto of the play, published in 1599, has 'Shee hath not seen the chaunge of fourteen yeares'.[30] In both

Q1 and Q2 the assertion of the daughter's immaturity is followed by a phrase that opens up a hypothetical future of anticipation, of mellowing towards the proposed occasion of marriage, though with a slightly more richly figured expression in Q2:

> Q1   'Let two more sommers wither in their pride
>   Before she can be thought fit for a Bride' (sig. B2ᵛ)

> Q2   'Let two more Sommers wither in their pride,
>   Ere we may think her ripe to be a bride'. (sig. B2ᵛ)

This exchange, following swiftly on the opening scenario of sexual aggression, adolescent frustration, and habitual feuding, condenses complex temporal effects. The futurity of deferral introduced here is metaphorically suggestive, in the evocation of a summer's burgeoning and withering, while the girl approaches readiness as a bride. More importantly, this subjunctive does not conclude but inaugurates the negotiation—the scene opens up that leisured temporal space of courtship required by the ecclesiastical insistence on mutual consent: 'But wooe her gentle *Paris*, get her hart, | My will to her consent, is but a part' (Q2, sig. B2ᵛ). The expansive future of the proposed courtship is then made dramatically immediate with a invitation '[t]his night' to an imagined first of many opportunities, an 'old accustomed feast' at the Capulets' house (Q2, sig. B2ᵛ). In the evocative *ekphrasis* of the yet-to-come feast, the motif of seasonal change and conflict between age and youth is glimpsed again. Young men enjoy the sight of 'well apparaild Aprill' treading on winter's heels, and such comfort, Capulet promises, Paris will 'inherit' in the 'fresh female buds' (Q1) (or Q2's less plausible 'fresh fennel buds') at the feast that evening. Then Capulet and Paris leave the stage, after which Benvolio and Romeo intercept letters of invitation and appropriate the feast's occasion for their own purposes. This second scene of the play has, in the short dialogue between Capulet and County Paris, introduced what Castelvetro might call an 'episode'—an implied series of actions which should follow on (*seguire*) from the present—but, of course, in this case, the future is not only implicit and extramimetic, it is also—and this is what accounts for the hint of pathos amid its bustle—merely hypothetical.

Although the relationship between Q1 and Q2 has been the subject of much controversy—once again, entertainingly deconstructed by

Randall McLeod in 'The Marriage of Good and Bad Quartos'—the sequence I have identified remains the same in both texts. The layered shifts of emphasis and aesthetic purpose witnessed by the variant texts, then, do not affect the conversation between Capulet and County Paris, which suggests that this dialogue is central to the whole play's temporal invention.[31] I use the word 'invention' here advisedly, because the shape of the dialogue inaugurating Capulet's wished-for future has clearly been invented from a circumstantial argument used in a different conversation in the Romeo and Juliet narrative as told by Pierre Boaistuau in 1559, and turned into English by William Painter and by Arthur Brooke.

It is a well-known and much discussed fact that Shakespeare altered Juliet's age, making her younger than in any of the earlier narratives—in Boaistuau *'elle n'auoit encores attainct l'aage de dix & huict ans'*, in Painter, likewise, 'she is not attained to the age of XVIII. yeares', while in Brooke, '[s]carce saw she yet full xvi. yeres'.[32] Critics have not, however, remarked that Juliet's age, in all these narratives, emerges not as an objective fact, but as part of a probable argument *pro et contra*—an argument proving reasons for and against the question of whether the present is a fit time for her marriage. And it is as a circumstantial argument that Shakespeare, too, introduces the topic, but with a difference that has enormous significance both for our sense of the 'characters' of Old Capulet and Juliet and for the temporal design of the whole play.

Shakespeare advances to the very inception of the play's action the shape of a conversation that, in the stories, only emerged at its crisis point. In the earlier narratives, parental conjecture over the question of Juliet's sexual maturity and readiness for marriage occurs late in the story, at a point when the parents also make their first appearance, after the death of Tybalt and Romeo's banishment. Julietta's mother assumes that distress for Tybalt's death is the cause of her daughter's grief, but when Julietta enigmatically denies this, her mother is plunged into an anxious quandary. Questioning household staff, she can find no positive information about the 'cause of care', so she finally conjectures to her husband, on probable grounds, that the cause is frustrated sexual desire and envy of her married friends. Julietta, seeing her friends all married, must feel impatient and envious, she suggests, 'To

see in wedlocke yoke the most parte of her feeres, | Whilst only she
unmarried, doth lose so many yeres'.[33] Having argued thus, she urges
her spouse to set about finding a husband for their daughter. It's at this
point that the argument borrowed by Shakespeare appears. Julietta's
father responds, in the manner of Old Capulet to County Paris, that
he has 'oft' considered her marriage but had always thought that a bit
more time should pass yet:

> Oft have I thought (deere wife) of all these thinges ere this,
> But evermore my mynd me gave, it should not be amisse,
> By farther leisure had, a husband to provyde;
> Scarce saw she yet full xvi. yeres: too young to be a bride. (ll. 1857–60)

The precise movement of mind traced here is clearly Shakespeare's
model. The difference is, of course, that in Boaistuau and Brooke,
the father's reiterated opinion that 'farther leisure' is required (or that
she is too young to marry) is presented as his memory of an argument with himself held within the recent past, while she still had not
attained a certain age limit—sixteen or eighteen years (*'i'auois plus-
ieurs fois pensé'*, 'oft have I thought'; *'voyant qu'elle n'auoit encores attainct'*,
'Scarce saw she').[34] In Shakespeare, the father's reiterated opinion
becomes the recollection of repeated responses to a suitor ('saying ore
what I haue said before' Q2, sig. B2ᵛ), while the conviction of Juliet's
immaturity is maintained as a current conviction, so that the decision
in favour of 'farther leisure' (in the sources part of a hypothesis of
the future entertained in the past) becomes the father's and the play's
subjunctive, or wished-for future: 'But *saying* ore what I haue said
before . . . Shee *hath* not seen the chaunge of fourteene years | *Let* two
more Sommers wither . . . | Ere we *may* think her ripe' (Q2, sig. B2ᵛ).
Thus Shakespeare has Capulet's subjective sense of time—the future
he desires, his project—shape the probable future of the play, our sense
of the play's time, at this moment. Even more significantly, where, in
the narratives, a 'real' Julietta exists and is known to the reader before
her parents make her the object of conjectures whether or not she is
sexually mature and impatient to marry, in Shakespeare's play these
conjectures—deliberately foregrounded as such in the rambling, lewd
testimony of the nurse—anticipate and affect our interpretation of
Juliet herself.

1.3. 'The very same book which Shakespeare consulted'

From this abbreviated discussion of the consequences of Shakespeare's transposition of a circumstantial argument from Boaistuau and Brooke, it is already evident that Shakespeare did not combine 'unnecessary circumstances' from the stories on which he drew, 'only because he happened to find them together'. Johnson was a bit disingenuous in suggesting that he knew this to be true because he had 'read the same story in the very same book which Shakespeare consulted'.[35] Johnson had not, in fact, trawled through the very volumes of Holinshed, Boccaccio, Cinthio, and Boaistuau consulted by Shakespeare, but had, rather, been involved in the publication of a collection of translations of Shakespeare's sources—a sort of Bullough's *Narrative and Dramatic Sources* of the eighteenth century. This collection was Charlotte Lennox's *Shakespear Illustrated: or the Novels and Histories on which the Plays of Shakespear are Founded* (1753).[36] Johnson furthered Lennox's project to the extent of composing, under her signature, the work's dedication to the Earl of Orrery; he evidently read quite thoroughly both her translations and her observations on the uses Shakespeare made of these sources. Indeed, Johnson's argument that Shakespeare's skill in human nature transcends his circuitous and cluttered plots is itself both indebted to and a critique of Lennox's observations, in which these shortcomings in Shakespeare's plays were unsparingly ridiculed. Lennox herself was a novelist—author of *The Female Quixote*—and her critique of Shakespeare was a defence of her own preferred genre, an argument against the contrivance of romance, made 'on behalf of the novel'.[37] Lennox distinguished between early modern romance and the modern novel, preferring the latter for its greater 'probability', which she defined, of course, in the post-Pascalian sense of empirical likelihood. Consequently, Lennox tended to prefer (anachronistically) the uncluttered, modern-seeming novellas of Matteo Bandello from which were derived the more argumentatively congested *histoires* by Pierre Boaistuau, whom English translators and whom Shakespeare followed in their turn. What Lennox disliked about Boaistuau and Shakespeare, we might say, was the presence in their texts of the sixteenth-century sense of 'probability' as the rhetorical testing or proving of arguments.

Dr Johnson almost certainly derived his sense that Shakespeare heedlessly followed his sources down circumstantial byways from reading Lennox's lament that in composing *Romeo and Juliet*, the playwright did not follow Bandello, but 'copied from a *French* Translation extant in his Time; or . . . from an *English* Translation of that *French* one, both very bad . . . many Circumstances injudiciously added, and many more altered for the worse'.[38] Where Bandello's hero and heroine spoke nothing but that which Lennox considered consistent 'with the Condition and circumstances' of the overwhelming passion of love and of sorrow at their love's losses, Boaistuau's and Brooke's Romeus and Julietta spend a great deal of time turning arguments over in their minds, conjecturing the forms of one another's intentions and motives, mentally levelling and retracting accusations against one another, or deliberating, in solitude, about ways and means of suicide.[39]

Lennox's views may seem quaintly irrelevant to us but in fact we still share them. The best of recent editions of *Romeo and Juliet* still offers an account of the narratives of Boaistuau and Brooke which, like Lennox's, is scathing about the stories' argumentativeness and which therefore, like Dr Johnson, is obliged to suggest that Shakespeare simply transcended them through his great skill in representations of life. Thus Jill Levenson, in her meticulous and excellent edition of *Romeo and Juliet*, argues that Boaistuau's and Brooke's narratives fail because while they use rhetorical figures of pathos to generate emotion, they contradict this emotion by aspiring to the verisimilitude of history, and including too many unnecessary circumstances, too many objective particulars. 'Sixteenth-century readers', Levenson writes,

> seem not to have noticed any failure of rhetoric or contradictions in the narrative's presentation, its measured account of boundless passion. Yet the lovers' story assumed the inconsistencies of its genre, which imitated both history and romantic literature. Aspirations to history account for the *circumstantiality* of the novellas which, like most Renaissance fiction, strain towards verisimilitude. As details fill out each res, slowing the tempo, they explain everything: Friar Lawrence's education; the use of rope ladders in Italy; Romeo's living arrangements in Mantua. Each act has a specific motive; each event, a distinct cause and inevitable results. At irregular intervals, however, the stock gestures of romantic love or anguish interrupt reasoned discourse.[40]

This sounds both very like Charlotte Lennox—these novellas are full of inappropriate 'circumstantiality', and the lovers should be impassioned, not busy debating and deliberating—and, on the face of it, this is all sensible and persuasive. And yet there is something wrong with Levenson's idea of a contradiction between reason and passion, just as there is with the idea that Shakespeare would somehow have read these narratives without being affected by, or interested in, their investigations of 'causes' and 'motives'. The problem with Levenson's analysis turns on her limitation of the emotional side of rhetoric to figures ('rhetorical figures of pathos') which makes her relegate 'circumstances' to the status of objective particulars lending historical verisimilitude. As topics to aid the invention of corroborative arguments of proof, however, circumstances contribute as much to the generation of emotion as do rhetorical figures of pathos.

Sixteenth-century readers, Shakespeare included, would not have found a 'contradiction' between rationality and passion in Boaistuau's and Brooke's tellings of the Romeo and Juliet story, for these readers shared the authors' understanding of probable argument as the rendering of emotionally engaged subjectivity. Both French and English stories—in common with many other fictions in verse and prose in this period—characterize people as continually engaged in conjecturing about one another's thoughts, deliberating about courses of action, or imagining possible scenarios in the most heightened, impassioned manner. In other words, people's thoughts are passionately argumentative, and the arguments highly imaginative. At every new turn of events, a character—whether Romeus, Julietta, Friar Laurence, or Julietta's mother—will suddenly be visited by 'a thousand thoughts' (l. 438) or 'an hugy heape of dyvers thoughtes' (l. 367) which will often take the form of explorations of the *causa* or cause—which means something like 'motive' or 'purpose'—by various kinds of probable argument. Thus, when Brooke's Julietta first learns of Romeus' identity as a Montague, she is oppressed by thoughts and spends seventy-six lines of verse conjecturing the 'cause' or motive behind his sudden show of love for her. Using proverbs, analogies, similes, and fictional examples of women abandoned by lovers, she finds it quite probable that he, as a Montague, intends to pursue the feud and to dishonour her father by seducing his only daughter. In a horrified, climactic envisaging

of this probability, she imagines Report trumpeting her defama-
tion through Verona, and she herself, though dead and entombed,
living on as a 'laughing stocke' (l. 401). But then, meditating the
arguments for the other side, she recalls probable signs—the look
in his eyes, his blushing and the faltering of his voice, his trembling
and near-ecstasy when they were together—and decides that these
are impossible to feign: 'Those arguments of love, craft wrate not
in his face' (l. 4210).

Brooke's Julietta is here doing what in the sixteenth century was
called 'meditating'. In the sixteenth-century rhetorical tradition,
'meditation' was the practice of running through topics in order
to rehearse the invention of arguments on either side of the case.[41]
Anyone who has read any prose fiction of the sixteenth century will
be aware of how frequently scenes of what seem at first to be private cogitation turn out to be scenes of the solitary and sometimes
vocal rehearsal of *pro et contra* arguments. So, for example, in Robert
Greene's *Pandosto*, Franion, the King's cupbearer, is asked by his master to commit treason. He withdraws to be 'secret in his chamber'
where he 'began to meditate with himself'. His 'meditations' take
the form of *sententiae*, offered as *pro et contra* arguments ('treason is
loved of many, but the traitor hated of all') and we are told that he
'muttered out these or suchlike words'.[42] Like Greene's and like so
many fictions of the period, Brooke's poem is fascinated by the way
in which the minds of those involved become imaginative by expe-
riencing doubts and inventing arguments to prove 'causes'. So, for
example, when Romeus first tries to see Julietta at her window, he,
not knowing when she'll be there, misses seeing her for about two
weeks, during which each of them entertains doubts about the other,
but, as Brooke is careful to note, she has greater 'cause' to imagine
more extreme horrors:

> Of greater cause alway is greater woorke ybred:
> While he nought douteth of her helth, she dreads
> lest he be ded. (ll. 479–80)

Sometimes, the work of hypothesis actually leads to hallucinations, as
when Julietta, about to drink the 'slepy mixture' given to her by Friar
Laurence, allows herself to doubt the latter's sincerity and the timing
of the plan and to ponder the horrors of waking in the vault. 'And

whilst she in these thoughts did dwell somewhat too long', Brooke writes,

> The force of her ymagining, anon dyd waxe so strong,
> That she surmysde she saw within the hollow vaulte,
> (a griesly thing to look upon) the carkas of Tybalt. (ll. 2378–80)

Nor are such probably imagined scenarios confined to the main characters. Almost everyone in the story engages in proving or refuting their doubts through argument and when they do not, this also calls for comment. Thus, when Julietta feigns an excuse to have her nurse sleep in another room, so that she can drink her mortifying potion, Brooke comments,

> And easely the loving nurse, dyd yelde to her desire,
> For she within her hed dyd cast before no doute. (ll. 2334–5)

Now, I do not deny that such detailed attention to the movements of the mind can make for tedious reading. Nor am I arguing that the imaginations of Shakespeare's characters in *Romeo and Juliet* are modelled after those in Brooke's poem (though there are indeed moments when this is explicitly the case, for example, in Act 4, scene 5, when Juliet hypothesizes doubtfully about the *motives* of Friar Laurence ('What if it be a poyson which the Frier | Subtilly hath ministered to haue me dead...?') or about the *time* ('How if when I am laid into the Tombe, | I wake before the time that *Romeo* | Come to redeem me...?'), culminating in a vision of waking horror ('Where bloudie *Tybalt* yet but greene in earth | Lies festering in his shroude' (Q2, sig. K1ʳ)).[43] My argument is, rather, that Shakespeare's characters are the product of a dramaturgy that innovates by employing similar circumstantial explorations of an implicit *conflictio causarum* or conflict of possible motives or purposes as a means of enabling us to imagine the transitions of time and place proper to narrative as if experiencing them subjectively in the 'now' of the stage. In other words, what makes times, places, and the events that occur in them seem more natural and vividly real in Shakespeare's plays than in those of contemporaries (whose stages are likewise dynamic or fluid) is that these times and places are already implicitly shaped as a part of people's having variously and dubiously 'cast before', imaginatively speaking, in just this way.

So the otiose 'circumstantiality' of Renaissance popular fiction, lamented by critics from the eighteenth to the twenty-first centuries, would be better appreciated and understood not as an artless excess of detail about *res* or 'the thing' (Levenson gives the example of Friar Laurence's education) but as the topics of rhetorical argument known as topics of circumstance (thus, Friar Laurence tells Julietta about his education—the topic of *educatio et disciplina*, a circumstance or accident of 'person'—as a confirmatory proof that the mixture he's giving her is genuinely going to work). Likewise, through the *ekphrasis* or description of the apothecary's shop, so puzzling to critics, the narrative (or, in Shakespeare's play, Romeo) anticipates the need for the artificial proof of *means* that will exonerate Friar Laurence in the hour of judgement. Boaistuau's '*Le paquet ouuert, ils trouuent entierement tout le contenu de l'histoire, mesmes le nom de l'apothicaire, qui luy auoit vendu le poison, le prix, & l'occasion pour laquelle il en auoit vsé*' becomes, in Shakespeare: 'This Letter doth make good the Friers words . . . And here he writes, that he did buy a poyson | Of a poore Pothecarie' (sig. M1ᵛ).⁴⁴

1.4. 'The true ground of all these piteous woes'

Shakespeare's knowledge of the *circumstantiae*, or the rhetorical topics of circumstance, has not been overlooked by critics. Indeed, *Romeo and Juliet* has, since the publication of T. W. Baldwin's *Shakspere's Small Latine & Lesse Greeke* (1944), figured as something of a *locus classicus* in the establishment of this fact. Baldwin observed that the denouement of *Romeo and Juliet*, in which the Watch discover and investigate the deaths at the Capulet tomb, closely follows the rules given in the pseudo-Ciceronian *Rhetorica ad Herennium* on the way to argue a 'conjectural' cause, or an issue of fact, by inventing arguments of suspicion from circumstances of place, time, duration, occasion, hope of success, and hope of escaping detection (*locus, tempus, spatium, occasio, spes perficiendi, spes celandi*).⁴⁵ The Watch, argued Baldwin, turn the mysteries of the slain bodies into a textbook investigation of the 'ground' or conjectural cause:

> *Watch.* The ground is bloudie, search about the Churchyard.
> Go, some of you, who ere you find attach.

> Pittiful sight, heere lies the Countie slaine,
> And *Iuliet* bleeding, warme, and newlie dead:
> Who here hath laine these two daies buried . . .
> We see the ground whereon these woes do lye,
> But the true ground of all these piteous woes
> We cannot without *circumstance* descry. (Q2, sig. L4ʳ)[46] (my italics)

'As the *First Watch* gathers the circumstances together, he finds that they argue "A great suspicion" against Friar Lawrence', writes Baldwin, and he concludes, from a detailed examination, that Shakespeare must have been closely following the text of the *Ad Herrennium*.[47] Quentin Skinner concurs. Quoting from the Watch's speech on the need for 'circumstance' to descry the 'ground' of the 'piteous woes' of the deaths, Skinner comments, 'With his pun on "ground"',

> The Chief Watchman reveals his understanding of the skills required to produce a confirmation in a conjectural issue. He knows he must focus not merely on the bloody ground but on what Thomas Wilson had called 'the chief title & principal ground' of the case. He also sees that this will require him, as he says, to descry the circumstances of the crime. He will need, that is, to enquire into time, place and persons, and thereafter consider the *argumentum* and *consecutio* in relation to what may have occurred.[48]

For Baldwin and Skinner, the scene bears witness to Shakespeare's technical knowledge in the representation of a judicial cause and in the use of 'circumstances' within that representation. This is right and illuminating as far as it goes, but we can extend this interpretation. '[T]he circumstances of the crime' as Skinner reads them slide too easily from forensic modes of enquiry into the objective facts of the situation. But the pun Shakespeare gives to the Watch discriminates between the visible 'bloudie ground' (blood being a sign) and the 'true ground' which *cannot be seen* without circumstance. This 'ground' might be glossed as *cause* or *explanatory* narrative, as Skinner's own example of Thomas Wilson's 'chief title & principal ground' suggests, or as Philip Sidney's reference to 'narration . . . as an imaginative ground-plot', or Shakespeare's own glossing of 'ground' as 'motive' in the 'grounds and motives of her woe'.[49] If we need 'circumstance' to *see the ground* in the sense of descrying motive or cause, this alerts us to the way in which circumstances, in Renaissance compositional theory, are forms of enquiry that themselves *constitute* the rhetorical probability and imaginatively visible reality of the motive or cause. In other words, it is not so much that Shakespeare represents an enquiry into circumstances as the objective facts of the case; it is, rather, that questions of circumstance, particularly the circumstance of Time, themselves shape and render imaginable the narrative and explanatory ground (as 'character', as 'motivation') of the 'piteous woes' we witness in *Romeo and Juliet*. So while Baldwin's and Skinner's insistence on the scene's adherence to a single source—the *Ad Herennium*—is illuminatingly precise, it prevents us appreciating, first, how pervasive references to the *circumstantiae* were in Renaissance compositional theory; second, how diverse were their recommended uses; and third and most important, how intimately they were related, through Cicero's and Quintilian's writings, to questions of descrying and distinguishing human intention and motive, or the 'cause' as an issue in dispute.

The classic seven circumstances were a set of questions—'*quis, quid, quando, ubi, cur, quem ad modum, quibus adminiculus*' (who, what, when, where, why, in what manner, with what help')—which, during the medieval period, were used in penitential enquiry as well as in rhetorical exegesis and in poetic composition—Chaucer, as Robert Watson has beautifully demonstrated, uses *circumstantiae* in *The Book of the Duchess* (*c*.1370).[50] By the second half of the sixteenth century, however, humanist texts on rhetoric and dialectic both varied the number of topics and greatly expanded their uses. Erasmus' *De copia* devoted a chapter to showing how 'circumstances' produce *copia*; he explains that they are what the Greek call *peristaseis* and, following Cicero and Quintilian, proceeds to divide them into two primary groups—the topics of *res* or deed and *persona* or person. Erasmus gives the first group as '*causa, locus, occasio, instrumentum, tempus, modus*' (cause, place, occasion, instrument, time, manner) and then adds the accidents of person, including '*natio, patria, sexus, aetas, educatio et disciplina*', and so forth.[51] Thomas Wilson's *Arte of Rhetorique* identified the classic 'seuen circumstaunces' (who, what, where, what help, wherefore, how), but in his rich commentary on Erasmus' *De copia*, the Wittenberg Professor of Rhetoric, Johannes Bernardi (known as Johannes Weltkirchius), observed that the numbers of circumstances vary, but that these topics supplied an 'incredible wealth of arguments and ornaments' for any case ('*ex qua incredibilis*

*Copia argumentorum atque ornamentorum in qualibet causa fere suppedita-
tur*').[52] Circumstances had a number of highly significant, fundamental uses for composition: Erasmus says they are valuable for
amplification, extenuation, vividness (*evidentia*), confirmation, and
probability.[53] In other words they have both aesthetic and ethical
force: as Weltkirchius notes, rhetoricians, dialecticians, theologians,
and jurisprudents all use them.[54] Weltkirchius, too, explicitly refers
the student to the connection between rhetorical circumstances
and the *applicita*, adjuncts and contingents of Rudolph Agricola's
dialectic.[55]

In elementary grammar school exercises the circumstances were
introduced first as topics from which to build probable narratives, then
as topics of proof, from which to confirm or refute (in Aphthonius,
'subvert') the probability of a narrative, and, finally, as topics
of vividness—*enargeia* or *evidentia*—with which to give narrative and
description imaginative presence.[56] So not only are circumstances
essential to establishing or questioning narrative credibility, they enable the bringing of a scene before the mind's eye. *Peristaseis* or *circumstantiae* thus represent, one classical scholar tells us, a point of contact
between the lessons of narration and description.[57] In the popular fiction of the period, a phrase like 'taking a survey of the circumstances'
means skimming the topics covered in a controversy.[58] And there is
no doubt, as we have seen, that Shakespeare was familiar with the
circumstantiae as topics; so, to take a knowing parody of their uses in
proving recognition, Shakespeare's Cymbeline goes methodically
through the 'Circumstantiall branches, which | Distinction should be
rich in', asking 'Where?', 'how . . .?, 'when . . .?' and 'Why . . .?', 'And
your . . . motiues . . .?' (5.5.3701–9).

Shakespeare was, however, more than merely familiar with the
circumstances as topics of invention; his wordplay on the relationship between 'circumstance' and the ability to see the occluded 'true
ground' of the tragedy's 'piteous woes' indicates his sense that *peristaseis* or *circumstantiae* were crucial to the making known of the inward
and always disputable question of human motive and human intention. The structural dependence of the legal 'issue' on a dispute over
intention that might only be discovered or made known by proving
the 'circumstances' lay at the heart of Cicero's rhetorical theory in
De inventione, as an important article by Michael Sloan has recently

revealed. Sloan shows that Cicero's source in *De inventione* is not, as has long been thought, Hermagoras, but Aristotle. It was Aristotle who, in the *Nicomachean Ethics*, first suggested that questions of 'the who', 'the what', the 'place', the 'time', the 'with what instrument', the 'how', and the 'for the sake of what' might be valuable in discriminating between voluntary and involuntary acts, and so establish degrees of responsibility. Following Aristotle, Cicero makes 'circumstances . . . the nucleus around which a speech of "dispute" (or one containing a "cause") is built'.[59]

One effect of the fundamental importance of circumstances to the rendering probable of the 'cause'—which in ethical, juridical, and rhetorical contexts is usually thought of as involving intention—is that the circumstances themselves can come to seem imbued with a potential intentionality and its associated affects. Thus, for example, Cicero, Quintilian, and the author of *Ad Herrenium* all write that in considering the place in which the act may have been done, account is taken of the opportunity that the place seems to have afforded for the act's performance. They offer several antitheses through which to question a place's opportuneness for an act, including questions of size and distance, and whether the place was remote or near, solitary or frequented:

> In connexion with the performance of the act . . . inquiry will be made about place, time, occasion, manner and facilities. In considering the *place* where the act was performed, account is taken of the opportunity the place seems to have afforded. *Opportunity*, moreover, is a question of the size of the place, its distance from other places, i.e., whether remote or near at hand, whether it is a solitary spot or much frequented.[60]

The 'opportunity' afforded by a place in being deserted or by a time in being secret thus comes to seem animate and voluntary itself; so, in *A Midsummer Night's Dream*, Demetrius effaces his own responsibility in an imagined scenario of rape, accusing Helena of laying her own modesty open to a guilty charge by, as it were, misguidedly *trusting* the opportuneness of the time, and *consulting* with the desertedness of the place:

> You doe impeach your modesty too much,
> To leaue the Citty, and commit your selfe
> Into the hands of one that loues you not,
> To trust the opportunity of night,

> And the illcounsell of a desert place
> With the rich worth of your virginity. (2.1.593–8)

This tendency to animate circumstances and diffuse ethical questions of intention, responsibility, and victimhood (being subject to malice or mischance) seems peculiarly Shakespearean; it is certainly present in different ways in both Q1 and Q2 of *Romeo and Juliet.* In Q1 Friar Laurence, stumbling across the corpses of Romeo and Paris, exclaims, 'what vnluckie houre | Is accessary to so foule a sin?' (Q1, sig.K2^{r}). Time's accessory guilt is intensified in Q2, and 'luck' is redefined as 'chance' in Q2: 'ah what an vnkind hower | Is guiltie of this lamentable chance?' (sig. L3^{v}). In a fascinating adjustment between Q1 and Q2 we see Shakespeare comment, through this quasi-animation of the circumstances, on their capacity both to prove guilt and extenuate. In Q1, after the Prince commands the Watch to 'bring forth the parties of suspition', Friar Laurence says:

> I am the greatest able to doo least.
> Most worthie Prince, heare me but speake the truth. (Q1, sig. K3^{r})

In Q2, however, this is transformed:

> I am the greatest able to do least,
> Yet most suspected as the *time* and *place*
> *Doth make against me* of this direfull murther:
> And heere I stand both to impeach and purge
> My selfe condemned, and my selfe excusde. (Q2 sig. M1^{r})

Here Friar Laurence acknowledges that the rhetorical circumstances of time and place animatedly 'make against' or impeach him.[61] Friar Laurence's use of the terms 'excuse' and 'purge' also reveals a knowledge—ostentatiously displayed in *Lucrece*—of the importance of circumstances in the issue of 'quality', that is, in the excusing or purging oneself of an accusation by pleading, for example, the necessity of circumstances beyond one's control.[62]

1.5. Juliet's Unconscious

Quentin Skinner has shown how Q2's version of Friar Laurence's speech forms a technically accomplished judicial *narratio*, proving his innocence. Skinner contends that Brooke's Friar appears, by contrast, unaware of the rules of forensic oratory.[63] We should not, however, overlook the way that Brooke in fact follows Boaistuau in shaping the entire denouement in a far more forensically attentive fashion than Bandello had done. This accounts, for example, for Boaistuau's invention of the apothecary's shop—deplored by Charlotte Lennox as an unnecessary circumstance—an *ekphrasis* which makes 'probable' or evident the poverty that motivates the apothecary and enables Romeo's purchase of means to kill himself. This forensically oriented proof of the topic of means (*instrumentum*) becomes important in Boaistuau, Brooke, and in Shakespeare, as Romeo's posthumous corroboration, by letter, of the Friar's innocence of murder.

My concern, however, is not the specifics of the forensic scene, but rather the way in which Shakespeare discovered, in his poetic adaptation of the forensic topics of circumstance, a way to make the fictional times and spaces of the theatre seem 'probable' by seeming to be experienced by the *dramatis personae*. In raising time-related questions, such as 'when' and 'how long?' and 'how old?', in dialogue, dramatic time becomes probable because of its being imbued with human intentionality and desire—time becomes a circumstance through which we think to descry the 'true ground' of passion and motivation animating the 'characters'. Shakespeare's dramaturgy is, then, a 'circumstantial dramaturgy' in the sense that it invents external circumstances of time, place, opportunity, means in order to invite us to imagine and argue for underlying, sometimes unconscious 'causes' of the sequence of action in the purposes and desires of the characters.

It is worth reminding ourselves that *Romeo and Juliet*, like all Shakespeare's plays, is *probable* in the sense that philosophical, sociological, and psychological interpretations of the action abound. Indeed, articles examining the characters of 'Romeo' and 'Juliet' for what they can tells us about the psychology of adolescence are still being written.[64] In the 1980s Edward Snow wrote a brilliant account of the lovers' language in which he noted that it is Juliet, not Romeo, whose imagination seems more 'open to the sexual act' and he attributed this to Juliet's link, through her nurse, with a primary realm of sexuality that is not subject to the phallic order that drives the Montague–Capulet feud and also structures Romeo's more limited sense of self in sexual relation. 'Her sexuality seems to issue spontaneously from a core of primary identifications, and in a form more

potentially disruptive to the male order of things than the anxious
phallic assertiveness . . . which produces "rebellious subjects".'[65] That
this powerful interpretation seems not only possible but illuminating
or *probable* is partly due to Shakespeare's transposition of the source
narratives' handling of the Capulets' debate over Julietta's age and
sexual maturity. Shakespeare transposes circumstantial arguments for
and against Juliet's sexual maturity to the beginning of the play. This
is a move of astonishing power, as it permits us to attach them both
to fate ('tragic irony' etc.) and to our sense of Juliet's own unconscious
through the topsy-turvy language associated with the stage Vice, here
embodied in the character of the nurse.

As many critics have observed, Old Capulet's vision of the expansive future of slowly ripening courtship between County Paris and his
own heir is linked to a reluctance to admit the passing of years and his
own ageing, expressed again in the form of the circumstantial question '*quando?*' ('when?' or 'how long is it now since?') in an exchange
with his cousin:

> 1. *Capu.* Nay sit, nay sit, good Cozin *Capulet.*
>   For you and I are past our dauncing dayes:
>   How long ist now since last your selfe and I
>   Were in a maske?
> 2. *Capu.* Berlady thirtie yeares.
> 1. *Capu.* What man tis not so much, tis not so much.
>   Tis since the nuptiall of *Lucientio:*
>   Come Pentycost as quickly as it will,
>   Some fiue and twentie yeares, and then we maskt.
> 2. *Capu.* Tis more, tis more, his sonne is elder sir:
>   His sonne is thirtie.
> 1. *Capu.* Will you tell me that?
>   His sonne was but a ward 2. yeares ago. (Q2, sig. C3ʳ)

As elsewhere, Shakespeare allows the circumstantial questions of time
and the accidents of age to assume a greater imaginative force by
remaining questions. And we see, characteristically, how the circumstances tend to become animate. In the phrase, 'Come Pentycost as
quickly as it will' the verb 'come' is used with a future date following as
a subject. This grammatical form gives the verb, which is really a subjunctive form, a latent anthropomorphism, a latent sense of desire.[66]
This is reinforced in that the phrase suggests, partly through the

submerged libidinal sense of 'come', that the feast day, the temporal limit of Pentecost, is hastening with desire into the present. That libidinal animation is stressed here, as Old Capulet challenges Pentecost to make him older: 'Come Pentecost as quickly as it will' (that is, 'no matter how fast Pentecost comes, it's still no longer than twenty-five years since we masked'). This grammatical form is frequent in *Romeo and Juliet*, as when Romeo later challenges 'after hours' of sorrowful consequence to prove stronger than the joy of the present minute, 'but *come what sorrow can*, | It cannot counteruaile the exchange of ioy, | That one short minute giues me in her sight' (Q2, sigs F1ᵛ–F2ʳ, my italics).

Old Capulet's rivalry with time is, as many critics have noted, plotted against the desire that seems, with a 'painful too-soonness' to propel Juliet herself into the fullness of sexuality and the pathos of early death.[67] Yet our earliest sense of this rivalry is the more powerful for being only diffusedly, immanently discernible through what Coleridge spoke of as the nurse's muddled 'memory of visual circumstances'. The famous scene, or circumstantially invented 'unscene', of the nurse's story of Juliet's weaning and fall, has been analysed variously as an 'all female scene', a premonition of tragedy, or most recently as a 'performance of memory' designed to counteract 'the isolating effects of part-based memorialisation'.[68] It, is, however, in a strictly formal sense, the inversion, by a fool or Vice, of circumstantial *confirmatio* (a use of circumstances to invent confirmatory proof) of Juliet's age. So when Juliet's mother challenges the nurse to 'know' her daughter's age, the nurse immediately confirms this by oath (fourteen of her teeth) then backs up this hilariously invalid proof (since she only has four teeth) by the diversionary question, '*how long is it now to* Lammas tide?' Juliet's mother answers, 'A fortnight and odd dayes', the slight imprecision of which answer the nurse proceeds to unravel into the defeat of all calculation, as follows:

Nurse. *Euen or odde, of all daies in the yeare come* Lammas *Eue at night shal she be fourteen.* Susan *and she, God rest all Christian soules, were of an age. Well* Susan *is with God, she was too good for me: But as I said, on* Lammaus *Eue at night shall she be fourteen, that shall she marrie, I remember it well. Tis since the Earth-quake now eleuen yeares, and she was weand I neuer shall forget it, of all the daies of the yeare vpon that day: for I had then laide worme-wood to my dug, sitting in the sun vnder the Doue-house wall. My Lord and you were then at* Mantua, *nay*

I doo beare a braine. But as I said, when it did taste the worme-wood on the nipple
of my dug, and felt it bitter, prettie foole, to see it teachie and fall out with the Dugge.
Shake quoth the Doue house, twas no need I trow to bid me trudge: and since that
time it is a leuen yeares, for then she could stand by lone, nay byth roode she could
haue run and wadled all about: for euen the day before she broke her brow, and then
my husband, God be with his soule, a was a merrie man, tooke vp the child, yea,
quoth he, doest thou fall vpon thy face? Thou wilt fall backward when thou hast
more wit, wilt thou not, Iule? And by my holydam, the pretie wench left crying,
and said I: to see now how a ieast shall come about? I warrant, and I should liue
a thousand yeares, I neuer should forget it: wilt thou not Iule quoth he? And pretie
foole it stinted, and said I. (Q2, sig. B4ʳ⁻ᵛ)

In this 'highly original piece of writing' we can also see the underlying
form of a parody of *confirmatio*—of confirmatory proof. The certainty
of the age that lacks two weeks and odd days comes apart with the
brilliantly nonsensical hyperbole: '*Euen or odde*, of all daies *in the yeare*',
while Susan's age, affirmed as the same as Juliet's, goes unspecified,
submerged in the ominous pathos of her death. Then we move into a
parody of circumstantial *evidentia* with the scene supposed to establish
eleven years since Juliet's weaning on the day of the earthquake. This
scene, often likened to a Dutch genre painting, encapsulates elements
that are inescapably interpreted symbolically and psychologically,
so the sun on the wall, the child's anger with the breast, the nurse's
abandonment and the old man's lecherous joke all come to signify
Juliet's crossing of the threshold of sexual initiation, her loneliness
in the vault, and the tragic accident of her death. But a too-overt
symbolism would have been a poetic and dramatic failure, and the
nurse's story works—is funny—as Coleridge noted, because of its
intelligibility as an attempt to prove, by evoking the circumstances of
the day of Juliet's weaning ('*of all the daies of the yeare*', again)—that
she actually does know Juliet's age. The extravagant irrelevance and
exuberant hints of beauty, pathos, and danger of her description of
the earthquake that shook the dovehouse and the little child that stood
'by lone' circle about what the rhetoricians would call the 'accident'
of Juliet's age, leaving it both as a question—we never know if she
should be fourteen come Lammas—and as the sense of 'accident'
in the other circumstantial sense of '*casus*', from '*cadere*' to fall—we
sense that something will fall out badly before she will reach that fourteen. The tragic plotting of the slowly ripening courtship desired by

Capulet against the 'love-performing night' impatiently awaited by Juliet is at the psychological and structural heart of the play, and is made possible by Shakespeare's creative attention to the dramaturgical possibilities of the *circumstantiae*.

Notes

1. 'Proposals for Printing, by Subscription, the Dramatic Works of William Shakespeare, 1756', in *Johnson on Shakespeare*, ed. Arthur Sherbo (New Haven: Yale University Press, 1968) 54–5, my italics. This pamphlet was given prominence as part of Malone's own preface in his edition of 1790 and in the Boswell–Malone edition of Shakespeare's works in 1821. See volume i of *The Plays and Poems of William Shakespeare with the Corrections and Illustrations of Various Commentators . . . by the late Edmund Malone* (London: J. Rivington, 1821) 198 (henceforward, *Boswell-Malone*).

2. *Johnson on Shakespeare*, 49.

3. 'chemsatain', 30 March 2013. See the comments to Dalya Alberge, 'Shakespeare Scholars unite to see off the claims of the "Bard deniers"', *The Guardian*, 30 March 2013, a review of Paul Edmonson and Stanley Wells, *Shakespeare Beyond Doubt: Evidence, Argument, Controversy* (Cambridge: Cambridge University Press, 2013) (<http://www.guardian.co.uk/culture/2013/mar/30/shakespeare-scholars-silence-doubters>).

4. Paul Yachnin and Jessica Slights (eds), *Shakespeare and Character: Theory, History, Performance, and Theatrical Persons* (New York: Palgrave Macmillan, 2009) 7.

5. See, for example, Harry Berger, 'What Did the King Know and When Did He Know It? Shakespearean Discourses and Psychoanalysis', *South Atlantic Quarterly*, 88:4 (1989) 811–62; Alan Sinfield, *Faultlines: Cultural Materialism and the Politics of Dissident Reading* (Oxford: Clarendon Press, 1992).

6. Margreta de Grazia, *Shakespeare Verbatim: The Reproduction of Authority and the 1790 Apparatus* (Oxford: Clarendon Press, 1991); Randall McLeod, 'Un "Editing" Shak-speare', *SubStance*, 10/11 (1981/2) 26–55.

7. Margreta de Grazia and Peter Stallybrass, 'The Materiality of the Shakespearean Text', *Shakespeare Quarterly*, 44:3 (1993) 255–83, 257.

8. It is, however, worth noting that in the 1623 Folio, a list at the end of *Measure for Measure* gives the names of the characters, although titled, 'The names of all the Actors'; see *The Norton Facsimile: The First Folio of Shakespeare*, ed. Charlton Hinman, second edition with an introduction by Peter W. M. Blayney (New York: W. W. Norton, 1996), 102.

9. Yachnin and Slights, *Shakespeare and Character*, 1.

10. Laurie Maguire, 'Actor–Audience Boundaries and *Othello*', *Proceedings of the British Academy*, 181 (2010–11) 132.

11. Maguire, 'Actor–Audience Boundaries', 132–3.

12. Tiffany Stern, *Documents of Performance in Early Modern England* (Cambridge: Cambridge University Press, 2009) 2, 11, 15.

13. Tiffany Stern and Simon Palfrey, *Shakespeare in Parts* (Oxford: Oxford University Press, 2007) 4.

14. Stern and Palfrey, *Shakespeare in Parts*, 78, 5.

15. Bart Van Es, *Shakespeare in Company* (Oxford: Oxford University Press, 2013) 98.

16. De Grazia and Stallybrass, 'Materiality of the Shakespearean Text', 283.

17. *Coleridge's Criticism of Shakespeare*, ed. R. A. Foakes (Detroit: Wayne State University Press, 1989) 36–7.

18. Ian Hacking, *The Emergence of Probability: A Philosophical Study of Early Ideas about Probability, Induction and Statistical Inference* (Cambridge: Cambridge University Press, 1975). On 'semantic revolutions', see Marc Cogan, 'Rudolphus Agricola and the Semantic Revolutions of the History of Invention', *Rhetorica*, 2.2 (1984) 163–94.

19. I owe this formulation to Peter Womack, 'The Comical Scene: Perspective and Civility on the Renaissance Stage', *Representations*, 101 (Winter 2008) 32–56.

20. T. W. Baldwin, *Shakespeare's Five-Act Structure* (Urbana: University of Illinois Press, 1947); Henry L. Snuggs, *Shakespeare and the Five Acts: Studies in a Dramatic Convention* (Washington: Vantage Press, 1960).

21. Nicholas Rowe, 'Some Account of the Life, &c. of William Shakespeare', in *The Plays of William Shakespeare, accurately printed from the text of Mr Malone's Edition*, 7 vols (London: J. Rivington, 1790) vii. xiii–iv.

22. *The Works of Shakespeare in Six Volumes Collated and Corrected by the former editions, by Mr Pope* (London: Jacob Tonson, 1725) i. ii–iii.

23. *Works of Shakespeare . . . Corrected . . . by Mr Pope*, i. ii–iii.

24. Random Cloud, '"The very names of the Persons": Editing and the Invention of Dramatick Character', in David Scott Kastan and Peter Stallybrass (eds), *Staging the Renaissance: Reinterpretations of Elizabethan and Jacobean Drama* (London: Routledge, 1991) 88–96, 88.

25. *The Most Excellent and lamentable Tragedie, of Romeo and Iuliet . . . As it hath bene sundry times publiquely acted, by the right Honourable the Lord Chamberlaine his Seruants* (London: Thomas Creede, 1599) sigs B4^{r-v}.

26. G. Thomas Tanselle, 'Time in *Romeo and Juliet*', *Shakespeare Quarterly*, 15:4 (1964) 349–61, 355.

27. *The Lamentable and True Tragedie of M. Arden of Feversham in Kent* (London: Edward White, 1592) sigs A2^r–B2^r.

28. *Lamentable and True Tragedie*, sigs A3^v, A4^v, B1^r.

29. *An Excellent conceited Tragedie of Romeo and Iuliet. As it hath been often (with great applause) plaid publiquely, by the right Honourable the L. of Hunsdon his Servants* (London: John Danter, 1597) sig. B2^{r-v}. Further references to Q1 will be given in the text.

30. *The Most Excellent and lamentable Tragedie, of Romeo and Iuliet. Newly corrected, augmented and amended: As it hath bene sundry times publiquely acted, by the right*

Honourable the Lord Chamberlaine his Seruants (London: Thomas Creede, 1599) sig. B2ᵛ. Further references to Q2 will be given in the text.

31. On the history of critical debate concerning the provenance and relationship of Q1 and Q2 of Romeo and Juliet, see Romeo and Juliet, ed. Jill L. Levenson (Oxford: Oxford University Press, 2000) 114–25.

32. See Pierre Boaistuau, Histoires Tragiques Extraictes de Oeuvres Italiennes de Bandel, & mises en nostre langue Françoise (Paris, 1559) fol. 64ʳ; William Painter, The Palace of Pleasure, ed. Joseph Jacobs, 3 vols (New York: Dover, 1966) iii. 104; Arthur Brooke, The Tragicall Historye of Romeus and Juliet [1562] in Narrative and Dramatic Sources of Shakespeare, ed. Geoffrey Bullough, i: Early Comedies, Poems, Romeo and Juliet (London: Routledge and Kegan Paul, 1977) 284–363, l. 1860.

33. Brooke, Romeus and Juliet, ll. 1845–6. Further line references will appear in the text.

34. Boaistuau, Histoires tragiques, fol. 64ʳ.

35. Johnson, 'Proposals for Printing', in Johnson on Shakespeare, ed. Sherbo, 54–5.

36. Shakespear Illustrated: or the Novels and Histories On which the Plays of Shakespear Are Founded, Collected and Transcribed from the Original Authors, 3 vols (London, 1753).

37. Jonathan Brody Krammick, 'Reading Shakespeare's Novels: Literary History and Cultural Poetics in the Lennox–Johnson Debate', Modern Language Quarterly, 55:4 (1994) 429–53.

38. Lennox, Shakespear Illustrated, 89.

39. Lennox, Shakespear Illustrated, 94–5.

40. Levenson (ed.), Romeo and Juliet, introduction, 13, my italics.

41. See Kathy Eden, Friends Hold All Things in Common: Tradition, Intellectual Property and the Adages of Erasmus (New Haven: Yale University Press, 2001) 74, who refers to Cicero, De oratore, 1.130.36, 'quid Crassus agitat, meditandi aut dicendi causa' ('observing what Crassus was doing for the purposes of training or rehearsal'). See also John Brinsley, Ludus literarius: or, The Grammar Schoole (London: Thomas Man, 1612) 182, glosses 'Meditation' as 'to runne through those places curiously in their mindes' to 'inuent matter'.

42. Robert Greene, Pandosto. The Triumph of Time (1588) in The Winter's Tale, ed. Stephen Orgel (Oxford: Oxford University Press, 1996) 238–9.

43. Brian Cummings reads Juliet's 'How if . . . I wake before the time that Romeo | Comes to redeem me?' as a confrontation of mortal fear, taking 'poison as if in preference to a life'. This seems strained; her fear is not of death; nor does she 'take poison'. See Mortal Thoughts: Religion, Secularity and Identity in Shakespeare and Early Modern Culture (Oxford: Clarendon Press, 2013) 183.

44. 'When they opened the letter, they found the whole contents of the story, even the name of the apothecary who had sold him the poison, the price and the use he had for it', Boaistuau, Histoires tragiques, fol. 84ᵛ.

45. T. W. Baldwin, *William Shakspere's Small Latine & Lesse Greeke*, 2 vols (Urbana: University of Illinois Press, 1944), ii. 76–81. See [Cicero], *Rhetorica ad Herrenium*, tr. Harry Caplan (Cambridge, Mass.: Harvard University Press, 1954) 2.2.3–2.8.12.

46. Baldwin, *Small Latine*, 77–8.

47. Baldwin, *Small Latine*, 77–8.

48. Quentin Skinner, *Forensic Shakespeare* (Oxford: Clarendon Press, 2014) 271.

49. Thomas Wilson, *Arte of Rhetorique* (London: 1585) 89, 'A state [*status*] generally, is the chiefe ground of a matter'; Philip Sidney, *An Apology for Poetry*, ed. Geoffrey Shepherd, rev. R. W. Maslen (Manchester: Manchester University Press, 2006) 103.31; Shakespeare, *A Lover's Complaint, in Complete Sonnets and Poems*, ed. Colin Burrow (Oxford: Oxford University Press, 2002) l. 63.

50. See D. W. Robertson, 'A Note on the Classical Origin of "Circumstances" in the Medieval Confessional', *Studies in Philology*, 43 (1946) 6–14; Rita Copeland, *Rhetoric, Hermeneutics, and Translation in the Middle Ages* (Cambridge: Cambridge University Press, 1991) 66–86; Robert Watson, 'Dialogue and Invention in the "Book of the Duchess"', *Modern Philology*, 98:4 (2001) 543–76.

51. Desiderius Erasmus of Rotterdam, *Copia: Foundations of the Abundant Style*, tr. Betty I. Knott, Collected Works of Erasmus (Toronto: University of Toronto Press, 1974–) [hereafter *CWE*] xxiv. 591; Erasmus, *De copia*, ed. Betty I. Knott, *Opera omnia* (Amsterdam: North Holland, 1969–) ordinis I, tome 6 [hereafter *ASD*, I:6] 218.

52. Wilson, *Arte of Rhetorique*, 18–24; *D. Erasmi Roterodami de duplici copia verborum ac rerum* (London: Henry Middelton, 1573) fols 134^{r-v}.

53. Erasmus, *ASD*, I:6:218, ll. 521–2.

54. Erasmus, *De copia* (1573), fol. 134^r.

55. Erasmus, *De copia* (1573), fol. 134^r; on Agricola's interest in literature, see Peter Mack, 'Rudolph Agricola's Reading of Literature', *Journal of the Warburg and Courtauld Institutes*, 48 (1985) 23–41.

56. *Aphthonius Sophistae Progymnasmata, partim a Rodolpho Agricola partim a Ioanne Maria Cataneo Latinitate donate, cum . . . Scholijs Reinhardi Lorichii* (London: Thomas Marsh, 1575) fols 17^{r-v}; fols 192^{r-v}, 194^v. Agricola's translation of Aphthonius, with commentary by Reinhard Lorichius, further spread Agricolan and Erasmian influence, as Lorichius imported extensive material from the *De copia*. In this edition, the circumstances form part of the second lesson, on narrative. In lessons five and six students are given exercises in *refutatio* and *confirmatio*: the confirmation and refutation of a narrative's likelihood, for which the *circumstantiae* provide topics. Finally, in lesson twelve, the elements of *ekphrasis* or *descriptio* are identified with the circumstances of 'person, thing, time, place' and linked, through reference to Erasmus, with *enargeia*.

57. Ruth Webb, 'The *Progymnasmata* as Practice', in Yun Lee Too (ed.), *Education in Greek and Roman Antiquity* (Leiden: Brill, 2001) 312.

58. Barnabe Riche, *The Adventures of Brusanus, Prince of Hungaria*, ed. Joseph Khoury (2013) 225.

59. Michael Sloan, 'Aristotle's Nicomachean Ethics as the Original Locus for the Septem Circumstantiae', *Classical Philology*, 105 (2010) 236–51; 248.

60. Cicero, *De inventione*, tr. H. M. Hubbell (Cambridge, Mass.: Harvard University Press, 1949) I.xxvi.38. Note the question of Cicero's subjunctive ('*in quo res gesta sit*', which is translated as an indicative, 'in considering the place where the act was performed'). See also Quintilian, *Inst.*, 5.10.37.

61. Quintilian, *Inst.*, 7.2.42–4, discusses how to argue that a deed was planned. First you ask whether the accused *wished* to do it, but then you consider whether they *could have done it*, and for that you discuss 'Place and Time. For example, theft: was the place inaccessible or frequented? Was the time day, (when there are more witnesses), or night, (when there is more opportunity?)'.

62. See Chapter 2, section 2.4.

63. Skinner, *Forensic Shakespeare*, 178–83.

64. Marjorie Cox, 'Adolescent Process in *Romeo and Juliet*', *Psychoanalytic Review*, 63:3 (1976) 379–92; Hyman L. Muslin, 'Romeo and Juliet: The Tragic Self in Adolescence', *Adolescent Psychiatry* (1982) 106–17; Paul Schwaber, 'For Better and for Worst: *Romeo and Juliet*', *Psychoanalytic Study of the Child*, 61 (2006) 294–307.

65. Edward Snow, 'Language and Sexual Difference in *Romeo and Juliet*', in John F. Andrews (ed.), *Romeo and Juliet: Critical Essays* (London and New York: Garland, 1993) 371–401; 388, 390–1.

66. See *OED*, '*come* (verb) . . . is used with a future date following as subject, as in French *dix-huit ans vienne la Saint-Martin,—viennent les Pâques*, "eighteen years old come Martinmas,—come Easter"; i.e. let Easter come, when Easter shall come.'

67. Barbara Everett, '*Romeo and Juliet*: The Nurse's Story', *Critical Quarterly*, 14:2 (1972) 129–39, 135.

68. Lina Perkins Wilder, 'Toward a Shakespearean "Memory Theater": Romeo, the Apothecary, and the Performance of Memory', *Shakespeare Quarterly*, 56:2 (2005) 156–75.

2

'Imaginary Work'

Opportunity in Lucrece *and in* King Lear

2.1. 'This weaues it selfe perforce into my businesse'

In the Folio text of *King Lear*, the second act opens with a transition of location for which little, if anything, has prepared the audience. Through the first five scenes we pick up hints of what is to come in exchanges that characteristically combine an impression of haste and immediacy with an implied hinterland of plotting, foresight, and policy. 'I thinke our Father will hence *to night*,' confides Goneril immediately after Lear's division of the kingdom; 'That's most certaine,' her sister replies, 'and with you: next moneth, with vs' (1.1.312–13).[1] Relocation to a new scene—Gloucester's house—neatly uses implied distance to constitute the immediacy of the King's departure as recent *news*, the stuff of political conjecture ('Kent banish'd thus? and France in choller parted? | And the King gone *to night*?', 1.2.358–9). In the brilliant third scene, which sketches in the disruptive habits of Lear as Goneril's house guest ('*By day and night*, he wrongs me, *euery howre* | He flashes into one grosse crime, or other' 1.3.510–11, my italics), Goneril urges her steward to exacerbate the situation so as to propel her father towards Regan in Cornwall: 'If he distaste it, let him to my Sister,' she seems to shrug, while doing all she can to ensure that this crisis will come to pass: 'let his Knights haue colder lookes among you . . . Ile write straight to my Sister to hold my course' (1.3.521–7). The row that breaks out in the following scene as Goneril confronts her father produces the expected reaction like clockwork.

> *Lear.* Darknesse, and Diuels.
> Saddle my horses: call my Traine together.
> Degenerate Bastard, Ile not trouble thee;
> Yet haue I left a daughter. (1.4.762–5)

After Lear has stormed offstage we experience the first of many temporal sleights, as it were, of *trompe l'œil*. An event which has just happened (the row over the hundred knights) has somehow already become part of the previous scene's future planning ('Ile write straight to my Sister'). 'What he hath vtter'd I haue writ my Sister,' Goneril now tells Albany, 'If she sustaine him, and his hundred Knights | When I haue shew'd th'vnfitnesse . . .' (1.4.853–5), the unfinished conditional is interrupted by the entry of her steward. 'What', Goneril asks him, 'haue you writ that Letter to my Sister?' (1.4.858). R. A. Foakes, the editor of the third Arden edition, calls this (quoting G. K. Hunter) Shakespeare's 'foreshortening the action'.[2] This phrase names the scene's temporal oddity, the impossibility of the steward, Oswald, having had time to incorporate the effects of the most recent row in any letter to Regan. The dramatic effect, Foakes observes, 'is to hint that Goneril has planned more in advance than the scene shows'. Hints that the letters have been brought up to date even as the events occur onstage produce a sense of the offstage world as one of continuous forethought, of preparation to strike in the heat of the moment ('We must do something, and i'th'heate,' as Goneril earlier said). It is not just a 'foreshortening of action' in the sense of a dramatic economy. Rather, this particular analeptic effect is one of implication—the folding into the present moment of a temporal and spatial elsewhere of forward planning, an impossible *then* and *there* which only exists in the form of a readiness to seize the *here* and *now*: 'Take you some company, and away to horse . . . Get you gone, | And hasten your return.'

The kind of here and now that can be seized, of course, has a special quality, that of fittingness or instrumentality. In the early modern period it was known as *Occasio* or *Opportunity*. Opportunity is a way of perceiving the present moment from the vantage of foresight—a concept vividly expressed in ekphrastic and emblematic traditions as the seizing of Occasion's forelock—hence the hints of advanced planning.[3] Many critics have commented on the temporal distortions of *Lear* noted by G. K. Hunter and R. A. Foakes, as well as on the play's geographical/topographical imprecisions. These apparent warpings of both time and place contribute to the impossible sequences whereby letters appear to deliver intelligence of events that have had scarcely time to occur, let alone be textually transferred with such alacrity. Explanations have been offered: A. C. Bradley thought geographical vagueness compensated by the universalizing 'vastness' of the tragedy as a consequence; W. W. Greg thought the play's temporal and topographical vagueness was 'designed to prevent topographical difficulties impeding the action'.[4] Jonathan Goldberg deconstructively pointed to the 'foundational illusoriness' of a play in which 'letters can arrive before they were sent'; alternatively, the social history of letter-carrying informs Alan Stewart's suggestion that we see the action as unlocated, 'a play of purely interpersonal relations . . . in which letters brought by personal bearers are crucial'.[5]

Yet all these critical approaches to spatio-temporal oddities of *Lear* proceed from the assumption that the dramatic norm is a *fabula* that may be coherently inferred from the temporal and spatial indicators of the *sjuzhet*. The outline of the play is, says Bradley, quite clear and 'anyone could write an "argument"' of it, but the attempt to 'fill in the detail' would produce confusion.[6] For Goldberg, *Lear*'s preposterous temporalities of Act 2 register illusoriness as a textual condition, acknowledged in the way Edgar's illusionistic description of 'Dover cliff' in Act 4 invokes annihilation and 'nothing' as the founding of all representation.[7] If, however, we consider Shakespeare's use, in *Romeo and Juliet*, of the circumstantial topic of *tempus*, Time, as a way of organizing dialogue so as to imply a *fabula* that seems both coherent and located in subjective experience, we can see that the topics of circumstance offered Shakespeare a range of ways to imply, along with the coherence of the *fabula*, different kinds of ethical or 'character' distinction (if we use 'character' as the translation of Latin, *mos, moris*, or Greek, *ethos*). It is often observed that the 'characters' of *Lear* are not very particularized or psychologically interesting. Bradley observed that they are more like 'the powers of good and evil in the world'.[8] Peter Womack has linked the 'good' characters in the play to the dialectical function of negation; they all at one time or another assume the role of 'Nobody', whereas, as he puts it,

> The political action of *Lear* takes place in the realm of Somebody, with its deceptions, its cruelty, its flatly literal contests for power. The effect of the unremitting self-interest of this sphere is to drive more and more of the characters into varieties of non-existence.[9]

The very broad ethical distinction that the spatio-temporal circumstances of *Lear* might be inviting us to draw, then, would be that between those struggling to be 'Somebody' and those exiled by them into the state of being 'Nobody'. This very distinction is implied in the forensic conception of *Occasio* or Opportunity as a source of arguments for the ease with which crime or oppression manipulates the resources of temporal and spatial contingency. 'Opportunity' in the forensic tradition describes the fitness of both place and time for the plotting of crime: Cicero thus invokes *opportunitas* as part of the consideration of a place's fitness, but also uses the term to distinguish 'occasion' from 'time'—'Time' (*tempus*). 'Occasion', he says, is 'a period of *time* offering a convenient opportunity' (*opportunitatem*).[10] In Erasmus' *De copia*, students were taught that *occasio*, also called 'opportunity', was to be understood as a topic of 'arguments and conjectures about ease and possibility', for example that it is easier for 'those without foresight to be oppressed by the cunning, the poor by the rich' (*'vt facilius est . . . improuidos ab insidiosis, pauperes a diuite opprimi'*).[11] As such, *occasio* or *opportunity* represents time, space, messengers, letters alike as aspects of the amoral ease with which a certain, usually oppressive, purpose or undertaking may find out or discover new resources.

In *Lear*, the first scene of Act 2 offers the most striking instance of the dramatization of the unexpected coinciding of time, place, and news being turned into Opportunity when the entrance of the Bastard Edmund signals to us that we are back at Gloucester's house. Edmund greets a servant (Curran) who tells him that 'the Duke of *Cornwall*, and *Regan* his Duchesse | Will be here . . . this night' as well as hinting of 'likely Warres toward' between Cornwall and Albany (2.1.931–2, 938–9). Nothing in the first five scenes has prepared an audience for this news: apart from Lear's 'Go you before to *Gloster* with these Letters' (which editors tend to emend or explain away, 1.5.875) indications have been that all the actors in this drama (letters, messengers, even Lear himself) have been heading towards Cornwall. Now Cornwall, it seems, is heading towards Gloucester. The sense of sudden, unexpected reversal is deliberate: Lear comments on his arrival at Gloucester's, ''Tis strange that they should so depart from home, | And not send backe my Messengers,' and a Gentleman replies, 'As I learn'd, | The night before, there was no purpose in them | Of this remoue' (2.2.1273–7). If we scarcely notice the bizarre detour that has messengers and royalty making it all the way from Albany to Cornwall and thence to Gloucester in 'this present euening'

(2.1.1040), this may be because what is first immediately apparent to us is the fittingness of the opportunity it presents to Edmund; that is the *ease* with which means make themselves available, through this unexpected diversion and its appropriated motives, to his purpose of incriminating Edgar. 'This weaues it selfe perforce into my businesse' (2.1.944), he says gleefully, and proceeds, with astonishing facility and success, to persuade Edgar that Cornwall's arrival somehow targets him, that the darkness itself counsels him to escape ('You haue now the good aduantage of the night', 2.1.952). He uses Curran's rumour of political difference to hint that inadvertently dangerous words have precipitated Cornwall's arrival ('Hee's comming hither, now, i'th'night, i'th'haste,' 2.1.954) or even, mysteriously, Albany's anger ('haue you nothing said . . .'gainst the Duke of *Albany*?' 2.1.956). Edmund's improvisation is magically effective: all the circumstances of time and place and even motive coalesce as Regan steps in smoothly to supply, from Goneril's letters, the disreputable history that explains and proves the parricidal charges against Edgar: 'Was he not companion with the riotous Knights | That tended vpon my Father? . . .'Tis they haue put him on the old mans death, | To haue th'expence and wast of his Reuenues. | I haue this *present euening* from my Sister | Beene well inform'd of them' (2.1.1033–41, my italics).

The scene ends with an emphasis on the affection generated by a shared awareness of opportunities to exploit, of shared understanding how events may be made 'fit for purpose'. Regan admits to Gloucester that they have turned up unexpectedly 'out of season, thredding dark-ey'd night' in order to be advised by him on 'Occasions . . . of some prize' (2.1.1062–3). The disturbing image of the night's eye-sockets as needle-holes instrumentally threaded by their mysterious 'occasions' is superficially dispelled in the warmth with which they beg Gloucester, 'our good old friend', to comfort himself and turn his attention to the 'businesses' arising from the 'differences' in the letters from Lear and Goneril (2.1.1067, 1070).[12] This business is urgent, it 'craues the instant vse' of Gloucester's counsel (2.1.1071). Once again, extreme temporal and spatial contingency—the urgency and unexpectedness of the Cornwalls' leaving home and arriving at Gloucester—is shaped so as to emphasize not its near-impossibility, but its *convenience*—its perception of 'Opportunity' or 'Occasion' arising from rivalry or 'differences' between others. The vagueness of

times and distances remarked by Bradley and Greg, the preposterous-
ness of intention and epistolary transaction noted by Goldberg: these
all contribute to a sense of the canny and uncanny shaping of time
and place as opportunity.

It is well known that Renaissance emblem books and collections
of adages took up the classical ekphrastic tradition of depicting
Kairos and *Occasio* as a figures (usually feminine) standing on an orb
or wheel, baldness at the back of the head contrasting with stream-
ing forelock.[13] I am proposing that the conception of Opportunity
implied in the verbal shaping of the action of *Lear*, however, has
less to do with this tradition (which stresses the positive ethical force
of grasping Occasion, and identifies its neglect with Remorse) than
with a forensic tradition of circumstantial argument in which conjectures of ease and ability are related to arguments proving sinister
and oppressive purposes.[14] I propose that the profoundly original
and moving way in which *Lear* makes inhuman atrocity banal and
ordinary—a matter of politic foresight and opportunity taking on, as
it were, a predatory life of its own—is anticipated in Shakespeare's
1594 narrative poem, *Lucrece*, where Opportunity is addressed
and accused as one of the conjectural 'circumstances' facilitating
Tarquin's rape. In arguing for the connection between the forensic
conception of Opportunity in *Lucrece* and the way time and place
are imagined in *Lear*, I want make a broader case for the association
between 'circumstances' and the 'imaginary work' of *ekphrasis* and
enargeia. Shakespeare worked on *Lucrece* during the near-suspension
of dramatic activity from June 1592 to October 1594. It may be
that this intense poetic re-engagement with the forensically derived
topics of circumstance (the questions of where, when, why, and so
forth) developed his sense of their potential, in theatre, to stimulate the imagining of an offstage, fictional world. In support of this
argument, I want to demonstrate the extent to which classical and
humanist treatments of the *circumstantiae* emphasized their role in
achieving *enargeia*, or vivid images of things unseen, and in arousing
the emotions. As the thought of 'circumstances' having anything
to do with emotion or imagination is likely to strike most readers
as thoroughly implausible, I will first turn to the question of why
it is that this ancient rhetorical association has become generally
obscure to modern English speakers.

2.2. Circumstances before the Emergence of Statistical Probability

Ancient and humanist writers associated the topics of *peristasis* or circumstance with the achievement of powerfully imaginative and emotional effects. This is not an association that is generally recognized. The reason for this, I suspect, has to do with the stubbornly and exclusively empirical sense in which the word 'circumstance' has been used since the eighteenth century. Eighteenth-century English common law developed a doctrine of circumstances as infallible proofs by attenuating the rhetorical tradition. In the eighteenth century, circumstances were held to be the extra-rhetorical, objective conditions of a crime and were accordingly opposed to the rhetorical contrivances of witness testimony; 'circumstances that tally with one another are above human contrivance', as it was famously said in a trial in 1752.[15] Partly as a result of this legal inheritance, our residual rhetorical understanding of the topics of circumstance—the 'five W's (and one H)' of journalism—tends to be thought of in terms of enquiry into objectively ascertainable facts. The transformation of the meaning of 'circumstance' from that of a topic to that of an objective material condition is part of the larger epistemological upheaval around 1660 that Ian Hacking has famously described as 'the emergence of probability'. It makes sense at this point to revisit the debate over Hacking's foundational genealogy so as to clarify some of the murkiness around accounts of what probability and circumstances looked like before probability was said to have 'emerged'.

'Probability', in our modern, habitual sense of the word, means something like 'likelihood' and, while the word has an informal adverbial sense that we use all the time (when we say something is 'probably' the case), the noun, 'probability', tends to connote the more authoritative philosophical regime of calculations, risks, norms, and statistics that governs our lives. So absolute has been the triumph of statistical probability—Hacking describes it as '*the* philosophical success story of the first half of the twentieth century'—that it is very difficult for us to imagine what the term used to refer to before statistical calculation came into being.[16] And the difficulty is compounded by the fact that all scholarly accounts of the rise of modern probability—whether influenced by Hacking's brilliant Foucauldian archaeology or reacting against it—overlook the vastly expanded domain of rhetorical and dialectical invention (that is, the finding out of figures and arguments in order to speak and write movingly and convincingly) that constitutes the dominant semantic field, in the sixteenth century, of the Latin noun *probabilitas* and its adjectival and adverbial cognates, *probabile* and *probabiliter*, as well as the English adjectival form 'probable'.[17]

Ian Hacking says that in its pre-1660 use, the word 'probability' had no connection with numerical ideas of randomness, but meant, essentially 'worthy of approval' in relation to the domain of *opinio* or 'opinion', which was incommensurable with *scientia* or 'knowledge'.[18] In a move indebted to Foucault, Hacking looked for the opening up of a conceptual space in which the ancient idea of probability as testimony of approval might encounter the modern idea of probability as numerical frequency. He found it not, as might be expected, in Blaise Pascal's moral and mathematical attack on Jesuit probabilism, but in sixteenth-century alchemical and hermetic texts.[19]

Hacking's thesis found some critics, among them the immensely erudite literary scholar Douglas Patey, who has maintained that there was no need to posit a conceptual revolution, since the mathematical idea of probability as frequency was essentially continuous with the ancient and medieval idea of probability as approved opinion.[20] But though Patey's alternative history of probability acknowledges the sixteenth-century rhetorical tradition, the focus of his argument is eighteenth-century literary criticism. Patey sees no distinction between sixteenth-century and eighteenth-century uses of the word 'circumstances' because he understands probability as relating primarily to inartificial proof (degrees of credibility of witnesses) rather than to the poetics of artificial proof (strategies of argument). '[T]he Renaissance paradigm for explaining probability', he writes, 'comes . . . from the "place" of "external" or "inartificial" proofs, that is, proofs that come from the testimony of more or less authoritative (and hence *probable*) witnesses.'[21] Within this framework, 'circumstances' are limited to their function as signs of objectively modifying conditions that help enquirers ascertain 'probability'.[22] Both the schools of Hacking and of Patey thus ignore the explosion of rhetorical and dialectical teaching in the sixteenth century, in which the object was not to draw up a canon of evaluative probabilities based either on authority or on empirical observation, but rather to enable the resolution of a *conflictio*

causarum, or conflict of motives, by deploying an array of argumentative techniques known as 'artificial proof'.[23]

This matters for our understanding of the 'circumstances' in
English literature pre-1660 because the transformation of the meaning has made it very hard indeed for us to reconstruct the *imaginative* scope that the pre-1660 sense of that word represented for
Shakespeare and his contemporaries. We think of 'circumstances'
as *external* and *objective* conditions that resist analytical generalization.
'[T]he external conditions prevailing at the time' as the *OED* puts it,
quoting Samuel Johnson's definition: 'the condition or state of affairs'.
The *OED* then offers phrases from the eighteenth century onward
which reinforce this sense of circumstances as material conditions,
exercising an objective force on our lives: we are 'governed by circumstances' (1768), man is the 'creature of circumstances' (1827), we
act by 'the force of circumstances' (1875).[24] In the wake of statistical
probability's philosophical dominance, 'circumstances'—now always
in an undifferentiated plural—have been assimilated to the idea of
'chance' itself, signifying the resistance of circumstances to any kind
of analysis other than that which pertains to the random, and, consequently, to statistical calculation. So, for example, Hacking's sequel
to *The Emergence of Probability* is called *The Taming of Chance*, while a
Foucauldian study of Stendhal and Balzac by the literary critic David
Bell is called *Circumstances: Chance in the Literary Text*.[25]

We are, in fact, so used to thinking about 'probability' as having to
do with statistical frequency rather than argument and about 'circumstances' as irreducibly random material particulars, that it is difficult
for us to recover a mentality in which the term 'circumstances' can
refer to a repertoire of questions that give depth, shape, and substance
to a figuratively expressed idea, often animating it and giving us the
sense that it is visually, tangibly, and audibly present, or emotionally
intelligible. Yet it is this latter, broader field of mental image-making
that is covered by the concept of the 'circumstances' in the rhetorical
textbooks with which Shakespeare would have been familiar.

Patey shows that eighteenth-century critics understood 'circumstances' to be empirical conditions affecting 'character', so their definition of the 'probable' in a literary work had a great deal to do
with the idea that characters should behave in a manner consistent
with their 'circumstances'. Charlotte Lennox's criticism of Romeo's

description of the Apothecary's shop as being 'inconsistent with the Condition and Circumstances of the Speaker' perfectly illustrates Patey's thesis.[26] Where Patey is misleading, however, is in backdating this kind of eighteenth-century aesthetic empiricism to the sixteenth and seventeenth centuries, where circumstances have a much more expansively imaginative role. Of seventeenth-century casuistry, Patey writes that '[r]ules for the application of circumstances cannot be made more specific than the standard lists of who, what, where, when, etc., for to do so would be to ignore the reason for which circumstances were devised'.[27] This is reductive and simply wrong. Even in forensic roles, in casuistry, and in law, the model was rhetorical, not logical, discourse, and was therefore concerned with artificial as well as inartificial proof (that is, with strategies of *argument* as well as with testamentary authority).[28] A few critics have discussed the role of circumstances in literary hermeneutics and in Shakespeare's plays.[29] But none of these accounts has broached the connection, made emphatically by Quintilian and his Renaissance followers, between circumstances, the arousing of emotions, and the creation of vivid mental pictures—the 'imaginary work' of circumstances.

2.3. Circumstances as Sources of Emotion and Imagination

Since the connection between the places of circumstance and the arousal of emotion through mental image-making is so clearly apparent to Quintilian, as well as to his Renaissance followers Erasmus and Rudolph Agricola, what is really remarkable is the extent to which we have been unable to perceive it. Influenced by Patey, perhaps, readers of Quintilian will come across his comprehensive list of the circumstances in book 5, on proofs, and assume that this 'standard list' is all there is. The work of circumstances in Quintilian is not confined to book 5, however, but builds cumulatively, providing intricate connections between books. Circumstances are first introduced in book 3, chapter 6, as part of the foundational theory of *status* or issue—the theory of how to analyse what's at the heart of a dispute—it's from this *status* that everything else derives (3.6.23–8).[30] In book 4, on narrative, Quintilian recommends adumbrating the topics of proof and sampling the circumstances of person, motive, and so on (4.2.55).

And while chapter 10 of book 5 is indeed the most expansive, detailed, and indispensable treatment, it's more of a repertoire of generative arguments than a list of enquiries. Circumstances are here defined as 'places of argument' (*argumentorum loci*) and considered the richest source of argument as artificial proof. Following Cicero, Quintilian divides them into accidents of person and circumstances of thing, and covers each topic in detail, suggesting, in every case, the different kinds of 'status' or issue in which arguments drawn from the topic might be relevant and powerful. Thus, though he does indeed list the *places* (*loci*) of circumstance as: '*causa tempus locus occasio instrumentum modus et cetera*' (5.10.23), he also shows how, when judiciously and appropriately applied, they cast the putative matter or event into the hypothetical or subjunctive mode, enabling an audience to *imagine* what something similar *might have been like*, but never, in any objective or calculating sense, to *know* it. The subjunctive links circumstantial enquiry to imaginative activity.[31] Moreover, the list of circumstances is followed by a classification of rhetorical and dialectical strategies for the application of the circumstances to any argument. This classification derives from Cicero's *Topica* and follows Cicero's own later integration of the topics of *persona* and *res* of his early work (*De inventione*) into the more comprehensive argumentative strategies of the *Topica*.[32]

Quintilian's book 5 is just the beginning—the imaginative applications of the topics of circumstance come later, in books 6, 7, 8, and 9. Book 6, for example, is concerned with teaching how to convey emotion (*adfectus*). Quintilian opens the book with a moving account of the death of his elder son, in whom, after the passing of the boy's younger sibling and his mother, the father had placed all his hopes. There's a powerfully affecting and particularized description of the boy's sinking eyes and his body turning cold and bloodless as his last breath fled (6, Prooemium, 12). Then, somewhat unnervingly, Quintilian goes on to teach his readers how to produce such emotional effects by using circumstances. If a prosecutor wants to make a charge seem outrageous or pitiable, these emotions are enhanced 'by considering what was done, by whom, against whom, with what intention, when, where and how, all of which admit an infinite variety of treatment' (6.1.15). In chapter 2 of the same book, he connects genuine feeling with the production of feeling in oratory by explaining that some people are good at forming what the Greeks call *phantasiai*, and the Romans 'visions', that is, scenes of detailed, quasi-hallucinatory imaginary power:

> Suppose I am complaining that someone has been murdered. Am I not to have before my eyes all the circumstances which one can believe to have happened during the event (*omnia quae in re praesenti accidisse credibile est*)? Will not the assassin burst out on a sudden, and the victim tremble, cry for help, and either plead for mercy or try to escape? Shall I not see one man striking the blow and the other man falling? Will not the blood, the pallor, the groans, the last gasp of the dying be imprinted on my mind? The result will be *enargeia*, what Cicero calls *illustratio* and *evidentia*, a quality which makes us seem not so much to be talking about something as exhibiting it. Emotions will ensue, just as if we were present at the event itself. (6.2.31–2)

In this passage, as critics have noted, it is circumstances (here rendered as 'accidents') that are chief among the means of achieving '*enargeia*' or '*evidentia*'.[33] In book 8, too, Quintilian associates *enargeia* with circumstances, when he identifies the former as being made up of a number of telling details (*ex pluribus*) which invite the listener to fill in others, as if actually seeing the scene. Cicero, says Quintilian, is able to make anyone, no matter how 'incapable of forming images of things', suddenly able to feel that he is seeing the scene described, and mentally to add details that are not there (8.3.64–5).[34] From Cicero, Livy, and Virgil Quintilian quotes unforgettable descriptions—of the morning after a luxuriously convivial gathering, where the guests are unsteady with wine and the floor tacky and littered with the evening's detritus; of the sack of a city, where flames rush through buildings, roofs crash in, and clamorous cries form a single wailing; of the moment of shivering fear as bloodstains drip uncannily from a torn tree. These examples, he says, show how vividness can be an effect of the 'accidents' of a situation: '*contingit eadam claritas etiam ex accidentibus*' ('the same vividness can even be obtained [by describing] the accidents') (8.3.70). In between books 6 and 8, in book 7, Quintilian treats the topic of 'division' or order and here, again, he returns to the theory of issues, showing in great detail and by way of worked examples, how topics of circumstance, such as 'person' or 'motive' or 'design' (*consilia*), dictate further lines of questioning, and involve other topics, such as that of time and place (7.2.39). So circumstances have both analytical and argument-generating power (as associated with proof and status theory in books 3, 5, and 7) and the power to conjure up vivid mental images so as to arouse emotion (books 6 and 8); they also embody a power inherent in their very unobtrusiveness and capacity to grow in the mind, as we see in Quintilian's reference to them as *semina . . . probationum* 'seeds of proof' sown in the narrative (4.2.54).

Erasmus' *De copia*, much indebted to Quintilian, draws attention to the twin powers of circumstances as contributors to vivid mental imaging and as generators of arguments. Erasmus' emphasis on the connection between circumstantial proof and *enargeia* is richly supplemented by Johannes Weltkirchius' extensive commentary. Circumstances are central to three important chapters in book 2 of the *De copia*: the fifth chapter on *evidentia* or *enargeia* (spelt *energeia* in the 1573 text), and the eighth chapter entirely devoted to circumstances and the long eleventh chapter on proof and argument, in which, after Quintilian, Erasmus identifies probable arguments as a type of artificial proof, and says that 'most of these are derived from . . . circumstances'.[35] Circumstances also figure in the ninth chapter on amplification by *incrementum*, where Erasmus borrows Quintilian's example from Cicero of the indecorous circumstances of Antony's vomiting (*Inst.*, 8.4.8) and in the tenth chapter on multiplying rhetorical propositions, where Erasmus borrows Quintilian's example of the Thebans' case of debt against the Thessalians as an example of how to select places of argument (*Inst.*, 5.10.111–18). On propositions, Erasmus shows how general propositions can be varied by '*circunstantiis*' [*sic*], 'specific circumstances'.[36]

In his chapter on *evidentia* or *enargeia* Erasmus' opening definition paraphrases Quintilian's words from book 6 on arousing emotion by picturing details, and from book 8 on bringing a scene before the mind's eye.[37] He then goes on to quote at length from Quintilian's examples of the sack of the city, and the sordid aftermath of the luxurious dinner party. Immediately he links these examples with the sensational narrative descriptions of messengers in the tragedies of Euripides, Seneca, and Sophocles, and with similar descriptions in Cicero. '[D]escriptions of this sort', he concludes, 'consist mainly in the exposition of circumstantial details (*circunstantiarum*), especially those which make the incident particularly vivid and give the narrative distinctiveness' [or 'character'] (*ac moratem reddunt narrationem*).[38] Weltkirchius' commentary on this chapter opens with an explicit linking of *enargeia* and the dialectical topic of 'accidents'. *Enargeia*, he says, is a mode of rhetorical representation 'born of dialectical defi-nition, especially that they call "of accidents"'.[39] Thus, in the most influential rhetorical textbook of the Renaissance, the poetic illusion of presence is identified with finding arguments from the accidental or contingent features of a thing or event.

In his own brief but rich chapter 8 on circumstances, Erasmus sums up their multiple uses, referring back to chapter 5 on vividness and forward to chapters 9 and 10 on amplification and chapter 11 on *con-firmatio* and on proof: 'Timely and appropriate use of circumstances has many advantages: first, in amplifying and diminishing (*ad amplifi-candum atque extenuandum*) about which we will speak briefly soon; then in vivid presentation (*ad evidentiam*) about which we spoke just above; and in addition, in confirmation and credibility (*ad confirmationem et probabilitatem*).' The whole composition, he says, should be dense and thick with arguments, everywhere crowded together and participating in one another.[40] This very pervasiveness however, makes it impossible for Erasmus to give a textbook example of how circumstances work. They are unobtrusive and merely implicit—you do not unfold or expli-cate circumstantial proofs, says Erasmus, 'they fight on their own'.[41]

Supplementing Erasmus' brief chapter, Weltkirchius' commentary offered students a comprehensive, detailed, and wide ranging discus-sion of each of the circumstances in turn. Weltkirchius, as we have seen, emphasizes the affinity between rhetorical circumstances and dialectical 'accidents' and '*applicita*'—these are topics that give a cer-tain character or quality to a thing, such as time, place, or the '*connexa*' of relationship.[42] Weltkirchius' commentary is throughout illuminat-ing, but I will here confine my attention to his treatment of *causa*, a topic of particular importance for Shakespeare's distinctive and inno-vative way of imbuing dramatic time and space with human purpose and emotion.

Causa is the second of the topics Weltkirichius discusses, placing it after *persona*, because 'person' has its own set of circumstantial top-ics, known as 'accidents'. This is all perfectly standard in Cicero and Quintilian—but no less illuminating for that. Because, of course, this arrangement means that *causa* can't be directly linked to *persona*, but can only be known by means of the other circumstances of *res*, time, place, manner, and so on. Yet *causa* always, as Weltkirchius defines it, involves human intention:

> The second circumstance is *causa* which here straightforwardly means the purpose of a willing producer, the plan, the intention which strives towards an intermediate goal or final object, and which also means the use or goal set for a task, i.e., the end of which someone does this or something else. Here we should think of causes that have to do with the will, not natural causes.[43]

So *causa* is both exclusively associated with human will and intention and, at the same time, only imaginable through inferences from the manner, time, or place of a deed's performance. Thus open manner argues a good *causa*, but secrecy its opposite, and so forth.

We see here, incidentally, why the *causa* of the circumstances can't be translated as 'cause' in Douglas Patey's sense of circumstances as signs leading to 'causes'.[44] For sixteenth-century readers *causa* here means something much more like Aristotle's 'οὗ ἕνεκα', which Monte Johnson translates as 'that for the sake of which', a phrase which corresponds to the meaning of the English word 'cause' as 'purpose' when used in locutions such as 'the cause of nuclear disarmament'.[45] '*Causa*' and 'cause' are thus always both anterior to any rhetorical enquiry (the question of why something was done) and, at the same time, the product of it (the 'purpose' as argued or justified in speech). Moreoever, if '*causa*' in one of its senses is a circumstances of the thing or deed (*res*) and the other circumstances are (for example) *tempus locus occasio instrumentum modus*—'time, place, occasion, instrument, manner'—then both senses of '*causa*' are only made known through the other circumstances, while these other circumstances themselves will only be invoked to the extent that they are to be manifestations or signs of human motives, purposes, and passions. Thus we may say that in sixteenth-century literary composition 'circumstances' are very often less like objective particulars or factual details than they are like arguments for the human uses of contingency. Thus what we think of as the 'external circumstances' of weather, season, time, location, or mode of doing are only ever imagined in relation to a conjecture about the motives and feelings that explain a human action. So, in turn, these conditions and details of weather or location or a room's furniture seem to acquire human characteristics—night is 'secret'; the road 'lonely'; the hearth or the marriage bed 'sacred' or 'defiled' or 'sorrowful'. This is not so much a matter of pathetic fallacy, as a constitution of time, place, means, instrument, and opportunity as arguments for the *causa*, or motive, behind the act in question.

At the same time it is important not to overstress the prevalence of this imaginative use of what is essentially a forensic habit of rhetorical invention. In most legal contexts, such as the examinations of Justices of Peace, any imaginative or emotive potential inherent in the topics of circumstance was necessarily ignored or suppressed. Peter Mack gives the example of Nathaniel Bacon investigating the circumstances of an alleged English attack on Dutch fishing boats in 1577:

> [t]he depositions relate a large number of facts and circumstances (how many prizes and of what value, where they were captured, how many were wounded in the fight, what amount of fish was on board, what meat was supplied to the ships for the soldiers) which are usually checked against another's testimony.[46]

Here the topics are run through to establish as much detail as possible as a means of testing and corroborating competing witnesses' accounts. In poetic and dramatic narrative, by contrast, the topics may be used to imply a motive, or *causa*, by conjuring the impression of detailed external conditions from which inferences may be drawn.

Between the sixteenth and the eighteenth centuries, there was a gradual fading of the rhetorical association of circumstances with *phantasia* and emotion. I have mentioned that the development of a law of evidence in the eighteenth century produced a discourse which opposed the objective reliability of 'circumstances' to the uncertainty of witness testimony, as if circumstances could exist outside a narrative frame: William Paley's complacent assertion, in 1812, that '[c]ircumstances cannot lie' became a commonplace.[47] In this context it is not surprising to find Romantic poetry tending to loosen the old rhetorical connection between imagination, powerful feeling, and the particulars of proof. As an epigraph to the *Lyrical Ballads* of 1802, Wordsworth quotes from a passage in Quintilian's tenth book in which Quintilian links the emotional power of oratorical improvisation to that capacity to produce mental images or *phantasiai* which had earlier, in book 6, linked to the topics of circumstance. The sentence quoted by Wordsworth, however, illustrates the importance of emotion to eloquence by noting that 'even the unskilled, so long as they are stirred by some emotion, are not short of words'.[48] So for Wordsworth, the *phantasia* or mental image that arouses strong emotion appears more spontaneous, less trammelled by an oratorical practice of running through the topics of proof. Indeed, in an earlier text, Wordsworth had consigned that very practice to the dullness of a legal routine. In the 1797–9 manuscript of his play *The Borderers*, Wordsworth has the hypocrite Rivers, who longs to visit violent summary justice on the saintly Baron Herbert, express his impatience with his companions for organizing a trial of the baron where 'His crimes shall be proclaimed' before 'the good and just | Of every age'.[49] The thought of all those 'dull particulars' or circumstantial proof seem, to Rivers, desperately boring:

> . . . Proof!
> Nay, we must travel in another path
> Or we're stuck fast for ever—passion, then,
> Shall be a unit for us—proof, oh no,
> We'll not insult her majesty by time,
> And place—the where, the when, the how, and all
> The dull particulars whose intrusion mars
> The dignity of demonstration.[50]

By the turn of the eighteenth century, these 'dull particulars' of where, when, and how no longer seemed able to conjure images before the mind's eye. Sixteenth-century readers of Cicero and Quintilian, by contrast, emphasize the ways in which artificial proof—arguments derived from the topics of circumstance—is essential to *enargeia*, to the arousal of emotion, and to the confirmation and refutation of arguments relating to inwardness, or motive. Shakespeare, like other educated Englishmen, learned from books that taught how pupils the topics of circumstance might be productive of inwardness, or '*causa*'. And instead of simply deploying circumstances so as to imply motives, Shakespeare would attribute human motives and feelings to the circumstances themselves.

2.4. Lucrece's Circumstances

The 'imaginary work' of circumstances as it emerges from Quintilian and Erasmus is essentially twofold. On one hand, as part of *confirmatio* and *refutatio*, and tending to establish or undermine probability as likelihood, enquiring into circumstances encourages us to imagine explanations and make inferential connections. On the other hand, as metonymic details that evoke a whole scene (the blood, the pallor, the groans, the last gasp of the dying) circumstances encourage the vivid fantasizing or quasi-hallucinating of a scene, the sense that one has experienced it. In a theatre where the plots were increasingly requiring audiences to make complex narrative connections across dynamically shifting locations and times, this twofold imaginary work would come in very handy. Ekphrastic uses of circumstance would enhance the imaginative reach of the theatre; uses of circumstance in *confirmatio* and *refutatio* to encourage inferences of motive would sharpen plot connections, and produce *dramatis personae* as interiorized characters. Shakespeare must have come to recognize the potential of rhetorical circumstances at some point fairly early in his career.

From June 1592 to October 1594 the public theatres suffered several suspensions of activity amounting to almost complete closure, due to disputes with the civic authorities and repeated plague orders. In 1592 Shakespeare was already writing plays, probably in collaboration with other writers.[51] During the months of intermittent playing activity between 1592 and 1594, however, his immersion in the composition of the narrative poems *Venus and Adonis* (1593) and *Lucrece* (1594) involved him in profound reflection on questions of emotion and rhetorical scene-painting and on the relation of both to the topics of circumstance and to arguments of guilt and innocence. We cannot know whether these reflections stimulated him to think in new ways about the circumstantial evocation of imagined times and places in drama, the diegetic supplementation of mimetic action. What we can know for certain, however, is that in writing *Lucrece*, Shakespeare was able to turn the venerable textbook exercise of debating the heroine's motive for killing herself into a contemplation of the extraordinary and morally ambivalent capacity of circumstantial rhetoric to arouse imaginative sympathy.

In *Lucrece* the narrative action is very simple. Tarquin, having been aroused by Collatine's praise of his wife, hurries from Ardea to Rome and revolves in his mind the shameful consequences of raping his hostess, Collatine's wife, then rapes her anyway. She then 'breathes . . . forth her spite' accusing the circumstances of Night, Opportunity, and Time as accessories to Tarquin's fact (sig. F3^r, l. 762).[52] She resolves to kill herself, but only after her husband will '[h]aue heard the cause' of her untimely death (sig. I1^r, l. 1178). Having written to send for her husband, she spends the interval contemplating the skill exhibited in a painting of the destruction of Troy and 'feelingly' weeping for 'TROYES painted woes' (sig. K4^v, l. 1492). On her husband's arrival, accompanied by other lords, she narrates her case, and they clamour to acquit her, but she kills herself nevertheless, prompting a vow of revenge against the Tarquins from the assembled Roman lords.

If the apparent disproportion of speech to action is no longer a source of outright critical dismay (as in F. T. Prince's description of Lucrece's speeches as 'endless tirades'[53]), there's still a sense in which it is misunderstood. Indeed, the more recent identification of Lucrece's speeches as belonging to Heroidean 'complaint' has contributed to this misunderstanding. For, as William Weaver has recently shown in a revolutionary interpretation of the poem, Lucrece's speech denouncing the guilt of Time, Opportunity, and Night as Tarquin's accessories is not ineffectual 'introspection and complaint', as critics have thought, but forms part of what I referred to in the previous chapter as a 'meditation'—that is, a private rehearsal of proofs for a forensic oration.[54] 'From the time Tarquin leaves her until she kills herself', writes Weaver, 'Lucrece speaks as if practicing to confirm a charge of rape and refute a charge of adultery.'[55] The key point here, of course, is that the *alleged* rape—which so many critics have assumed to be a transparently objective 'fact'—does not have any reality for Collatine and the Roman lords except that which Lucrece can give it in her forensic speech. Adultery is always the more probable explanation for a woman's alleged rape, as is evident from the very threat by which Tarquin persuades Lucrece to consent, as well as from the long afterlife of the Augustinian dilemma.[56] Moreover, as everyone knows, the distinction between adultery and rape turns on evidence that must perforce remain 'unseen, save to the eye of mind'—that is, the evidence of Lucrece's own motives and desires, her own *causa*.

The reason that Lucrece addresses Night, Opportunity, and Time, then, is because these temporal circumstances were standard topics for the invention of arguments that proved ability to do the deed. Because she cannot deny that the unacceptable act took place, Lucrece is obliged to contemplate a defence based on the *status* or issue of 'quality' in which she does not attempt to deny the offence, but uses circumstances to show how she was forced to act as she did (Quint., *Inst.*, 7.4.13).[57] Thus appealing to the *time* of Tarquin's visit to her, showing that it was at *night*, and she was *opportunely* alone and helpless, would form part of a narrative of the fact, or deed, which would help prove Tarquin's premeditated design. Her narrative before the Roman lords thus economically and vividly deploys, in its first three lines, the circumstances of time, instrument, place, and manner:

> 'For in the dreadfull dead of darke midnight,
> With shining Fauchion in my chamber came
> A creeping creature with a flaming light . . .' (sig. L3ᵛ, ll. 1625–7)

This is the moment, as Weaver explains, that the usefulness of her earlier apostrophe to the circumstances becomes clear: the earlier speech is thus not otiose but purposeful, it 'anticipates her rhetorical situation as that of a pleader in a criminal case'.[58]

Weaver's identification of Lucrece as a forensic speaker marks a very important and consequential shift in criticism of Shakespeare's poem. It breaks decisively with previous accounts that more or less uniformly disparage the heroine's ineffectual and hence exasperating solitary lamentation. Such accounts are Jonathan Bate's, who feels that, 'there is potentially something tasteless about giving so much rhetorical copiousness to a person who is supposed to have been raped', preferring Shakespeare's solution to this 'problem' in *Titus Andronicus*, where the raped Lavinia is tongueless.[59] Yet, while Weaver's reading of Lucrece as effective pleader seems infinitely preferable to Bate's fastidiously cruel distaste, it is worth, nevertheless, asking why Weaver's has seemed the less obvious reading. Why have critics assumed the redundancy of Lucrece's lamentations? Weaver says her speech's *usefulness* as a meditation on the circumstances of the crime is not apparent until she pleads before the lords, but one might argue that 'useful' doesn't seem quite the right term for a speech accusing Time which proceeds at length in this sort of manner (I am picking a couple of verses at random):

> Times glorie is to calme contending Kings,
> To vnmaske falshood, and bring truth to light,
> To stampe the seale of time in aged things,

To wake the morne, and Centinell the night,
To wrong the wronger till he render right,
To ruinate proud buildings with thy howres,
And smeare with dust their glitring golden towrs.
To fill with worme-holes stately monuments,
To feede obliuion with decay of things,
To blot old bookes, and alter their contents,
To plucke the quils from auncient rauens wings . . . (sig. G3ᵛ, ll. 939–49)

This meditation is full of *enargeia*, of vivid mental image-making through the use, recommended by Quintilian and Erasmus, of the exposition of detailed circumstances to bring the object before the mind's eye. You'll remember that Erasmus said that this kind of description 'consists chiefly in an exposition of circumstances, of those in particular that bring the thing most forcefully before one's eyes' and 'give character to the narrative' ('*ac moratam reddunt narrationem*'), and he includes in its scope descriptions of such personifications as Calumny, Hunger, and Opportunity.[60]

What is very striking in the example I've just given—apart from the anaphora—is the way a tendency to animate and personify inhabits every verb, as well as the way in which powerful generalizations or commonplaces are conveyed by vivid metonymies, material details that suggest the whole by the part. Time 'wakes' the morning, for example, and 'smears' obscuring dust on the play of light on metal that is both power (gold) and transience (glitter), but Time also 'feeds' the loss of human memory with meaning turned into material decay: blotted books, old quills. Effectively, here, familiar proverbs and sayings about Time have taken on a mesmerizingly vivid and emotionally charged life.

So far, so copious, one might think. This is nothing more than the outpouring of Shakespearean fancy. But there is something more to this. Not only are the circumstances animated through metaphor, but subtending this level of personification we have the forensic characterizations of Night, Time, and Opportunity through epithets and periphrases that suggest incriminating histories and relationships. Thus, Night is a passive 'register' and 'notarie' of shame, a location ('Blacke stage') for tragedies, but Opportunity, more active, puts time and place together and 'sets the wolfe where he the lambe may get' (sig. F3, ll. 765–6; sig. G2ʳ, l. 878). Opportunity is characterized in relation to Time as a servant, but in acting as accessory to Tarquin's lust, this servant has betrayed Lucrece. Lucrece then discovers the paradox that Time, whose office is ruin, decay, oblivion, should nevertheless have allowed his servant, Opportunity, to reverse his work by enchaining Lucrece to a limitless sorrow, an 'endlesse date of neuer-ending woes' (sig. G3^r, l. 935).

Lucrece's speech races indignantly through dazzlingly capacious fictions of this kind that, in multiplying the *mores* or characteristics of the circumstances themselves, also diffuse and distribute *causae* or motives. Her inventive thoughts, '[m]uch like a presse of people at a dore' (sig. I4^r, l. 1301), seem to exist in excess of their usefulness in her forensic *narratio* to the lords. Their apparent excess is part of a threefold puzzle in the poem, whose other two parts involve, secondly, the apparently unrelated episode of *ekphrasis*, or Lucrece's contemplation and description of the skilful painting of Troy's destruction, and, thirdly—though this is not Shakespeare's invention, of course—the fact that though Lucrece is successful in persuading the Roman lords that she has indeed been 'constrayn'd with dreadfull circumstance' (sig. M1^v, l. 1703), she nevertheless refuses this defence, and kills herself anyway.

Key to this threefold puzzle is the relation between circumstances as *confirmatio*, or arguments of proof, and circumstances as the metonymic details that stimulate emotion by urging the supplementary work of *phantasiai*—the mental imagining of absent things (Quintilian, *Inst.*, 6.2.29). If we understand Lucrece's meditation of the arguments for her defence as an example of the first, her contemplation of the painting of Troy is a rhetorical exercise in the second. It is an exercise in *ekphrasis* understood as a 'discourse of viewing' preparative to emotive speaking.[61] Once she has meditated the circumstances of the offence and resolved to let Collatine know her *causa*, Lucrece writes a letter, but withholds from it 'the life and feeling of her passion' which 'she hoords to spend, when he is by to heare her' (sig. I4^v, ll. 1317–18). Whereas her maid weeps simply at the sight of her mistress's tears without being persuaded the eloquence of her 'cause' ('No *cause*, but companie of her drops spilling' (sig. I2^v, l. 1236, my italics)), Lucrece knows that she must practise to achieve *enargeia* and perform *adfectus* or emotion if a male audience is to feel compassion for her *cause*, the argument for her innocence.

The two forms of practice are complementary. We have already seen how *adfectus* or emotion is aroused, in Quintilian's influential account, by enlisting our capacity to make absent things present by practising how to set before our eyes all the circumstances ('accidents') of the scene (*Inst.*, 6.2.32). Lucrece seeks, in the painting of Troy, images of those in distress and forlorn, in order to 'lend them words' and 'borrow' their looks—that is, in order to practice performing the effect of deep feeling (sig. K4ᵛ, l. 1498). But the ekphrastic language in which the painter's skill is conveyed is simultaneously one in which the capacity to animate, or to give 'lifeless life', is associated with the capacity to select circumstantial details so that a viewer is able to see the very sweat and dust begriming the foot soldiers, and the 'ashie lights' in the eyes of the dying (sig. K1ᵛ, l. 1378). So effective is the painter's selection of circumstantial details that rhetorical metonymy is expressed as perspective, a technique whereby the 'eye of mind' supplies what is not there:

> For much imaginarie worke was there,
> Conceipt deceitfull, so compact so kinde,
> That for ACHILLES image stood his speare
> Grip't in an Armed hand, himselfe behind
> Was left vnseene, saue to the eye of mind:
> A hand, a foote, a face, a leg, a head,
> Stood for the whole to be imagined. (sig. K3ʳ, ll. 1423–8)

As Colin Burrow notes of the preceding stanza, Shakespeare seems to have derived these scenes from the *ekphrasis* or description of a siege of Thebes in the *Imagines* of Philostratus where the part similarly stands for the whole: 'some are seen in full figure, others with the legs hidden, others from the waist up, then only the busts of some, heads only, helmets only and finally just spear-points.'[62] Ekphrastic collections such as that of Philostratus were part, as Simon Goldhill writes, of a highly developed discourse of viewing for which 'the notion of *phantasia*—impression—is crucial'. This discourse had its own theoretical handbooks, among the most prominent of which were the *progymnasmata* (elementary textbooks on rhetorical composition) and Quintilian's book 6.[63] Both these texts treat 'circumstances' pervasively. As P. H. Schrijvers notes, Quintilian's treatment of *phantasia* and of the achievement of *enargeia* in 6.2.31 (imagining a scene of murder) and in book 8.3.67–70 (giving examples from Virgil and from Cicero's *In Verrem*) involves '*l'application du système des* circumstantiae *ou—en grec*—περιστάσεις'.[64] Quintilian's most famous example of *enargeia*—that of the sack of the city at 8.3.68, borrowed by Erasmus—is likewise the effect of circumstances:

> Ensuite, grâce à l'élaboration des circonstances du sac d'une ville, apparaîtront les flammes, les toites qui s'écroulent, les cris, la fuite, les lamentations etc., etc. . . . Quintilien ajoute que l'on atteint à la même clarté en décrivant les particularités accidentelles (en latin: accidenta), qui sont propres aux personnes. (Thus, thanks to the elaboration of the circumstances of the sack of a city, the flames appear, the roofs which collapse, the cries, the lamentations, etc., etc. . . . Quintilian adds that one achieves the same vividness by describing accidental particulars which are proper to persons.)[65]

The same terminology, Schrijvers points out, is found in Philostratus' *Imagines*, where the Greek term for 'accidental details'—συμβαίνοντα is said to engage the '*phantasia*', '*cette faculté de représenter ce qu'on n'a pas vu*' ('that faculty of representing what one has not seen'). It is in the work of Philostratus, according to Gerard Watson, that the word '*phantasia*'

> is extended in its meaning from a term practically confined to a technical philosophical debate in epistemology to something more like 'phantasy' in our modern English sense, which can include in its range of meanings, the notion of the creation of an unreal and even ideal world, visualized by the artist and shared with others for their pleasure and enlightenment, the world of the 'imagination'.[66]

Emphasized in both Philostratus and Quintilian, then, is the importance of 'accidental details' (συμβαίνοντα, *accidentes*, circumstances) which, in Quintilian's words, make a listener work to supply what is missing, so that he feels that the scene has been 'displayed to his mind's eye' (*oculis mentis ostendi* (8.3.61).[67] Shakespeare's phrase, 'the eye of mind', is a clear allusion here to Quintilian. There is no evidence that Shakespeare knew Philostratus' work directly, but, as Colin Burrow observes, it was required reading at St John's, Oxford, where the later principal master of Stratford grammar school, Thomas Jenkins, studied.[68]

These two parts of Lucrece's preparation for her forensic oration thus represent each aspect of that twofold quality of the imaginary work of circumstance that I outlined earlier. The speech personifying and animating Night, Opportunity, and Time represents (in brilliant excess) the work of *confirmatio* by which the circumstances of the *res*, or thing, are considered from the point of view of human motives and feelings. The contemplation of the painting of Troy, on the other hand, draws on a classical discourse of viewing (*ekphrasis*) to show how the rhetorical depiction of circumstances or '*accidentes*' engages the mind of a viewer or auditor to represent to him or herself what he or she has not seen: this process is in itself a part of an innovative identification of 'imagination' as '*cette faculté de représenter ce qu'on n'a pas vu*'. The second part of Lucrece's preparation, then, reveals the power of the first as the power of well-chosen verbal details (circumstances) to call up supplementary mental images and the emotions associated with them—the power that we call 'imagination'.

That Lucrece must kill herself is a given, but the reason she gives in Shakespeare's poem appears to be intimately related to the poem's interest in the 'imaginary work' of circumstances, their capacity to activate the imagination so as to make a given conjectural *narratio* seem so vivid as to be true. Lucrece, as William Weaver has explained, appeals to the *status* or issue of 'quality' which involves the transfer of blame to another individual, or to circumstance (*in rem*) (Quintilian, *Inst.*, 7.4.14, gives the example of Tiberius Gracchus, accused of making the treaty of Numantia, defending himself by saying he was under orders, and so coerced).[69] So Lucrece deploys six topics of circumstance in her *narratio* (who, what, where, when, how, and why) to establish that Tarquin had the motive, opportunity, and ability to rape her against her will ('Mine enemy was strong, my poore selfe weake', sig. L4^r, l. 1646).[70] As Weaver notes, however, she fails to confirm this narrative, asking merely, 'What is the qualitie of my offence | Being constrayn'd by dreadfull circumstance? | May my pure mind with the fowle act dispence . . .?' (sig. M1^v, ll. 1702–4). They clamour to acquit her, 'With this they all at once begin to saie | Her bodies staine, her mind vntainted cleares' (sig. M1^v, ll. 1709–10). But she refuses to allow an acquittal based on the 'excusatio' of the issue of quality: 'No no, quoth shee, no Dame hereafter liuing | By my excuse shall claim excuses giuing' (sig. M1^v, ll. 1714–15).

In imagining a woman as a forensic speaker, Shakespeare highlights the danger to patrilineage in allowing the *enargeia* of circumstances— the capacity of circumstances to persuade us to believe what appears before our mind's eye—to serve as proof of innocence (that is, all adulterous wives might thus allege rape, given even a modicum of Lucrece's eloquence). Indeed, the capacity of the artist's circumstantial *enargeia* to deceive has already become apparent to Lucrece when, seeking to practise her sympathy on figures in the Troy painting who are most 'forlorne', she comes across 'a wretched image bound', to whom the painter had given 'An humble gate, calme looks, eyes wayling still | A brow vnbent that seem'd to welcome wo' (sigs. K4ᵛ–L1ʳ, ll. 1500–1, 1508–9). This figure is Sinon, the Greek whose deceit betrayed Troy. Critics have attended to Sinon as Tarquin's analogue, and have traced the comparison to Renaissance commentaries on Ovid's *Fasti*.[71] But Sinon was better known in Renaissance textbooks on rhetoric and dialectic as an exemplar of the power of the topics of circumstance to enable deceit by encouraging readers and auditors to infer connections that do not exist, to imagine, that is, the coherence of the *fabula* as proof of its truth.[72] Rudolph Agricola's *De inventione* gives Sinon's narrative in 2.57–198 of Virgil's *Aeneid* as a perfect example of how circumstances, in Erasmus' words, 'fight by themselves' to persuade listeners of the truth of the cause. Listeners to Sinon's narrative, says Agricola, invent the truth of the story themselves, by 'collecting and comparing' details that, though not true in themselves, agree well with one another:

> [A]lthough there is nothing in the speech to prove the truth of what is being said, the listener himself, through collecting and comparing these things, as well as their order and agreement among themselves, persuades himself that it is so. (*quanquam nihil sit in oratione, quo uera quae dicuntur probentur, ipse tamen auditor collectione collationeque rerum, & earum inter se ordine & congruentia, si esse sibi persuadet.*)[73]

'Lucrece's critique of Sinon', as Weaver says, 'also reflects her dissatisfaction with rhetorical persuasion, for she finds in Sinon the master of the art she has hitherto practised.'[74] In refusing to allow her circumstantial narration to succeed in proving Tarquin's rape, Lucrece acknowledges the dubious precedent her oratorical success would set, since the 'imaginary work' of circumstance is effective irrespective of the narrative's truth. In this sense, the perspectival work in the painting of Troy—the way in which a shield, a hand, a face, a head 'stood for the whole to be imagined'—becomes a metaphor not just for the metonymic work of circumstances as vivid details, but for their capacity to imply plausible narrative causality. Regan's improvised history of Edgar's parricidal character—'Was he not companion with the riotous Knights | That tended vpon my Father? . . . 'Tis they haue put him on the old mans death' (2.1.1033–41)—is a perfect example of how the *enargeia* of circumstance works not just through ekphrastic description, but through narrative causality.

Depressing as it is for a history of the judicial recognition of rape as violence against women, Lucrece's ethical refusal to accept the acquittal that relies on the *enargeia* of circumstance represents a powerful new artistic discovery. In the very excess of her rhetorical preparation lie the elements of a new imaginative resource for the plotting of time and place, and the production of motive and character on the English stage. The very fact that her meditations on the circumstances seem, in Burrow's word, 'overstocked' is itself indicative of their thesaurus-like function in relation not to Lucrece's forensic speech, but to Shakespeare's dramatic composition. Shakespeare's most extraordinary breakthrough was his discovery of a way of endowing a whole play with something like an 'unconscious' dimension by expressing the qualities of motivation and desire that are attributed to circumstances in the course of forensic speech.

Nothing characterizes Lucrece's meditation on the circumstances of her rape more than its proliferating diffusion of motive and feeling, *causa* and *adfectus*. Lucrece's personifications of the circumstances seem 'overstocked' partly because they multiply *causae*, or motives, in an ambiguous and inclusive profusion. This both works against unequivocal proof of guilt or innocence but also, more importantly, registers a sceptical awareness of the repertoire of cultural narratives inherent in the merest epithets and, hence, an awareness of the ease with which circumstantial questions themselves adumbrate and invite us mentally to picture ('imagine') our own culture's familiar stories.

2.5. Timing Is Everything: The Death of Cordelia

When Regan, having just arrived at Gloucester's, responds to the 'news' of Edgar's parricidal attempts by identifying him as 'my Fathers Godsonne' and 'He whom my Father nam'd', her speech is

an image of Opportunity as art of rhetorical timing. For Occasio/
Opportunity was not just one of the topics of circumstance. It was
also a way of describing the power of circumstances—considered
rhetorically and casuistically—to alter the qualities of things in
themselves, to effect ethical transvaluation, to alter consequences.
Writing of the adage '*Nosce Tempus*', Erasmus wrote, 'Such is the force
of Opportunitas, of Timeliness, that it can turn what is honourable into dishonour, loss into gain, happiness into misery, kindness
into unkindness, and the reverse; it can, in short, change the nature
of everything.'[75] In his commentary on the *De copia*, Weltkirchius
notes that while dialecticians consider circumstances to be 'extrin-
sic', theologians and lawyers recognize that circumstances actually
'change the quality of an event or thing' (dancing, for example, is
one thing at a wedding, another in the forum). Weltkirchius refers
the student to the well-known passage in *De officiis* where Cicero
writes of the need to take account of 'the opportunity of time' and
of 'occasio'. '*Tanta vis est et loci et temporis*,' Cicero writes, 'So great
a force is there, of both place and time,' as one sixteenth-century
translation runs.[76] Shakespeare's Lucrece puts it rather more nega-
tively: 'We haue no good that we can say is ours, | But ill annexed
opportunity, | Or kils his life, or else his quality' (sig. G1ᵛ, ll. 873–5).
'Timing is everything,' we might say.

But to say 'timing is everything' is to state an ethical position that
assumes a material distinction. People who are in the right place at
the right time are not just lucky: timing depends on forethought and
a certain access to power. Or we could put it another way: what looks
like lucky timing usually conceals a range of behavioural compro-
mises to secure the advantage. In *Lear*, these carefully concealed com-
promises are dramatized as the lack of resistance put up by temporal
and spatial contingency, the collapsing distances between Albany and
Cornwall, between Cornwall and Gloucester. Topographical obsta-
cles dissolve before the magical knack that the unscrupulous have of
being in the right place at the right time.

Thus it is that the very form of Regan's, Goneril's and Edmund's
desires begin to be shaped by the opportunities they see arise. 'Let his
knights haue colder looks among you . . . I would breed from hence
occasions,' as Goneril says, in Q1 (Q1, sig. C3ʳ); when Edmund weighs
up his options between the widow Regan and the married Goneril, he

contemplates not so much the loveliness of either as the lovely shape of possibility itself: 'Neither can be enioy'd | if both remaine aliue' (5.1.2894–5). Goneril's letter to Edmund expresses as sexual challenge and invitation the *opportunities* available for killing Albany: '*You haue manie opportunities to cut him off: if your will want not, time and place will be fruitfully offer'd*' (4.6.2716–18). And when the steward Oswald demurs about letting Regan unseal the letter he bears from Goneril to Edmund, her offer of preferment to the man who kills blind Gloucester prompts him to a more provisional answer: in Q1, 'Would I could meet him, Madam, I would shew | What Lady I doe follow' (Q1, sig. I2ʳ).[77]

To say this is different from saying that Goneril, Regan, Cornwall, Edmund, and the steward behave opportunistically. *Lear* is not, that is to say, the Queen's Men's *True Chronicle Historie of King Leir and his three daughters* (1605) where we have 'psychological motivation' on display in explicitly staged scenes of intrigue in which the sisters, speaking the language of foresight, occasion, and occlusion, find 'fit occasion' to be avenged on Cordella 'unperceyv'd'.[78] In *Lear* the psychology of opportunity is perceptible in the very preposterous form of its offstage events, its impossible transactions of letters and intelligence. So, for example, Kent's so-called 'report' of the unstaged event of his delivery of letters to Regan is a striking example, both in its belated ineffectuality and in the story it tells, of Kent's exile, as Lear's servant, from the brave new world of rhetorical and political opportunity. From shameful incarceration in the stocks, Kent explains to Lear and to the puzzled audience precisely why he struck and slandered Oswald:

> My Lord, when at their home,
> I did commend your Highnesse Letters to them,
> Ere I was risen from the place, that shewed
> My dutie kneeling, came there a reeking Poste,
> Stew'd in his haste, halfe breathlesse, painting forth
> From *Gonerill* his Mistris, salutation;
> Deliuer'd Letters, spite of intermission,
> Which presently they read; on those contents
> They summon'd vp their meiney, straight tooke Horse
> Commanded me to follow, and attend
> The leisure of their answer, gaue me cold lookes

> And meeting here the other Messenger
> Whose welcome I perceiu'd had poison'd mine . . .
> Hauing more man then wit about me, drew; (2.2.1303–18)

Two features of this account stand out. The first is the vivid *enargeia* of the description of how the steward appropriated a moment of reception clearly belonging to Kent, taking advantage of the latter's courteous pause, the instant between kneeling and rising. The rush of the main verb to anticipate its subject's arrival *there*, in Kent's very position of dutiful priority, defines the seized upon time and space of Opportunity: '*Ere* I was risen from *the place* | That shewed my dutie kneeling, *came there* a reeking Poste'. But the second striking feature is the speech's *bad timing*. The speech eloquently explains the apparently gratuitous abuse that Kent had earlier heaped on Oswald and amply justifies that abuse. Yet although Oswald's epistolary queue-jumping looks like a clear breach of postal etiquette, Kent's belated account of it to Lear makes us appreciate that he could not have been so vivid, or lucid, in the protracted interrogation before Cornwall. The muffling of the incident and its preposterous revelation before Lear thus dramatizes the impossibility, for the newly disempowered Kent, of speaking in a timely fashion, or of being timely.

'Such is the force of Opportunitas, of Timeliness, that it can . . . change the nature of everything,' wrote Erasmus; Weltkirchius wrote, however, that *Occasio* names the ease with which 'the poor are oppressed by the rich, the off-guard by the cunning'. In *Lear* we experience both of these truths. As Womack has said, in *Lear* it is the raw struggle to be Somebody that drives many of the play's characters into being various kinds of Nobody—unnamed servants, wandering beggars, the blind outcast, and the mad:

> This serial nullification of the play's high-born characters opens it up
> to the enormous absent presence of the wretches whose 'looped and
> windowed raggedness' they all come to share—stocked, locked out,
> naked, mutilated.[79]

I would add that the oddly mutable quality of the play's offstage world, the apparent distortions and deliberate vagueness of its distances and locations, are a part of this dispossessing 'nullification'. If opportunity is the 'fit' of time and place with human purpose, then those who, as Lucrece puts it, 'ne'er meet with opportunity'—that is, the 'soul whom wretchedness hath chained', and 'The poor, the lame, the blind' (sig. G2^{r-v}, ll. 876–903)—are those for whom the right time and place are *not to be found*. The dispossessed aristocrats of *Lear* become the wretched, the poor, and the blind of Lucrece's speech, for whom the right time never comes, the right place will not be.

Thus we might understand the significance of the perceived lack of adequate tragic 'motivation' for Cordelia's death which, as Bradley says, 'seems expressly designed to fall suddenly like a bolt from the sky'.[80] Where distance and length of time seemed, in Acts 1 and 2, opportunely obsequious to the purposes of rapid epistolary transaction and unimpeded domestic relocation, the action of Act 5, scene 3 designedly slows time down, fatally protracting the interval in which Edmund's commission for Cordelia's death might have been reversed. Stephen Booth has excellently explicated the scene as one in which Albany, distracted by the contents of the letter delivered to him by Edgar, completely bungles the opportunity—and there seems ample time for it—to save Cordelia's life. The scene opens with Lear and Cordelia being led away as captives and in urgent danger of death at the hands of Edmund's henchman. Though Albany promptly demands them as prisoners from Edmund, he proceeds with inexplicable leisure to allow the playing out of the 'interlude' of obliquely revealing what he knows about his wife's adultery; Edgar's triumph in combat over Edmund follows, with revelations of his identity and a narrative of the death of their father. Q1 includes a further delaying narrative about Kent, followed in both texts by the entrance of a Gentleman proclaiming 'O she's dead'; audience relief that this refers to Goneril and not Cordelia is short-lived. Only at this point of exhaustion does Kent come on to bid the King 'good night'. 'Great thing of vs forgot', exclaims Albany, 'Speake, *Edmund*, where's the King? and where's *Cordelia*?' (5.3.3192–3). 'The frustration of the audience', Booth writes, 'is scrupulously intensified by Shakespeare; his care is epitomized by the parenthetic plea for haste with which Edmund delays the syntactic completion of "quickly send to the castle":

> *Edmund.* I pant for life. Some good I mean to do,
> Despite of mine own nature. Quickly send –
> Be brief in it – to th'castle, for my writ
> Is on the lives of Lear, and on Cordelia
> Nay, send *in time* . . .

A moment later: *Enter Lear, with Cordelia in his arms*, and the most terrifying five minutes in literature have begun for the audience.'[81] Booth thus brilliantly attributes the emotional shock of Cordelia's death to its shocking *untimeliness*: 'If the power and intensity of our responses to the last moments of *King Lear* do not result from *what* happens,' he has written, 'they may result from *when* and *where* it happens.'[82] 'When' and 'where', of course, are the circumstances that, together, define the presence or absence of Opportunity.

Notes

1. I quote mainly from the Folio text of *Lear*, noting differences from Q1 (1608) where relevant. In the 1980s differences between the two texts of *Lear* became exemplary of the need to break with editing as the realizing of authorial intention. However, the broad observations I make about the plotting of *Lear* apply both to Q1 and to F, texts whose similarities are, for my argument, more important than their considerable differences. On the differences, see Michael Warren's excellent parallel text, *The Complete* King Lear *1608–1623* (Berkeley and Los Angeles: University of California Press, 1989) and *The Division of the Kingdoms: Shakespeare's Two Versions of King Lear*, ed. Gary Taylor and Michael Warren (Oxford: Clarendon Press, 1983).

2. *King Lear*, ed. R. A. Foakes (London: Arden, 1997) 211, note to 1.4.325.

3. See n. 13.

4. A. C. Bradley, *Shakespearean Tragedy: Lectures on Hamlet, Othello, King Lear and Macbeth* (Harmondsworth: Penguin, 1991) 238–42; W. W. Greg, 'Time, Place and Politics in "King Lear"', *Modern Language Review*, 35:4 (1940) 431–46, 432.

5. Jonathan Goldberg, 'Shakespeare Writing Matter Again: Objects and Their Detachments', *Shakespeare Studies*, 28 (2000) 248–51, 250–1; Alan Stewart, *Shakespeare's Letters* (Oxford: Oxford University Press, 2008) 220.

6. Bradley, *Shakespearean Tragedy*, 240.

7. Jonathan Goldberg, 'Dover Cliff and the Conditions of Representation: King Lear 4:6 in perspective', *Poetics Today*, 5:3 (1984) 537–47.

8. Bradley, *Shakespearean Tragedy*, 241.

9. Peter Womack, 'Nobody, Somebody and *King Lear*', *New Theatre Quarterly*, 23:3 (2007) 195–207, 205.

10. Cicero, *De inventione*, tr. H. M. Hubbell (Cambridge, Mass: Harvard University Press, 1949) i. 38–40.

11. *D. Erasmi Roterodami de Duplici Copia Verborum ac Rerum . . . cum commentarijs M. Veltkirchij* (London: Henry Middleton, 1573) fol. 135[r–v]: '*Tertia circunstantia est occasio, quam facultatem & opportunitatem & auxilia vocant alij, vt facilius est paucos a multis, improuidos ab insidiosis, pauperes a diuite opprimi, & ex hoc loco sumuntur argumenta et coniectura a facili, possibili, difficili.*'

12. In Q1, Regan speaks not of 'thredding' but of 'threatning darke ey'd Night'; the 'Occasions' are 'of prise' and the letters contain not 'differ-ences' but 'defences'; see *M. William Shak-speare his True Chronicle Historie of the life and death of King LEAR and his three daughters* (London, 1608) sig. D4ᵛ.

13. See Erasmus, 'Nosce Tempus/Consider the due time', in *The Adages of Erasmus*, ed. William Barker (Toronto: University of Toronto Press, 2000) 106–9; Andrea Alciato, *Emblemata* (Lyons, 1550), tr. Betty I. Knott (Aldershot: Scolar Press, 1996) 133–4.

14. Kelly A. Myers, 'Metanoia and the Transformation of Opportunity', *Rhetoric Society Quarterly*, 41:1 (2011) 1–18. Even Christian moralizations of this emblem tradition tended to stress Opportunity's positive value; see John Mulryan, 'A Parochial Twist on a Secular Proverb: Occasio's Bald Pate and the "Opportunity" to be Good in Joannes David's *Typus Occasionis* and *Occasio Arrepta*', *Emblemata*, 16 (2008) 133–50.

15. See Alexander Welsh, *Strong Circumstances: Narrative and Circumstantial Evidence in England* (Baltimore and London: Johns Hopkins Press, 1992) 18–31, 30.

16. Ian Hacking, *The Taming of Chance* (Cambridge: Cambridge University Press, 1990), 4.

17. I don't mean to suggest that critics working on Renaissance texts are unaware of the Renaissance meaning of 'probability', but only that this meaning is not generally acknowledged by the majority of Shakespeare critics. Examples of specialists in the Renaissance who have contributed to our understanding of probability in this period include Lisa Jardine, 'The Place of Dialectic Teaching in Sixteenth-Century Cambridge', *Studies in the Renaissance*, 21 (1974), 31–62; Victoria Kahn, *Rhetoric, Prudence and Skepticism* (Ithaca, NY: Cornell University Press, 1985); Peter Mack, *Renaissance Argument: Valla and Agricola in the Traditions of Rhetoric and Dialectic* (Leiden: Brill, 1993); Joel Altman, *The Improbability of Othello: Rhetorical Anthropology and Shakespearean Selfhood* (Chicago: Chicago University Press, 2010).

18. Ian Hacking, *The Emergence of Probability: A Philosophical Study of Early Ideas about Probability, Induction and Statistical Inference* (Cambridge: Cambridge University Press, first publ. 1975, 2nd edn 2006) 22–3.

19. Hacking, *The Emergence of Probability*, 43.

20. Douglas Lane Patey, *Probability and Literary Form: Philosophic Theory and Literary Practice in the Augustan Age* (Cambridge: Cambridge University Press, 1984) 266–73.

21. Patey, *Probability and Literary Form*, 4.

22. Patey, *Probability and Literary Form*, 35–6. '[C]onjecturing, as probable inference was called . . . must take account not only of clear signs, that might indicate a conclusion, but also of the modifying "circumstances" of each case.'

23. On 'artificial proof', see Kathy Eden, *Poetic and Legal Fiction in the Aristotelian Tradition* (Princeton: Princeton University Press, 1986) 12–21.

24. *OED*, circumstance, n, 4 a.

25. David F. Bell, *Circumstances: Chance in the Literary Text* (Lincoln: University of Nebraska, 1993).

26. Patey, *Probability and Literary Form*, 87; Charlotte Lennox, *Shakespear Illustrated: or the Novels and Histories On which the Plays of Shakespear Are Founded*, 3 vols (London: 1753), i. 93.

27. Patey, *Probability and Literary Form*, 61.

28. See, for example, D. W. Robertson, 'A Note on the Classical Origins of "Circumstances" in the Medieval Confessional', *Studies in Philology*, 43 (1946) 6–14.

29. On circumstances and hermeneutics, see Kathy Eden, *Hermeneutics and the Rhetorical Tradition: Chapters in the Ancient Legacy and its Humanist Reception* (New Haven: Yale University Press, 1997); Rita Copeland, *Rhetoric, Hermeneutics and Translation in the Middle Ages* (Cambridge: Cambridge University Press, 1991) 63–86. On Shakespeare's knowledge of circumstances from the pseudo-Ciceronian *Ad Herennium*, see T. W. Baldwin, *William Shakspere's Small Latine & Lesse Greeke*, 2 vols (Urbana: University of Illinois Press, 1944) ii. 76–81. On probability in Shakespeare, see Altman, *Improbability of Othello*.

30. Quintilian, *The Orator's Education*, ed. and tr. Donald A. Russell, 5 vols (Cambridge, Mass.: Harvard University Press, 2001), 3.6.23–8. Further references to book, chapter, and paragraph of this edition will be in the text. Quintilian's first mention of the circumstances as part of status theory is noted by Weltkirchius' note to Erasmus in *De copia*, 1573, fol. 134ᵛ: 'Out of the . . . last six Aristotelian predicaments Quintilian creates the circumstances in book 3 chapter 8' ('*Fab. ex. decem . . . ex posterioribus sex praedicamentis Aristotelicis facit circumstantias in lib. 3 cap. 8*').

31. When Cicero and Quintilian treat time, place, manner, etc., they always use a subjunctive mood—so for 'manner' (*modus*), Quintilian says, 'we ask how something *might be done*' (*quo quaeritur quem ad modum quid* sit *factum*).

32. See Marc Cogan, 'Rudolphus Agricola and the Semantic Revolutions of the History of Invention', *Rhetorica*, 2:2 (1984) 163–94, 168.

33. For discussions of the importance of this passage in Quintilian for Renaissance drama, see Eden, *Poetic and Legal Fiction*, 88–90; Baldwin, *Small Latine*, ii. 204.

34. See Ruth Webb, *Ekphrasis, Imagination and Persuasion in Ancient Rhetorical Theory and Practice* (Farnham: Ashgate, 2009) 109.

35. Erasmus, *De copia*, ed. Betty I. Knott, Opera omnia (Amsterdam:, North Holland, 1969–), ordinis I, tome 6 [hereafter *ASD*, I:6], I:6:202–15, 218, 230; Erasmus, *Copia, Collected Works of Erasmus* (Toronto: University of Toronto Press, 1974——) (hereafter *CWE*), 24:577–89; 591–2; 605; Erasmus, *De copia* (1573), fols 121ʳ–130ʳ, 133ᵛ–136ʳ, 148ᵛ–149ᵛ.

36. Erasmus, *De copia*, *ASD*, I:6:218–29, 222, l. 626; 223, l. 665; Erasmus, *Copia*, *CWE*, 24: 592–605; 596, l. 14; 597, l. 30; Erasmus, *De copia* (1573) 136ʳ–148ʳ.

37. Erasmus, *De copia, ASD*, I:6:203.

38. Erasmus, *De copia, ASD*, I:6:204, ll. 215–16; Erasmus, *Copia, CWE*, 24:579, ll. 9–11.

39. Erasmus, *De copia* (1573) fol. 127ʳ. '*nascitur ex definitione Dial. praesertim illa quam accidentariam [sic] descriptionem vocant.*' Books on dialectical invention, in turn, cross-refer accidental or contingent topics and rhetorical circumstances. Cf. Alardus on Agricola's dialectical topic of 'contingents'; he links these to Quintilian's 'circumstances', such as evidence of an altercation before the murder, or stammering and bad conscience after. Rodolphus Agricola, *De inventione dialectica lucubrationes*. Facsimile of the Edition Cologne, 1539 (Nieuwkoop: B. de Graaf, 1967) 113.

40. Erasmus, *De copia, ASD*, I:6:218, ll. 522–3: '*Facit enim vt tota oratio densis ac crebris argumentis vndique differta sit et communita*'; Erasmus, *Copia, CWE*, 24:592, ll. 2–3.

41. Erasmus, *De copia, ASD*, I:6:218, ll. 523–5: '*Quae tametsi non explices . . . tamen pugnant per sese*'; Erasmus, *Copia, CWE*, 24:592, l. 4.

42. See Mack, *Renaissance Argument*, 165.

43. Erasmus, *De copia* (1573), fol. 135ʳ, '*Secunda circunstantia est causa, quae hic significat prorsus efficientis voluntaria intentionem, voluntatem, propositum, consilium, quod tendit in aliquem finem medium aut ultimum, & significat etiam vsum aut finem negocij propositum, propter quem finem quisquam facit hoc aut illud. Huc ergo refertur causa voluntaria non naturalis.*'

44. Patey, *Probability and Literary Form*, 94.

45. Monte Johnson, *Aristotle on Teleology* (Oxford: Clarendon Press, 2005) 64–6.

46. Peter Mack, *Elizabethan Rhetoric* (Cambridge: Cambridge University Press, 2002) 127; see *The Papers of Nathaniel Bacon of Stiffkey*, i: *1556–1577*, ed. A. Hassell Smith (Norfolk Record Society, 1978 and 1979) 214.

47. Welsh, *Strong Circumstances*, 16.

48. See Wordsworth, *Lyrical Ballads* (London: Longman and Rees, 1802) LXV, '*Pectus enim id est quod disertos facit, & vis mentis; ideoque imperitis quoquo, si modo sint aliquo affectu concitati, verba non desunt*' ('It is the heart and power of the mind that make us eloquent. That is why even the unskilled, so long as they are stirred by some emotion, are not short of words'). See Quintilian, *Inst.*, 10.7.15 and 6.2.29. Thanks to Colin Burrow, who alerted me to this reference.

49. William Wordsworth, *The Borderers*, ed. Robert Osborn (Ithaca, NY, and London: Cornell University Press, 1982) 2.3.431–3, p. 180.

50. Wordsworth, *The Borderers*, 3.1.5–16, p. 182.

51. The play referred to by Philip Henslowe as 'harey the vj' was first played by Strange's Men on 3 March 1592 and its success is reported by Thomas Nashe in *Pierce Pennilesse* (August 1592). A month later, Robert Greene parodied a line from *1 Henry VI* in his mocking portrait of a 'Shake-scene'. It is usual to assume that 'harey the vj' refers to *1 Henry VI* as we know it from the Folio and that Shakespeare contributed to its composition. See *Henry VI part 1*, ed. Edward Burns (London: Arden, 2000)

8, 69–70. Bart Van Es, *Shakespeare in Company* (Oxford: Oxford University Press, 2013) describes Shakespeare as a 'conventional poet-playwright' in 1592–4 whose writing is 'alive with the presence of other writers, both as co-authors and as a transformative influence', 27. I think the notion of what is 'conventional' begs several questions and am reluctant to assume, as Van Es does, that the Folio *Taming of the Shrew* is an example of such 'early' and 'conventional' writing, but I share with Van Es the sense that something in Shakespeare's compositional habits changed around 1594.

52. References to *Lucrece* (London: Richard Field, 1594) will be given in the text by signature. I have also made extensive use of Colin Burrow's edition of *Lucrece* in William Shakespeare, *Complete Sonnets and Poems* (Oxford: Oxford University Press, 2002); references to line numbers in this edition will also be given in the text.

53. *The Poems*, ed. F. T. Prince (London: Methuen, 1960) xxxv.

54. For 'introspection and complaint', see Katherine Duncan-Jones, 'Ravished and Revised: The 1616 *Lucrece*', *Review of English Studies*, NS 52:208 (2001) 517.

55. William Weaver, ' "O teach me how to make mine own excuse": Forensic Performance in *Lucrece*', *Shakespeare Quarterly*, 59 (2008) 424–30, 423.

56. On the Augustinian dilemma, see Ian Donaldson, *The Rapes of Lucretia: A Myth and Its Transformations* (Oxford: Clarendon Press, 1982) 21–39.

57. On the issue of quality, see also Heinrich Lausberg, *Handbook of Literary Rhetoric: A Foundation for Literary Study*, tr. Matthew T. Bliss, Annemiek Jansen, and David E. Orton (Leiden: Brill, 1998) §§171–96.

58. Weaver, 'Forensic Performance in *Lucrece*', 441.

59. Jonathan Bate, *Shakespeare and Ovid* (Oxford: Clarendon Press, 1993) 81.

60. Erasmus, *De copia*, 204, ll. 215–16, p. 206, ll. 279–3; tr. p. 48, p. 50.

61. Simon Goldhill, 'What is Ekphrasis for?', *Classical Philology*, 102 (2007) 1–19, 2.

62. Philostratus, *Imagines*, tr. Arthur Fairbanks (Cambridge, Mass.: Harvard, 1931) book 1, 4, 'Menoeceus', the siege of Thebes, 16–17. *Complete Sonnets and Poems*, ed. Burrow, 318.

63. Goldhill, 'What is Ekphrasis For?', 2–4; Goldhill cites Quintilian, 6.2.29.

64. P. H. Schrijvers, 'Invention, imagination et théorie des émotions chez Cicero et Quintilien', in J. den Boeft and A. H. M. Kessels (eds), *Actus: Studies in Honour of H. L. W. Nelson* (Utrecht: Instituut voor Klassieke Talen, 1982) 395–408, 402–3.

65. Schrijvers, 'Invention', 403.

66. Gerard Watson, *Phantasia in Classical Thought* (Galway: Galway University Press, 1988) 59.

67. See Philostratus, *Imagines*, book 2, 1, 'Singers', 130–2; Quintilian, *Inst.*, 8.3.62. Shrijvers discusses the importance of this theory of *phantasia* to the Younger Philostratus' *Apollonius of Tyana*; for more on this, see Watson, *Phantasia in Classical Thought*.

68. *Complete Sonnets and Poems*, ed. Burrow, 318.

69. See Weaver, 'Forensic Performance in *Lucrece*', 435–7; for the issue of quality, see also Lausberg, *Handbook*, §§171–96.

70. Weaver, 'Forensic Performance in *Lucrece*', 435.

71. *Complete Sonnets and Poems*, ed. Burrow, 48–9.

72. Weaver, 'Forensic Performance in *Lucrece*', 444; Mack, *Renaissance Argument*, 193–5.

73. Mack, *Renaissance Argument*, 193–4; Agricola, *De inventione dialectica*, 262–3.

74. Weaver, 'Forensic Performance in *Lucrece*', 444.

75. Erasmus, 'Nosce Tempus', *Adages of Erasmus*, ed. Barker, 106; '*Tantum vim habet opportunitas, vt ex honesto inhonestum, ex damno lucrum, ex voluptate molestiam, ex beneficio maleficium faciat et contra breviterque rerum omnium naturem permutet*', *Adagia, ASD*, II:2:196.

76. Erasmus, *De copia*, 1573, fol. 134ʳ; Cicero, *De officiis*, tr. Walter Miller (Cambridge, Mass.: Harvard University Press, 1913) 1.40.142, '*locum autem actionis opportunitatem temporis esse dicunt; tempus autem actionis opportunitatem Graece εὐκαιρία, Latine appellatur occasio*', 'By "place of action", moreover, they mean "opportunity"; and the "opportunity" for an action is called in Greek *eukairia*, in Latin *occasio* (occasion)'; Nicholas Grimalde, 'And place, they saye, concerneth the doyng, opportunitie the time. And time conuenient for the doing, in Greeke εὐκαρία, in Latine is called *Occasio*', *Marcus Tullius Ciceroes thre bokes of duties*, ed. Gerald O'Gorman (Washington: Folger Shakespeare Library, 1990) 104.

77. See Stewart, *Shakespeare's Letters*, 212.

78. Geoffrey Bullough (ed.), *Narrative and Dramatic Sources of Shakespeare* (London: Routledge and Kegan Paul, 1973) vii. 341, ll. 166, 169–70; Grace Ioppolo, 'A Jointure more or less: Re-measuring *The True Chronicle History of King Leir and his three daughters*', *Medieval and Renaissance Drama in England*, 17 (2005) 165–79, 176–8.

79. Womack, 'Nobody, Somebody and *King Lear*', 206.

80. Bradley, *Shakespearean Tragedy*, 233–4.

81. Stephen Booth, *King Lear, Macbeth, Indefinition and Tragedy* (New Haven: Yale University Press, 1983) 10–11.

82. Booth, *King Lear, Macbeth, Indefinition and Tragedy*, 6.

3

Where and How?

Two Gentlemen of Verona *and* The Maid's Tragedy

3.1. 'Tant d'actes particuliers'

In these chapters I have been talking about the way in which Shakespeare's plays use the topics of circumstance to establish a sense of the play's outer 'world'—its spaces, distances, temporality, architecture—as already shaped by the psychology or ethics of a particular human story. The mark of this circumstantial dramaturgy's success has been its invisibility. So effective has Shakespeare's circumstantial plotting of the play world been that generations of readers and audiences have assumed that the inwardness and psychological depth of Shakespeare's characters is separable from the play world's 'objective' coherence (the character of Othello is separate from the 'time scheme' of *Othello*; Hamlet is separable from the 'Denmark' of *Hamlet* and from 'the revenge plot'). But the Shakespearean play world, of course, not only has no objective coherence—it is not even composed to persuade us of the illusion that it has. That is not the nature of its 'probability'. Its inferred times and places are the product of highly emotive dialogues and soliloquies that are structured, however playfully, as clever ways of proving arguments about questions of human value. It is from the emotive and ethical 'probability' of these arguments that we infer both the contours of the dramatic world and characters' motives, anxieties, and desires. So the times and places we infer in a Shakespearean play are already ethically charged: charged, that is, with the potential for imagining and analysing the particularized personal dramas that constitute 'character'.

Critics have recently written a great deal about the collective and collaborative dimensions of Shakespearean theatre as explanatory of

Shakespearean effects of 'psychological depth' or 'inwardness'. Some have emphasized continuities between Shakespearean theatre and the participatory ritual of forgiveness known as the sacrament of penance, celebrated in the theatre of Corpus Christi; others have stressed Shakespeare's working with known actors and developing an intensely relational dramatic practice. Persuasive as these accounts are, they take no account of the argumentative texture of plot composition, of the way in which a dramatic world of histories, households, places, and distances may be implied and made 'probable' by the tropes and figures used in a dramatic dialogue. The neglect of this topic is part of a general underestimation of the difference made by rhetoric and dialectic in transforming the ways in which arguments seem probable or believable or transforming the ways in which people came, in the sixteenth century, to trust and believe in knowledge about one another.

In the 1980s, Stephen Greenblatt wrote a thoughtful and provocative essay on why Renaissance stories about crises of 'identity' or the unmooring of the self's bearings seemed not adequately explained as the products of a 'psychic condition' or not amenable to psychoanalytic analyses. Taking his cue from Natalie Davis's rich socio-historical analysis of the famous French imposture case of Martin Guerre (in which a look-alike, Arnaud du Tilh, successfully impersonated Guerre for years in the village of Artigat, enjoying Guerre's wife and patrimony), Greenblatt pointed to the way in which English dramatists returned again and again to tell the story of similar impostures. 'In Renaissance drama, as in the case of Martin Guerre, the traditional linkages between body, property and name are called into question,' he noted. Yet in both, 'identity is conceived in a way that renders psychoanalytic interpretations marginal or belated'.[1]

> For what matters most in the literary texts, as in the documents that record the case of Martin Guerre, are communally secured proprietary rights to a name and a place in an increasingly mobile social world, and these rights seem more an historical condition that enables the development of psychoanalysis than a psychic condition that psychoanalysis itself can adequately explain.[2]

Greenblatt here argued that it was no coincidence that the drama of the Renaissance so often 'invites reflection on the extent to which it is possible for one man to assume the identity of another', for this drama of deception, playful in the theatre, punishable in life, was a part of the long cultural process by which an identity established by 'communally secured proprietary rights to a name and place' was transformed into an identity established by the disciplinary narratives of psychoanalysis.[3] Greenblatt's terminology is that of performance ('Every theatrical performance at once confirms and denies this possibility').[4] The word 'performance', however, may distract us from the textual condition of probability, the fact that, for an imposture to be successful, a man must speak as if he has 'inward' or intimate knowledge, he must use trivial circumstances to speak *probabiliter*, convincingly. Part of what was so troublingly effective about Arnauld du Tilh's performance as Martin Guerre was his apparent mastery of innumerable domestic details, names of villagers, locations of items of furniture and clothing; the lawyer Jean de Coras remarked that he had never known a man with a memory '*si heureuse*', so happy, '*de se souuenir de tant d'actes particuliers, des lieux, & des propos, de si long temps, & a l'endroit de tant & tant de personnes*'.[5] Du Tilh was apparently able to say to each villager he met, 'Don't you remember, when we were at a certain place, ten or twelve, fifteen or twenty years ago, that we did this or that thing, in so-and-so's presence?'[6] For the humanist Coras, Du Tilh was comparable to the great generals of Persia, Greece, and Rome, who memorized all the names of their soldiers in order to be able to seem familiar and friendly with them. He was an untaught master of the art of memory, able to deploy the topics of circumstance credibly in a thousand little narratives of domestic life in Artigat. If dramas of deception and imposture are evidence of a long cultural upheaval in modes of thinking about identity and how it is secured, they may also speak less of a fascination with performance per se than of a fascination with the emotive productivity and *enargeia* of such circumstantial proofs, which so skilfully constitute or simulate the contours of intimate knowledge and personal 'inwardness'.

Shakespeare's *Two Gentlemen of Verona* is not exactly one of the myriad Renaissance plays turning on imposture and impersonation. Proteus does not assume his friend's clothing or trick anyone into thinking that he is Valentine. Yet he imitates him in everything. He attempts to appropriate Valentine's social and erotic success and happiness, following him to Milan, taking his place in the Duke of Milan's affections, and trying his best to lay claim to the Duke of Milan's daughter and heir, Silvia, whose love Valentine by this time possesses. Such a theft of the proprietary markers of Valentine's (gentlemanly) identity requires, as the play explicitly shows, emotive and persuasive skill. Having successfully betrayed Valentine to the Duke's anger and to banishment, Proteus needs to wipe Valentine from Silvia's memory and affections. This he proposes to do by slandering him 'With falsehood, cowardize and poore discent: | Three things, that women highly hold in hate' (3.2.1476). When the Duke (to whom Proteus outlines one part of this plan) objects that Silvia would be sceptical of the motives of one making such a speech, Proteus concedes the importance of circumstantial proof, 'it must with *circumstance* be spoken, | By one, whom she esteemeth as his friend' (3.2.1481). Proteus' 'circumstance' is, implicitly, Arnaud du Tilh's mastery of '*tant d'actes particuliers, & tant de personnes*', the details of white taffeta stockings left in a certain coffer. It is the deployment of these circumstantial proofs that turn 'property' into 'psyche' or that tread the line between the social and the inward markers of identity.

I am not, however, trying to argue that Proteus 'is' Arnauld du Tilh, or that the play is even concerned with the plausibly circumstantial detail of the slanders Proteus might have dredged up against his boyhood friend, Valentine. The play takes no interest in dramatizing the probability of these, referring only generically—whether in Proteus' voice or Silvia's—to the 'falsehood', 'vowes', and 'flattery' of Proteus' courtship of Silvia (4.2.1630–1,1719–20). My interest is, rather, in the way circumstantial invention begins, in this early Shakespearean comedy, to turn markers of social identity—the definition of a 'gentleman'—into a drama of inwardness, character, psychology. In this process, the identities of 'Valentine' and 'Proteus' are distinguished precisely so that the latter can realize the potential loss or theft of a deeper 'truer self' that is already implicit in the former's—that is, in Valentine's—materialistic model of love as courtly ambition. What Proteus does, in other words, is to realize the logic of the value system Valentine embodies, to push it to the point where, from being a social code to secure the identity of a gentleman, it becomes a drama of the betrayal of one's faithful self by one's ambitious self. This is why Proteus seems to have marginally more 'depth' than Valentine (though admittedly, there is not much in it). 'Where' and 'how' are, as

I will show, the circumstantial questions which shape both the play's materialist critique of gentlemanly behaviour and an emergent inwardness: that is, a sense of unconscious motives anticipating a conscious act of betrayal. Circumstantial arguments shape a play world of differentiated locations that are simultaneously 'real' and ethically charged.

3.2. Where Should a Gentleman Spend His Time?

Nevertheless, *The Two Gentlemen of Verona* will still seem an outrageous choice of play for a demonstration of the importance of circumstantial argument to our 'belief' in the fictional world or to our sense that any ethical import attaches to the fidelity of either gentleman. For *Two Gentlemen* is notorious for being utterly careless to establish any consistency of place and for having no serious ethical concerns: we are never quite sure *where* the action takes place—the title says Verona, and the young men seem to head for Milan, but confusion abounds. The first location in which we meet our 'gentlemen' is never named as such; in 2.5 the 'Milan' to which they have both relocated seems temporarily to have become Padua, and in 3.1 the Duke of that city confusingly refers to 'here' as 'Verona', not Milan ('There is a Lady in *Verona* heere', 3.1.1150). Besides this, there is all the boarding of ships to inland destinations—the two gentlemen seem continually to be embarking at harbours for Italian cities whose connecting routes were well known to be overland. Clifford Leech, editing the play in 1969, listed over forty such contradictions of detail.[7] On the question of the play's ethics or characterization critics are equally scathing. In an early and influential study Stanley Wells commented on the failure of characterization in the play. Our impressions of both gentlemen are at first sympathetic, but Valentine turns out to be 'downright stupid' while Proteus behaves 'in the most caddish manner imaginable' deciding to betray both his betrothed and his friend.[8] Even earlier, Arthur Quiller-Couch concluded that the behaviour of both Valentine and Proteus towards Silvia meant that, by the end of the play, 'there are . . . *no* gentlemen in Verona'.[9] Adrian Kiernander's response to the apparent lack of both locational and ethical referentiality is to retitle the play, 'Non-Consensual Sex Somewhere in the Vicinity of Milan'.[10]

Critics have taken the play's failings to indicate Shakespeare's youthful inexperience, but it is precisely this sense of the play's relatively sketchy composition that makes it so illuminating as an example of a circumstantial technique that Shakespeare would go on to develop with greater complexity. (I am assuming that the 1623 Folio text of *Two Gentlemen of Verona* substantially represents the play likely to have been composed around the same time as *Romeo and Juliet* and in circulation before 1598.[11]) Montemayor's story of Felix and Felismena provides Shakespeare with a proof of the inconstancy caused by '*ausencia*' or absence, in the form of a separation from the beloved. Montemayor's Don Felix, who leaves his beloved Felismena, seems to be the clear antecedent of Shakespeare's changeable Proteus, who leaves Julia.[12] In Montemayor, Felismena dresses as a young man and rides the twenty miles to the imperial court at which Felix now serves, only to hear her beloved singing love songs to a new mistress, just as Shakespeare's Julia, leaving Verona for Milan to follow Proteus, hears him singing songs to Silvia (4.2). Felismena learns from Felix's page, Fabius, that Don Felix did have a beautiful mistress back home, but she's *absent* now, he says, and 'this mischievous absence doth violate and dissolve those things, which men thinke to be most strong and firme'.[13] Critics assume Proteus is a changeable 'character', that he *is* Don Felix.[14] His movement from Verona to Milan apparently makes him inconstant (because absence violates and dissolves things that are firm) but he is destined to be so, since his name derives from the shape-changing sea god, a byword for changeableness.[15]

But Shakespeare does nothing so simple as to replace Don Felix with Proteus. Rather, he turns the premise of Montemayor's narrative—the '*ausencia*' or absence occasioned by the young man leaving home to seek profit at a foreign court—into a dialectical *proposition* the circumstantial proving of which generates the two main characters (the two gentlemen) and explains the motif of their friendship, intimacy, and identical education ('I knew him as my selfe: for from our Infancie, | We have converst, and spent our howres together,' says Valentine of Proteus, 2.4.712-13). It is worth recalling that the invention of propositions and their proving by circumstances was one of the methods of '*copia*' discussed by Erasmus and Weltkirchius.[16] Erasmus, indeed, said that the invention of propositions required particular ingenuity (*ingenium*). Shakespeare applied such ingenuity to Montemayor, where he read that Don Felix's father, hearing of Felix's seduction of Felismena, dispatched his son to a royal court twenty miles away so he could employ the arts of amorous speech with better advantage. The father moralized his decision thus: '[I]t was not meete that a yoonge Gentleman, and of so noble a house as he was, should spende his youth idly at home, where nothing could be learned, but examples of vice, whereof the very same Idelnes (he said) was the onely Mistresse.'[17] Here was Shakespeare's proposition, the basis of his play. He imagined the voices of Valentine and Proteus arguing on opposite sides of it, then a reprisal of the same argument by Proteus' father and his friend Pantino in Act 1, scene 3, and then Proteus succumbing to patriarchal imperative and Valentine's example. It is the emotive and parodying process of inventing and acting on the arguments of either side that constitutes both the play's fictional 'world' (the 'where?' that distinguishes Verona from Milan, 'home' from 'abroad') and its sharply ethical scrutiny of the motivating desires (the 'how?' of manner or behaviour) that characterize the gentlemen defined by this proposition.

The play opens with the dismissal of an implied argument against travelling abroad, an implied entreaty to stay at home. 'Cease to perswade, my louing *Protheus*,' says Valentine,

> Home-keeping youth, haue euer homely wits,
> Wer't not affection chaines thy tender dayes
> To the sweet glaunces of thy honour'd Loue,
> I rather would entreat thy company,
> To see the wonders of the world abroad,
> Then (liuing dully sluggardiz'd at home)
> Weare out thy youth in shapeless idlenesse. (1.1.1–11)

As an illocutionary speech act, this operates as a (somewhat backhanded) gesture at invitation, indicating Valentine's leave-taking and confirmed by Proteus' reply: 'Wilt thou be gone? Sweet *Valentine*, adew' (1.1.14). In rhetorical or dialectical terms, however, the invitation is clearly a form of 'proof', a refutation of Proteus' unheard argument by insulting it as the product of a 'homely wit' (the neatly vacuous circularity of the proof does not make it less effective). The speech act of leave-taking continues both to constitute dramatic action (Valentine preparing to travel) and dialectically to define and evaluate the locations of 'home' and 'abroad' by associating the latter with seeing 'wonders' and improving one's wits, while the former lapses into the 'shapeless idlenesse' of loving and living 'dully sluggardiz'd'. By way of a series of puns on 'boots'—as a synonym for shoes, 'ouer-bootes in loue'; 'giue me not the Boots' ('don't mock me'); 'it boots thee not' ('it's not *profitable*'), Valentine is able to introduce a definition of home-bound love as a bootless or *unprofitable* exchange:

> *Val.* To be in loue; where scorne is bought with grones:
> Coy looks, with hart-sore sighes: one fading moments mirth,
> With twenty watchfull, weary, tedious nights;
> If hap'ly won, perhaps a haplesse gaine;
> If lost, why then a grievous labour won;
> How euer: but a folly bought with wit,
> Or else a wit by folly vanquished. (1.1.28–41)

'Being in love' becomes a series of antitheses understood as bad material bargains: you pay up in groans, and heart-sore sighs, multiple watchful, weary nights, and you get scorn, coy looks, and maybe—if you are very lucky—a fading moment's mirth. This definition, of course, has nothing to do with whether or not 'courtly love' is honourable or profitable in itself; after all, Valentine's own thoroughly profitable courtship of heiress Silvia in Act 2 is rhetorically identical to Proteus' of Julia. Valentine's definition moves Proteus not because it is true but because it is probable; it possesses the *enargeia* which Erasmus' *De copia* identified with dialectical definition by means of 'circumstances'.[18] One of the objects of dialectical argumentation was, as Rudolph Agricola insisted, emotional manipulation.[19] Rhetorical figures—techniques of patterning and repetition—heighten argumentation's emotional effect—here by the omission of conjunctions (*asyndeton*), a figure used, as Quintilian says, when 'we are particularly insistent on something' (*Inst.*, 9.3.50). Valentine's particular insistence is the proof, by circumstance, that only unambitious fools stay at home. This, at least, is how Proteus understands him:

> *Pro.* So, by your circumstance, you call me foole.
> *Val.* So, by your circumstance, I fear you'll proue. (1.1.40–1)

Valentine's exit is followed by a short, dejected soliloquy in which Proteus reiterates Valentine's antitheses: honour and love are equated, respectively, with going abroad and staying at home; leaving one's friends 'dignifies them' while staying at home to love is merely undignified self-leaving or self-loss. Then Speed enters as a clown/Vice figure initiating the familiar dramatic routine of the tardy servant looking for his master. This routine quickly becomes another game of dialectical definition by circumstance: Proteus tells Speed that his master has embarked; Speed redefines 'embarque' as 'ship'd' and punningly defines himself as a 'Sheepe'; Proteus offers to prove him a sheep, which the latter argues he will deny 'by a *circumstance*' (my italics), but Proteus wins, arguing by analogy that as a sheep follows the shepherd for food, so Speed follows Valentine for wages (1.1.75–97). The pastoral vocabulary, with its mercenary reduction of courtship to pounding sheep, flows on through Speed's satirical account of the tight-fisted prostitute ('lac'd-Mutton') who gave him nothing for delivering Proteus' letter (1.1.101). It is clear by the end of the first scene that the circumstantial definition of propositions is both constitutive of the 'where' of the play world (its imaginary locations of home/ Verona and abroad/Milan) and subversively analytical of the social stakes of its own processes of 'proving'.

In Montemayor's *Diana*—and presumably in the Queen's Men's now lost play *Felix and Philomena* (1585)—Don Felix's very name proves that gentlemen thrive by foreign travel, since '*feliz*' in Spanish means 'successful, lucky, happy'. Shakespeare transposes the name which identifies 'happiness' with 'moving' onto the servant, Speed, who exposes, both verbally and actively, the material gains that define a successful investment of effort in courtly lovemaking. (To 'speed', of course, is 'to succeed or prosper, to meet with success or good fortune, to obtain one's purpose or desire'.[20]) Nevertheless, lexical variants on the word 'happy' and 'success' pervade the opening exchange between Valentine and Proteus in such a way as to leave us in no doubt that travel and courtship are projects in which a gentleman hopes to thrive, to enjoy good hap. Proteus hopes that when Valentine 'haply' sees some noteworthy object on his travels, he will be 'partaker in thy happinesse | When thou do'st meet good hap' (1.1.15–18); Valentine mocks that Proteus will 'pray for my successe' on some book of love (1.1.22) and exhorts 'To *Millaine* let me heare from thee by Letters | Of thy successe in loue' (1.1.61–2), while Proteus concludes, 'all happinesse bechance to thee in *Millaine*' (1.1.65).

Ever since Robert Weimann's brilliant theorization of the distinction between the medieval *locus* and *platea* as a distinction between the mimetic acting of a fiction, and the acting that subverts mimesis by reaching out to the audience, it has been commonplace to say that Shakespeare's clowns disrupt the illusion of the play world and subvert its values, just as the Vice subverted the serious spiritual concerns of the allegorical morality play. On Speed's asides during Valentine's courtship of Silvia in Act 2, scene 1, Weimann thus observes,

> The object (Silvia's and Valentine's high-flown addresses) is part of the play world, but the perspective of his comic 'asides' links the clown with the real world of everyday experience.[21]

Yet, oddly enough, this is not really true. The materializing wordplay by which Lance and Speed mock Valentine's and Proteus' hyperbolic rhetoric and expose its lack of reference to anything 'real' is in fact as constitutive of the play's imaginary world of travel and courtship as any other language in the play. And if the clowns' language is subversive of Valentine's high-flown addresses, the pretext of these (as the play's opening debate shows us) hardly needs subverting.

Speed's asides and mocking replies to Valentine in Act 2, scene 1, expose the material objectives that move his eloquence as well commenting on the thoroughly generic nature of the language of courtship. When Valentine tells Speed that Silvia's 'beauty is exquisite | But her favour infinite', Speed's down-to-earth version ('the one is painted and the other out of all count . . . Marry, sir, so painted to make her faire that no man counts of her beauty', 2.1.448–54) merely extends the irony of the opening sequence, in which Valentine's competitive proofs elevated the status of happiness and good success 'abroad' by talking down 'home'. Materially speaking, the beauty of Valentine's new love is an effect of location, a circumstantial proof of the originating proposition. Courting heiress Silvia in Milan ('abroad') is simply the opposite of 'spending youth idly at home' by courting non-heiress Julia. When Speed comments to the audience on Valentine's failure to perceive that Silvia has commissioned him to be the scribe of a love letter to himself the effect is to strengthen the audience's sense of the merely generic quality of the textual content of courtly wooing—both Valentine and Proteus can produce the necessary language of sighs, tears, and vows to order.

René Girard's reading of the play as an instance of 'mimetic desire' clearly shows the way in which Valentine's epideictic rhetoric proceeds, by means of its relentlessly comparative proofs, to endow certain objects with value by devaluing others. In Girard's reading it is not Proteus whose selfish ambition trumps some Renaissance formula of ideal friendship, but Valentine whose comparative rhetoric *forces* Proteus to desire to imitate and finally rival and betray him.[22] Proteus' sudden passion for Silvia comes about as a result of the comparative mode of proof that requires that Valentine debase Julia to elevate Silvia, just as he earlier insulted 'home' to prove the worth of 'abroad'. Valentine ignites Proteus' desire by vaunting his good fortune and commanding Proteus to praise Silvia:

> *Val.* Call her diuine.
> *Pro.* I will not flatter her.
> *Val.* O flatter me: for Loue delights in praises . . .
> *Pro.* Haue I not reason to prefer mine owne?
> *Val.* And I will help thee to prefer her to:
> Shee shall be dignified in this high honour,
> To beare my Ladies traine . . . (2.4.799–813)

'As he listens to this', Girard drily observes, 'Proteus must picture the dismal future that awaits him in the company of his pathetic Julia.'[23] Proteus' soliloquy at the beginning of Act 2, scene 6 justifies his perjury by invoking Valentine's own conviction of the transcendent value of Silvia:

> O sweet-suggesting Loue, if thou hast sin'd,
> Teach me (thy tempted subiect) to excuse it.
> At first I did adore a twinkling Starre,
> But now I worship a celestiall Sunne. (2.6.936–9)

It is clear that Silvia's greater desirability as a mistress is an effect of the proving of the circumstantial question 'where?', that is 'where should a gentleman spend his time?' ('Silvia happens to be the daughter of the reigning Duke,' Girard notes.[24]) It is also clear that the really profitable 'moving' that advances gentlemen's fortunes is not the moving from Verona to Milan or from home to abroad, but the *emotional* moving wrought by eloquence—including eloquence in the deployment of circumstantial proofs to create believable fictions. In the scene of Valentine's fictional movement towards Milan the real action involves

Proteus' being *moved* to self-doubt by Valentine's 'circumstance'. The implicit pun is on the Latin *movere*, to move, which literally means 'to set in motion' and figuratively 'to affect, excite, inspire, make an impression on'. Shakespeare, then, uses circumstantial proofs to constitute the rudimentary fictionality of the imagined world (movement between its local habitations, the distinction between its names) while, at the same time, asking us to scrutinize the ideological work performed by such 'proving'.

3.3. 'How did thy Master part with Madam *Iulia*?'

Shakespeare's splitting of Montemayor's lucky and inconstant Don Felix into two gentlemen produced the second gentleman as a kind of simulacrum or parody of the first. Sensing this, critics liken Proteus to 'the medieval Vice' or express exasperation that the soliloquies in which he deliberates on his serial betrayals seem, outrageously, 'to invite our sympathy with what he takes to be a moral dilemma'.[25] Yet the shallowness and inauthenticity we sense in Proteus is not the limit of Proteus as a 'character'; it is, rather, an analytical and critical parody of the social 'character of a gentlemen' that we see in his model, Valentine. We sense this not only in Proteus' grosser blunders (the substitution of Lance's cur for a courtly lap-dog) but in comically crass locutions (urging Thurio to compose sonnets 'full fraught with serviceable vowes' (3.2.1514), which conjures lovers as shipping merchants totting up bills of lading). These moments of crudeness are funny and hapless versions of the bullying social competitiveness that characterized Valentine's tactics in courtship; for example, when he nastily equates Thurio's inarticulacy with bad faith, implying in the phrase 'bare words' that he fails to pay his servants (2.4.695).[26] As well as doubling his gentleman-hero, however, Shakespeare made another significant change to Montemayor's story. In Montemayor, Felix slipped away from Felismena without a word ('his great grief would not suffer him to acquaint me with his departure,' said Felismena, whether naively or ironically).[27] In *Two Gentlemen*, by contrast, Shakespeare devotes an entire short scene to the exchange of rings, handfasting, and vow that transforms the parting of Proteus and Julia into a betrothal. The staging of this spousal is deliberately designed to call the ethics of gentlemanly eloquence—its simulated emotional inwardness and its speaking 'with circumstance'—into question. The handfasting turns the play's mockery of the gentlemen's repertoire of tears, sighs, and vows into a question of what distinguishes probable argument—the aim of which is *fides*, faith or belief—from actually keeping faith.[28] So the inauthenticity that has, from the first, haunted the generic language of the gentlemen's courtship begins to emerge, from parodic scenes involving Lance and Speed, as a question of '*causa*' or 'motive' which in turn begins to constitute Proteus as a character whose conscious or unconscious motives for deceiving his friend and betraying his lover become the object of our interest.

This is why, oddly enough, the verbal disorderings of the Vice or clown are not 'disruptive' of our faith or belief in the probability of the play world of *Two Gentlemen*, but are rather constitutive of its imaginative topography and also of our belief in what truth or inwardness its characters seem to possess. For our belief was never a belief in the objective 'probability' in the post-Pascalian sense (this is why, *pace* Coleridge, we don't need to suspend it) but rather a belief in or conception of the ethical stakes of what, in material terms, is being contested. Knowing about 'where', about home and abroad and inferring 'Verona' and 'Milan', does not mean suspending disbelief about the objective existence of these places: it means, as we perfectly well know, grasping something of what is at stake in the contest over definitions of gentility or social status.[29]

Travel by water to the Italian cities of *Two Gentlemen of Verona* is not, in other words, a careless mistake. It is a copious, circumstantial, and comic *proof* of the proposition, an effect of producing the external circumstances of the play as simultaneously human, inward, and affective and, by way of clowning subversions, interrogating the affective investments they imply. So, for example, the circumstance-creating vocabulary of 'ships' and 'shipping' generates and is generated by puns on 'sheep' and shepherding, with all the economic associations involved. Speed is thus proved a sheep by 'a circumstance' (1.1.88) in a dialogue that begins with shipping—'Twenty to one, then, he is ship'd already, | And I have plaid the Sheepe in loosing him' (1.1.76–7). When Lance starts replaying the 'ship' pun in Act 3, scene 1, as Valentine prepares to leave for his banishment from the city, critics complain of its impropriety, since the anticipated travel is by land, not sea. 'what newes with your Mastership?', asks Speed, and Lance answers, 'With my Mastership? why, it is at Sea' (3.1.1348). But this objection in itself pays tribute to a reader's or audience's disposition to interpret even punning subversions of meaning as contributors to the substantive fiction.

If the first act of the play was concerned with proving the circumstantial topic of *locus*, place, or answering the question 'where?', the second act shifts to a concern with *modus*, manner, asking the question 'how?', a question often linked, in forensic rhetoric, with conjectures about motive (so Quintilian, *Inst.*, 5.10.52, 'if, for instance, I were to say it was done with good intention, and so openly, or with bad intention, and so by ambush'). So Lance steps onstage with his dog immediately after we have witnessed the tearful betrothal of Proteus and Julia to describe the emotional 'manner' of his own farewell from Verona. Proteus' leave-taking of Julia glossed her tears and silence as probable signs; her tears were a 'tide' that would 'stay' him from his journey; her silence a sign that 'truth hath better deeds, then words to grace it' (2.2.582–6). Unable to find words adequate to the tidal wave of grief experienced by his family at his departure for Milan ('My Mother weeping: my Father wayling: my Sister crying: our Maid howling: our Catte wringing her hands', 2.3.598–600), Lance wrestles with the casting of his shoes, staff, and dog in various roles to 'shew' us 'the manner of it' (2.3.606), that is, to enact mimetically what he should convey by a verbal *ekphrasis*. For theatre critics the scene is famous. While the dog always steals the show, it does so, they say, by marking the limits of illusory stage mimesis: 'the illusion has suddenly become a field of play, of what if? . . . What if it barks? Urinates?'[30] But since Lance is trying to *describe an offstage event*, his whole miniature show, dog included, also works to critique the Protean *enargeia*, that is, the gentleman's investment in using vivid, circumstantial language to move his auditors into imagining what is not there (i.e. sincere feeling). Underlying the mockery of Proteus here lies a parody of Erasmus' citing of '*Proteo mutabilor*' ('more mutable than Proteus') as an example of how one might collect material under the heading 'inconstancy' and then turn it to the praise of 'versatility'.[31] You may say, Erasmus proposes, 'that senseless rock and brute earth alone are unmoved', or 'the basest element is earth, which does not move, but water moves' ('*stupida saxa ac brutam tellurem vnam non moueri . . . infima est, quae non mouetur, terra; at mobilis acqua*').[32] Lance's dog is Erasmus' '*stupida saxa*', 'a stone, a very pibble stone' for not being moved to weep, the 'vnkindest Tide that euer any man tied' (2.3.602, 631). Yet Lance also slyly aligns himself with the dog ('I am the dogge: no, the dogge is himselfe and I am the dogge' 2.3.613–15) and implicitly with Proteus in being *unmoved*. As a comment on Proteus' 'nay, not thy tide of teares, | That tide will stay me longer then I should' (2.2.582–3), Lance's scene exposes the facility with which Proteus' emotive proofs secure another's faith while he himself remains unmoved. Pantino warns Lance that in losing the tide, he will lose his master and his service: this 'real' tide is evidently of economic significance. But in a parody of Proteus, Lance bluffs that he is not worried: he is able to produce all the emotion necessary to power up faith and contract profitable bargains: 'Loose the Tide, and the voyage, and the Master, and the Seruice, and the tide: why man, if the Riuer were drie, I am able to fill it with my teares: if the winde were downe, I could driue the boate with my sighes' (2.3.643–6).

After these hyperbolic hydraulics, we arrive in Milan, where Proteus promptly falls in love with Valentine's Silvia. This happens with such alacrity, indeed, that again we experience the comedy of Proteus' 'shallowness'. The dialogue of Speed and Lance in the following scene, however, nicely troubles the apparent causality of the sequence, casting a retrospective uncertainty over the probability of Proteus' fidelity in the very moment of the lovers' earlier exchange of vows. John Kerrigan has proposed that Shakespeare 'uses binding language to create uncertainty, between shifting motives shown and withheld', suggesting that the attraction of staging of a formal oath or vow (such as Proteus' and Julia's) is that it 'can challenge the audience to make a judgement about motives and intentions. They put us close to the onstage witnesses or promisees.'[33] In *Two Gentlemen* we seem, at first, to be the only witnesses to the enacted betrothal, but it is less in our act of witnessing (which precedes Proteus' sight of Silvia) than in Lance's retrospective enquiry into the circumstances of the parting that we experience uncertainty about Proteus's intentions or unconscious feelings in making the vow. In other words Act 2, scene 5 has no purpose other than to activate, retrospectively, our uncertainty around the question of Proteus' *causa*, or intention. The scene is, technically speaking, parodically organized around a circumstantial topic, the topic of *modus* or 'how?', and a comic note of scepticism about how faith may ever be conveyed in words is struck from the moment of Lance's response, first, to Speed's opening oath, and second, to the emptiness of the promise implied in the word 'welcome' when unaccompanied by any hospitable act. So the scene opens like this:

> *Speed. Launce*, by mine honesty, welcome to *Padua*.
> *Laun.* Forsweare not thy selfe, sweet youth, for I am not welcome.
> I reckon this alwaies, that a man is neuer vndon till he be hang'd,
> nor neuer welcome to a place, till some certaine shot be paid,
> and the Hostesse say welcome. (2.5. 874–9)

Lance's 'forsweare not thy selfe, sweet youth, for I am not welcome' beautifully redefines 'welcome'—a deictic, as it were, a word defining the conditions of the present moment—as an *empty promise*, a speech act like Proteus' vow. As John Kerrigan puts it, '[t]he meaning of what we vow is mutable because relative. When I promise you *x* it is not *x* but the prospect of what *x* will be.'[34] Lance's reminder of such mutability underlying promissory words frames the question that intervenes between himself and the ale that Speed then reassures him will be his 'presently'. Before the exit that signals the real presence of ale, Speed asks, 'But sirha, how did thy Master part with Madam *Iulia*?' (2.5.881–2). Lance gives several obfuscating answers, playing on the implication that the bargain sealed between the lovers has been undone—'are they broken?', asks Speed, using the terminology of bankruptcy. 'No; they are both as whole as a fish,' equivocates Lance. A lewder equivocation follows, 'Why then, how stands the matter with them?', asks Speed, 'Marry thus', responds Lance, 'when it stands well with him, it stands well with her' (2.5. 889–93).

There follows a tour de force of semantic disordering which thematizes its own purpose of confounding intelligibility on the question of the probability of a marriage between Proteus and Julia. Keir Elam has analysed this exchange as a 'disjunctive echo', a variant on the patterns of anaphoric or epistrophic repetition that otherwise pervade *Two Gentlemen*:[35]

> *Speed.* What an asse art thou, I vnderstand thee not.
> *Lau.* What a blocke art thou, that thou canst not?

This immediately runs into Lance's mangling of the sound and sense of 'understand':

Lau.	My staffe vnderstands me?
Spee.	What thou saist?
Lau.	I, and what I do, too: looke thee, Ile but lean, and my staff vnderstands me.
Spee.	It stands vnder thee indeed.
Lau.	Why, stand-vnder: and vnder-stand is all one. (2.5.894–901)

Speed later mocks Lance for this dated dramaturgical practice: 'Well, your old vice still: mistake the word' (3.1.1349–50). But the verbal resistance Lance sets up in Act 2, scene 5 is clearly plot-productive in the characteristically Shakespearean way that will, in later plays, contribute implicitly to the sense we have that characters may behave in ways that are opaque to themselves, or may give hints of a changing inclinations before they appear conscious of these. This is not 'your old vice still', Lance's topsy-turvy language does not only offer the 'nonrepresentational element of festive release' characteristic of the Vice of moral and penitential drama, but includes a newer, deliberate introduction of rhetorical uncertainty around the circumstance of promissory *causa*, or intention.[36] The preposterous disordering of the word 'understand' enacts the scene's rudimentary temporal disordering, as it leaves the audience with the suggestion that Proteus' intention to be unfaithful to Julia might be implicit in the very form of his courtship of her, and might have antedated the arrival in Milan and the mimetic desire for Silvia that seemed to motivate it.

Complicated as the scene is to explicate, the audience is in no doubt, when Lance refers the matter of predicting the match to his dog ('if hee shake his taile, and say nothing, it will', 2.5.904), that Lance's purpose is to suggest that Proteus' heart was not in the word he spoke in Act 2, scene 2, the scene of parting. Sarah Beckwith has recently used the speech act theory of ordinary language philosophy to argue that Shakespeare uses the implication of wholeness in the speech act to repair the psychic losses of the Reformation, and, in particular, to recover the capacity of the body to signify to the community the desire of the heart to be loved and forgiven.[37] But Shakespeare's invention of the vow of faith in *Two Gentlemen* shows us a dramaturgy which does precisely the opposite: Proteus begins to seem like a 'character'—begins, that is, to seem more than a self-declaring medieval Vice—when we understand that the community (Lance and

Speed) think it *probable* that his heart and his words did not go together,
that the 'Proteus' of this story exceeds his speech acts, and that we
don't know whether his feelings of reservation on the matter were
conscious or unconscious.

Many critics have commented on the dismaying ending of *Two
Gentlemen*, whether reacting to Proteus' near-rape of Silvia, or to
Valentine's readiness to gift his title to Silvia to his friend, having forgiven him. Before this sobering denouement, however, one further
effect of Shakespeare's introduction of Proteus' spousal vow is worth
commenting on. When Silvia meets Julia disguised, like her antecedent Felismena, as a page, Silvia questions the boy ('Sebastian') about
the beauty of Proteus' former lover. Sebastian's description takes the
meta-theatrical form of foregrounding his own impersonation (as a
boy-player) of the resemblance between the abandoned female and
her male impersonator, recalling a festival at which she/he wore
'Madam *Iulias* gowne' in order to play Ariadne. 'How tall was she?',
Silvia asks, and Julia/Sebastian replies:

> About my stature: for at *Pentecost*,
> When all our Pageants of delight were plaid,
> Our youth got me to play the womans part,
> And I was trim'd in Madam *Iulias* gowne,
> Which serued me as fit, by all mens iudgements,
> As if the garment had bin made for me:
> Therefore I know she is about my height,
> And at that time I made her weepe a good,
> For I did play a lamentable part.
> (Madam) 'twas *Ariadne* passioning
> For *Thesus* periury and vniust flight;
> Which I so liuely acted with my teares:
> That my poore Mistris moued therewithall
> Wept bitterly: and would I might be dead,
> If I in thought felt not her very sorrow. (4.4.1976–91)

The boy Sebastian recalls a typical schoolboy exercise, the lessons
of *ethopoeia*, or of imitating speech and character. His imitation,
drawn from Ovid's *Heroides*, involved enacting Ariadne's letter to
Theseus. Lynn Enterline has well described other instances in which
Shakespeare contemplates the schoolboy technique of 'imitating *someone else*'s passion' as a way of producing 'the effect of inwardness, of

intense personal feeling'.[38] Her emphasis is on performance, but in this case, of course, the text underlying the performance is full of power-fully imagined particulars of the scene of Theseus' departure. In her letter to Theseus, Ovid's Ariadne evokes her feelings on discovering his absence from her bed, then describes the cliff-top she climbed to see the disappearing sails of his departing ship. Implicitly, the asso-ciations of merchant-venturing activated by the metaphors of lovers' tears as profitable 'tides' on while to set sail acquire a new dimension. Julia did not know, when Proteus left, that his words were not 'bonds', nor 'his oaths oracles', but Ariadne's vividly circumstantial *narratio* of the moment when Theseus' ship finally vanished from her straining eyes, and she wept, is here understood to convey Julia's secret feeling. In this moment of the feigned Sebastian's feigned memory of enact-ing the feigned woes of Ariadne, the emotional power of *enargeia* or the realization, through vivid circumstance, of invisible, secret grief, comes into its own.

3.4. Marlowe, Lyly, Jonson

I have been writing as if the idea of adapting the invention of circum-stantial arguments to the composition of a play was Shakespeare's. Yet this is hardly likely, given the importance assumed by the topics of circumstance in humanist textbooks on composition and in manuals of Justices of Peace. We have already seen, for example, how Thomas Norton and Thomas Sackville realized the imaginative and emotive potential of an argument of Time by having Porrex alight on the idea of 'fond delay' as a reason to attack his brother forthwith, without enquiring into his intentions. Did other dramatists use the topics of circumstance to imply other times and places and to encourage us to imagine secret feelings and unspoken motivations?

Christopher Marlowe is the obvious dramatist to consider first, as his stylistic novelty and widespread influence is generally con-ceded.[39] When the Admiral's Men secured the services of Christopher Marlowe in the late 1580s, what he seems to have brought to the thea-tre was a new *enargeia*—an imaginative power based in language—so effective that the Queen's Men struggled to compete by commission-ing a number of anti-Marlowe plays which nevertheless imitated Marlowe's style.[40] As Scott McMillin and Sally-Beth MacLean have shown, however, this Marlovian revolution took place strictly at the level of the blank verse line and what it did to the imagination. New vistas of wealth and violence, dominance and desire, opened up in Tamburlaine's boasts and promises, of 'bullets like Ioues dreadful Thunderbolts', or of ships that 'Plow up huge furrowes in the Caspian Sea', or of horses that 'sweat with Martiall spoile | Of conquered kingdomes and of Cities sackt'.[41] Yet Marlowe seems not to have thought of plotting his dramatic action around circumstantial arguments. His only mention of the topics of circumstance occurs in *The Massacre of Paris* (1594) when the newly crowned Henry III assures his minions that 'No person, place, or time, or circumstance' will 'slack' his affection for them.[42] Marlowe does not, then, seem to use circumstances forensically, as Shakespeare does, to imply human motive or investment in time, place, or opportunity, or to reflect ethically on the power of rhetorical *enargeia*. When, for example, in the first scene of *Tamburlaine*, the captain of the Persian army, Theridamas, promises to defeat Tamburlaine 'Before the Moone renew her borrowed light' (1.1.69), we have an emotive, lyrical image as an apparent argument of time, but the line implies nothing about Theridamas' motives or desires and exerts no further imaginative pressure on events as they unfold.[43] Contrast this with the opening of Shakespeare's *A Midsummer Night's Dream* and the difference is immediately apparent. Theseus announces the imminence of his wedding: it will take place in four days, with the advent of the new moon. But, he goes on,

> me thinks, how slow
> This old Moone wa[n]es. She lingers my desires,
> Like to a Stepdame, or a dowager
> Long withering out a yong mans reuenue.[44]

In Shakespeare's play an emotive use of *prosopopeia* or personification suffuses the temporal and spatial circumstances—specified as the night and the wood—which thus seem to collude with the fantasies of frustrated desire and anxiety about sexual humiliation played out before the audience through the rest of the action. For Theseus, the old moon slowly waning blocks sexual fulfilment while for Lysander, the time of erotic appointment, 'To morrow night', is marked by a narcissistic moon, who 'doth beholde | Her siluer visage' in the watery glass of the dew. For Titania, the moon and attendant flowers weep

over rapes and violations that the 'opportunitie of night', and solitari-
ness of the wood—'a desert place', according to Demetrius—actively
counsel.[45] This play of metaphor is integrated with a shaping of dramatic action according to passionate human motivations or 'causes'
that are implied by allusion to the incriminating *circumstances* of time
and place—to moonlight, darkness, the solitude of woods—but never
precisely explained or ascribed. Shakespeare thus retains the existing
dynamism and fluidity of stage time and space, while tightening and
sharpening emotional intelligibility, lending to the play what feels like
a realm of the 'unconscious'—a dimension of anxiety and desire that
is not located in any specific person.

    If Marlowe made no use of circumstantial arguments to structure
dramatic action, however, this was not because there was no prec-
edent at all for doing so. David Bevington has shown how indebted
Marlowe's dramatic structures were to popular morality play models.[46]
An alternative to the morality play's scenic form, however, existed in
the more forensically organized plots of Roman comedy. The plays
of Plautus and Terence might be described as amorous intrigues
structured around conjecture and inference. They are filled, as I have
shown elsewhere, with the work of evidence gathering and conjecture,
so that they encourage audiences to be aware of the deceiving *enargeia* of circumstantial inference.[47] In Terence's *Adelphoe*, for example,
Aeschines worries that his involvement in paying for the rescue of a
prostitute (his brother's lover) will cause his own girlfriend to infer that
he's been unfaithful to her. [B]ut this is that I feare', he writes,

> that they should beleeue their suspition of me to be true: there are so
> many probabilities concurring together. I my selfe tooke her from him,
> I my selfe paied the money, and she is brought home to mee.[48]

The 'probabilities concurring together' are arguments drawn from
the circumstantial questions 'who . . .?' and 'where . . .?' Aeschines
realizes with horror that their coherence has a verisimilitude more
vivid and powerful than the truth.

    The plays of Terence and Plautus tend to celebrate the decep-
tive verisimilitude of circumstantial arguments in a comic denouement in which the transgressive loves of the young are reconciled
with the legal regulation of marriage, kinship, and property. Early
Elizabethan adaptations of Terence and Plautus, however, preferred

to depict representatives of a reforming legal order—magistrates and Justices—employing the topics of circumstance to expose such deceptions and transgressions. A particularly benign example is *Gammer Gurton's Needle* (*c*.1550–60) in which Master Bailey, faced with an angry curate accusing his neighbour, Dame Chat, of attempted murder, calmly tries to establish the Time of the assault, 'Answer me to this, Master Rat, *when* caught you this harm of yours?' (my italics).[49] In George Gascoigne's much harsher *Glasse of Government* (1575) the Markgrave cross-examines the parasite Eccho to discover the designs behind his friendship with two young gentlemen of Antwerp. Disgusted with Eccho's evasive answers, he orders him to be whipped, 'untill he confesse the circumstances of all these matters'.[50] John Lyly's *Mother Bombie* (*c*.1588–91) takes this drama of intrigue, conjecture, and circumstantial proof in a more inward, dream-like direction which may have influenced Shakespeare. Four mercenary fathers all want to marry their offspring advantageously, and four wily servants plot to enable two of the young ones to marry for love, but in place of a patriarchal magistrate discovering all the deceptions by forensic questioning, Lyly substitutes Mother Bombie, a wise woman before whom people feel remorse of conscience and reveal their unacknowledged desires and wrongdoings. Nevertheless, the play abounds with the language of artificial proof and inference. In Act 1, scene 3, two of the ambitious fathers, Priscius and Sperantius, happen to interrupt a clandestine marriage between the children that they plan to marry more advantageously. 'It was happy', says Priscius to Sperantius, 'that we prevented that by chance, which we could never yet suspect by circumstance.'[51]

The Terentian comedy of intrigue and evidence-gathering, along with its Elizabethan imitation and reformation, certainly offered dramatists a model of plot composition based on mistaken inference and on the construing and misconstruing of circumstantial arguments. And while Shakespeare would seem to be the dramatist who went furthest in exploiting the contribution of circumstantial arguments to the implying of extramimetic times and places—the imagined 'world' of the play—he was not the only one to acknowledge the power of circumstantial arguments to conjure up plausible scenarios. References to circumstances abound, for example, in Jonson's plays. Jonson's emphasis tends to be on the way in which circumstantial coherence contributes to the success of a plot or to its narrative coherence. 'It cannot choose but take, if the circumstances miscarry not,' says Prospero, of his 'device' or plot in *Every Man in his Humour* (1598).[52] In that play's denouement, Doctor Clement (later 'Justice Clement') uncovers Prospero's device by asking, again and again, 'where . . .?' About what time . . .?', 'what time . . .?' and 'how . . .?' (5.3.6, 9, 11, 14). There are numerous other examples: in *Sejanus* (5.296–8), *Epicene* (5.2.65–6); *The Alchemist* (4.6.5–6), and *Bartholomew Fair* (4.6.25) Jonson uses the term 'circumstances' in the contexts of plotting a stratagem or of lending credibility to a narrative. In the *Devil is an Ass* (1616) Justice Eitherside concludes 'out of the circumstances' (5.8.99) that Fitzdotterel is demonically possessed partly because Meercraft and Everill give arguments of place and time to prove (quite fraudulently) that Wittpol, Manly, and Mistress Fitzdotterel conspired to bewitch Fitzdotterel to gain control of his property. The argument of *time* implies the property motive: 'Sir, they had giv'n him potions', begins Meercraft; 'Just to the *time* o'delivery o'the deed', chimes in Everill; 'And then the witchcraft gan appear', finishes Meercraft (5.8.2–5, my italics). In *The Tale of a Tub* (1633), Squire Tub can hardly believe that constable Toby Turf was taken in by the 'bald, half-hatched circumstance' of Justice Preamble's ruse to steal away his daughter (3.3.24); a few scenes later, Preamble himself cannot 'make conjecture by the circumstance | Of these events' to figure out how his secret plot came 'so quickly to the ears of Turf' (3.7.5–8).

   If these examples show Jonson's awareness of the contribution of circumstance and the theatrical *enargeia* of narrative coherence, he also seems, from early in his career, to have been interested in the psychology of circumstantial thinking. He evidently learned, as Shakespeare did, from Cicero's and Quintilian's association of circumstantial argument with the power to conjure up *phantasiai* or mental images, performing and arousing emotion. At the beginning of Act 3 of *Every Man In*, the merchant Thorello hesitates about leaving the house, weighing, through the circumstances of time, opportunity, motive, and place, the likelihood of being cuckolded in his absence (3.1.6–30). Finally, abroad in the city, he meets his neighbour, Cob, who brings him from his house alarming reports of the advent of numerous male visitors, apparently consorting with his kinswomen. Everything Cob says actually refutes Thorello's suspicions, but the merchant supplies all the evidence himself: he is sure, he says to Cob, that his sister and wife would welcome the young men. 'Like enough', Cob concedes, in a general way, 'yet I heard not a word of welcome' (3.3.25). From this reassuring denial, Thorello supplies a fantastic inference: 'No, their lips were seal'd with kisses, and the voice | Drowned in a flood of joy at their arrival, | Had lost her motion, state and faculty,' and then asks, desperately, 'Cob, which of them was't, that first kissed my wife? | My sister, I should say. My wife, alas, | I fear not her. Ha? Who was it, sayst thou?' (3.3.26–31). Cob's oaths of denial ('God's my judge, I saw nobody to be kissed,' 3.3.34) are in vain; Thorello dashes back to his house to confront the scene of debauchery he has conjured up merely by considering the circumstances under which a merchant like himself might be cuckolded.

Jonson's copy of Quintilian is now in Emmanuel College, Cambridge. In it, the very passage in which Quintilian describes how to use circumstances to conjure up *phantasiai* or *visiones* has been annotated in a seventeenth-century hand, possibly Jonson's. At the end of the section in which Quintilian describes how to stir up emotion in oneself and one's auditors by working up the circumstances of a scenario, he concludes with the commonplace of the actor moved to tears by merely speaking the dramatist's words—how much the more, Quintilian writes, should we orators be moved, who have to imagine the facts on our clients' behalf (*Inst.*, 6.2.34). Jonson—if it was he—has written, '*Histriones de posita persona illacrimasse*' ('actors having put aside their parts weeping').[53] The example of Thorello shows, however, that Jonson had absorbed Quintilian's lesson, whether or not he annotated his book.

3.5. 'About yᵉ How & Where Debate arose': *The Maid's Tragedy*

My argument so far has proceeded as if dramatists composed plays in majestic solitude but there has, especially of late, been a great deal of interest in the collaborative nature of theatrical production and play composition. Circumstantial invention, as I have been describing it, is both a part of the plotting of the play (imagining where the scenes are located, for example) and a part of poetic language (the significance, for instance, of metaphoric play with the idea of the 'tides' in

Two Gentlemen). Tiffany Stern has recently argued that the devising of a 'plat' or 'plot' in the early seventeenth century anticipated the writing of a whole play, and that 'plots' had a material and commercial existence separate from that of finished plays—they could be distributed between co-authors for writing, they could be sold or stolen.[54] Stern draws further conclusions, proposing more contentiously that contemporary criticism of plays reveals a conceptual 'separation amounting almost to a rivalry, between a play's plot and its language'. She also holds that the separation, in plot scenarios, of scene from scene dictates that 'scenic rather than narrative integrity is a source of generative and creative power'. Her overall position is that the evidence of plot scenarios should caution us not to read the 'unity' of a finished play into its compositional process: collaborators might write scenes out of narrative order, 'co-writing required multiply distributed plots'.[55] This argument is a corrective, from the perspective of theatre history, to the literary critics who insist on reading plays as if their printed state represented some kind of ideal or organic unity; plays, Stern suggests, are always merely provisional 'documents of performance'.

Juxtaposing Stern's evidence of playhouse practice with the no less plentiful evidence of the pedagogy of 'circumstances' produces interesting questions. To what extent did Shakespeare's contemporaries draw on the forensic and dialectical topics of circumstance in plotting the action of their plays? Is circumstantial plot composition possible as part of a collaboration between two or more playwrights? Is it really possible to separate poetic invention from both the imagined 'world' and serious ethical concerns of the plot, if these themselves arise from topics of circumstance?

There are not, as Stern observes, many seventeenth-century stories told about the plotting of plays. The one exception that she gives, a poem concerning Beaumont and Fletcher 'Moulding ye figure of an unborn play', happens to demonstrate that not only dramatists but some of their audience and readership were attuned to the importance of circumstances in plotting the action around pointed ethical and legal questions.[56] The poem, from a Restoration miscellany, probably refers to *The Maid's Tragedy* (1608–11), a play whose plot was commended by Dryden as an example of that marvellous 'labyrinth of design where you see some of your way before you, yet discern not the end until you arrive at it'.[57] The poem jokingly describes the hazards faced by Beaumont and Fletcher as they were mistaken for traitors by a 'Countrie-Fellow' who assumed their discussion of how to manage the king's death was an actual plot of regicide:

> Beaumont & Fletcher (y^t exalted pair)
> Once wth y^r Muse went down to take ye Air.
> Beneath a Hedge close by ye Road they Lay,
> Moulding ye Figure of an unborn play.
> At winding up of ye well-labord scene,
> It was resolv'd the King must die. But then
> About y^e **How & Where** Debate arose.
> One was for stabbing; th'other poison chose.[58]

For Stern, the anecdote serves to distinguish plotting from the poetic language of the play—the anecdote, as she writes, 'depends upon Fletcher being at the plotting (rather than writing) stage of play-writing'.[59] No less fascinating, however, is the way that the anecdote reveals the importance of the topics of circumstance in the plotting process. The choice of stabbing or poison is not just a choice of *what to stage* (as if the dramatists were asking themselves: would the audience rather see the King stabbed or poisoned? Which would be more sensational, more affecting?). It involves ethical and legal distinctions that generate further arguments and lead into the 'labyrinth of design' Dryden so praised.

In the manuscript (though not in Stern's transcription), the words 'How' and 'Where' have been capitalized, underlined, and written with thicker strokes of the quill to embolden the words. This seems to suggest that they're recognized as technical terms—that the choice between poison and stabbing is recognized as a choice involving the topics of *Modus* and *Locus*, manner and place, two of the standard topics of circumstance. One might be struck by the oddity of this—surely the choice between stabbing and poison is just a choice of how or how? What has the question 'where' got to do with it? The reason is illuminating, though, for it shows us how the topics are mutually implicated in legal argument. *Where* an action takes place can generate ethical arguments about the manner of the action and the intentions of the agent. So, for example, when Quintilian discusses *modus* (manner) in book 5, chapter 10, he says that the circumstance of 'how' something might be done can be generative of arguments of quality—that is, legal defences where the criminality of the act is not denied, but it is argued that there was justification for it in these circumstances (5.10.52). In the case of poison used to kill an adulterer, he observes, the *modus* would undermine the justice of the cause, because in Roman law it is lawful to kill an adulterer openly, *in flagrante*, but not clandestinely, with poison.[60] More generally, from the perspective of ethos or character, questioning the *modus* enables conjectures of intention (*causa*), which can be used in various ways: 'if, for instance, I were to say it was done with a good intention, and so openly, or with a bad intention, and so by ambush, at night, or in an isolated place'.[61] So it is possible to argue from the openness of someone's violent action that they are somehow justified or excusable because they did not even try to hide what they were doing. Thus the 'how' includes the 'where' in that a clandestine space, such as a bedroom, closet, or cabinet implies a clandestine manner and a purpose to remain unaccountable for the violence.

The poem about Beaumont and Fletcher plotting out their play is intriguing, then, because it registers at the level of a joke the way in which topics of circumstance lie at the heart of the intricate and highly emotive design of *The Maid's Tragedy*. The play is set in Rhodes, opening with the return of a patriotic war veteran, Melantius, who has been called back to attend the wedding of his best friend, Amintor. Melantius supposes Amintor to be marrying his betrothed, Aspatia, and is disquieted to find that this is not the case: the King of Rhodes has sinisterly forbidden Amintor to honour his promise to Aspatia and has ordered him to marry Melantius' sister, Evadne. Hints of the claustrophobic oppression of absolutism, present from the outset of the play, coalesce into full-blown horror on the wedding night, when Evadne reveals to Amintor that their marriage is fake, a cover-up for her royal concubinage. Amintor, stifled by the imperative to act the joyful newly-wed, slowly reveals the cause of his hidden grief to Melantius. Outraged, Melantius determines to kill both his sister, Evadne, and the King: 'My honestie | Shall steele my sword, and on my horrid point | Ile weare my cause,' he declares (3.2.192–3).[62] With brilliant concision, this image identifies the manner of killing (stabbing) with the openness of public justification, the sword's point declaring the honesty of the *cause*. But Amintor is distressed to think

what this openness will say about him: 'it will be cald | Honor in thee
to spill thy sisters blood | If she her birth abuse, and on the King |
A brave revenge, but on me that have walkt | With patience in it, it
will fixe the name | Of fearefull cuckold' (3.2.223–8). Already, then,
we can see the complex ethical dilemmas arising from the debate
'About yᵉ **How** & **Where**' of the king's death. For Melantius, the killing has to be public and openly attributed to prove the righteousness
of his *cause*, legally and politically speaking—if it is secret, he will be
a sordid criminal, not an honourable tyrannicide. For Amintor, by
contrast, honour depends on the punishment of the King remaining
a clandestine affair.

Melantius tells Aspatia's father, Calaniax, who has the keeping of
the King's fort, that he wants the latter to deliver it into his hands,
so that he can 'kill the King, that wrong'd you and your daughter'
(3.3.312). Melantius knows Calaniax loathes him: to be sure, Calaniax
goes straight to the King with these treasonous words and a scene
follows in which the sceptical King decides to test Calaniax's story
and Melantius's loyalty (4.2). The King probes Calaniax for artificial
and inartificial proofs, because the story sounds incredible: 'But did
he break without all circumstance | To you his Foe, that he would
have the fort | To kill me and then scape?', he asks, and then, 'You
have no witnesse?' (4.25–7; 23). Unable to gather anything more from
Calaniax except indignation at not being believed, the King proceeds
to invite Melantius to drink, testing his loyalty with a chilling jocular-
ity over the raising of a bowl of wine:

> *King.*   Give me the wine.
>   Melantius, I am now considering
>   How easie twere for any man we trust
>   To poyson one of us in such a boule. (4.2.54–7)

Melantius replies, 'I thinke it were not hard, Sir, for a Knave' (4.2.58).
Melantius' answer is precise: he deflects the King's general suspicion
of his own intentions by defining such clandestine killing as lowly
knavery. In this instance the pointed quality of this response preserves
the freedom of his thought without revealing it to the tyrant: implied
in the definition of poisoning lies the apparent condemnation of the
thought of king-killing, but it allows for the suggestion that a less

'easie' way of killing might be honourable and heroic. Once again the epigrammatic form of the language enacts and discloses the ethical and political stakes of the debate about *modus* and *locus*, the 'how' and 'where' of the plot.

In the event, a complex blend of public and private defines the manner and location of the King's death. He is stabbed, but not publicly. Melantius' sister Evadne kills her royal lover in the bedroom. She insists on publicity to the extent of waking the King and confronting him with his misdeeds as she stabs him, but the improbability in forensic terms of the whole scenario is registered by the terrified gentlemen of the bedchamber when they discover after Evadne's departure that the King, their master, lies murdered in bed: *2 Gentleman* cries treason and *I. Gentleman* says, 'This will be laid on us: | Who could believe a woman could doe this?' (5.1.125–6).

In the penultimate scene of the play the ambiguously clandestine manner of the King's murder temporarily becomes honourable tyrannicide with Melantius' extravagantly public claiming of responsibility '*on the wall*' of the royal fort. Lysippus, the dead King's brother, plans to pursue Evadne for justice, but Strato, a gentleman, deters him, defining Evadne as the mere 'instrument'—just another circumstance—of the 'act' that Melantius now justifies as his cause:

> Never follow her
> For she alas was but the instrument.
> Newes is now brought in that *Melantius*
> Has got the Fort, and stands upon the wall,
> And with a loud voice cals those few that passe
> At this dead time of night, delivering
> The innocence of this act. (5.1.136–42)

Strato then interprets Melantius's actions to Lysippus as justified in consideration of the provocation of the dead King's adultery:

> He lookes as if he had the better cause, Sir,
> Under your gracious pardon let me speake it . . .
> I do beleeve him noble, and *this action*
> *Rather puld on then sought,* his minde was ever
> As worthy as his hand. (5.2.14–21) (my italics)

Defences of 'quality'—arguments that the deed, though wrong, might be defended by adducing circumstances that excuse it—often depend on the accusing the victim of a crime that 'puld on' or provoked the violent act, as Orestes killed Clytemnestra because she had murdered Agamemnon. 'Our whole defence', says Quintilian of this issue of 'assumptive quality', 'rests on accusing the victim' (*Inst.*, 7.4.8). '[*O*]*ccisus est sed latro, excaecatus sed raptor*,' Quintilian instances: 'He was killed, but he was a thief, he was blinded, but he was a rapist' (7.4.7). In Melantius' case, of course, the defence on the issue of 'quality' would be '*occisus sed adulter*', 'he was killed, but he was an adulterer'. The crucial argument, however, stems from Melantius' honourable *intention*: 'He lookes as if he had the better cause, sir.' This argument is explicitly conjectural and is made on the grounds that Melantius' *modus*, or manner, is so 'open'—he is there on the walls of the royal fort, claiming responsibility for the King's death.

This defence does the work of persuading Lysippus, the new King, to pardon Melantius and accept his brother's death as a political warning '[t]o rule with temper' (5.3.293), but the murdered King's manipulations of his subjects' sexuality and honour have further tragic consequences and the last scene witnesses the suicides of Evadne, Aspatia, and Amintor. The play closes with Melantius scarcely being restrained from putting an end to himself: his determination to die does the ideological work of scapegoating him as 'curst' by his function in purging tyranny from kingship (5.3.295). That the poem on Beaumont's and Fletcher's plotting of the play jokes about treason and is found in a Restoration miscellany is telling: the play seems to have held the stage with great popularity through the 1660s, but to have suffered temporary prohibition in the wake of the Popish Plot and the Exclusion Crisis (1678–83), possibly because the subject of a king being killed by his mistress had taken on a new and troubling applicability at the court of Charles II.[63]

Whatever the subsequent fate of their tragedy, it is clear that Fletcher and Beaumont adapted, in composing their tragic plot, the Roman forensic tradition of using topics of circumstance to discover lines of argument in a legal case (Quintilian, *Inst.*, 7.1). Since Eugene Waith's *The Pattern of Tragicomedy in Beaumont and Fletcher* (1952), it has been well known, of course, that the authors drew on the elder

Seneca's *Controversiae* precisely for this purpose.[64] Quintilian's book 7, as Donald Russell observes, supplements the treatment of status theory in book 3, and concentrates on *divisio* or on plotting the main lines of argument—the elder Seneca's *Controversiae* conclude with analyses of the *divisio* followed by the orators.[65] Circumstances become essential generators both of the direction taken by the action, and of the epigrammatic arguments by which characters justify or veil their decisions. The author of the miscellany poem on Beaumont's and Fletcher's collaborative plotting recognized this: the debate over the 'How' and the 'Where' of the King's death was not just a discussion between playwrights, but the generator, within the play, of acute legal, political, and ethical controversy, as well as powerfully ambivalent emotional effects (as in the bedroom stabbing scene, for example, where Evadne '*Ties his armes to the bed*' (5.1.35)). But the example of both poem and play shows us that playwrights and audiences alike were used to thinking in circumstantial terms—thinking about the 'how' and 'where'—and that these circumstantial arguments were essential to debate both about what form the play's action should take, and what meanings the action would have.

It would be presumptuous to claim, for this chapter, the status of any kind of survey of the compositional uses of the topics of circumstance in sixteenth- and seventeenth-century drama. It may, however, serve as a first try at such a thing. To summarize, it would seem that the Terentian intrigue plot opened up one way for dramatists to think about the psychological and emotive power of circumstantial arguments. George Gascoigne, John Lyly, and Ben Jonson all recognized and exploited *circumstantiae* thus. Shakespeare's departure from his contemporaries lies partly in the distinctive way in which he uses *circumstantiae* to stimulate audiences and readers to imagine both the outer world of action and the inner world of motive and feeling simultaneously. Shakespeare innovates further by parodying circumstantial enquiry in the voice of the Vice or Clown in such a way as to create a sense of unconscious or unacknowledged motives and feelings. While Jonson was, like Shakespeare, fascinated by the capacity of circumstantial arguments to create illusion, his emphasis on deception and self-deception limits their conjectural potential. Beaumont and Fletcher plot dramatic action according the ethical and political arguments that can be drawn from circumstances, though their use of these topics lacks the copious, metaphorical dimension that, in Shakespeare, both conjures and critiques the imaginary world.

Notes

1. Stephen Greenblatt, 'Psychoanalysis and Renaissance Culture', in Patricia Parker and David Quint (eds), *Literary Theory/Renaissance Texts* (Baltimore: Johns Hopkins University Press, 1986) 210–24, 221; see Natalie Zemon Davis, *The Return of Martin Guerre* (Cambridge, Mass.: Harvard University Press, 1983).

2. Greenblatt, 'Psychoanalysis and Renaissance Culture', 221.

3. Greenblatt, 'Psychoanalysis and Renaissance Culture', 221.

4. Greenblatt, 'Psychoanalysis and Renaissance Culture', 219.

5. Jean de Coras, *Arrest memorable, du Parlement de Tolose* (Lyon, 1561) 51.

6. Coras, *Arrest memorable*, 51.

7. *Two Gentlemen of Verona*, ed. Clifford Leech (London: Arden, 1969) xv, xviii.

8. Stanley Wells, 'The Failure of the *Two Gentlemen of Verona*', *Shakespeare Jahrbuch*, 99 (1963) 161–73, 166–7.

9. *The Two Gentlemen of Verona*, ed. Sir Arthur Quiller Couch and John Dover Wilson (Cambridge: Cambridge University Press, 1921) xiv.

10. Adrian Kiernander, '*The Two* (?) *Gentlemen* (?) *of Verona* (?): Binarism, Patriarchy and Non-Consensual Sex Somewhere in the Vicinity of Milan', *Social Semiotics*, 4:1–2 (1994) 31–46.

11. On dating, see William C. Carroll's introduction, *Two Gentlemen of Verona* (London: Arden, 2004) 116–30; for Shakespeare's uses of Arthur Brooke, see Mozelle Scaff Allen, 'Broke's *Romeus and Juliet* as a Source for the Valentine–Silvia plot in *The Two Gentlemen of Verona*', *Studies in English*, 18 (1938) 25–46.

12. J. de Oliveira e Silva, 'Structures and Restructures in Montemayor's *Diana*, Books I–III, *Bulletin of Hispanic Studies*, 72:2 (April 1995) 165–73; See also *A Critical Edition of Yong's Translation of George de Montemayor's* Diana *and Gil Polo's* Enamoured Diana, ed. Judith M. Kennedy (Oxford: Clarendon Press, 1968) xxix.

13. George de Montemayor, *A Critical Edition of Yong's Translation of George de Montemayor's* Diana *and Gil Polo's* Enamoured Diana, ed. Judith M. Kennedy (Oxford: Clarendon Press, 1968) 93, ll. 24–6.

14. Kennedy comments, 'there is only one example of inconstancy in Felismena's story, but it was sufficiently striking for Shakespeare to dub his representation of Don Felix, Proteus', *Montemayor's Diana*, xxix.

15. See A. Bartlett Giamatti, 'Proteus Unbound: Some Versions of the Sea God in the Renaissance', in Peter Demetz, Thomas Greene, and Lowry Nelson, Jr (eds), *The Disciplines of Criticism* (New Haven: Yale University Press, 1968) 437–75.

16. Erasmus, *Copia, CWE*, 24:595–605, 595, ll. 15–16; *De copia* (1573), fols 144ʳ–147ᵛ.

17. Kennedy, *Montemayor's* Diana, 87.

18. Erasmus, *De copia* (1573), fol. 127ʳ: 'The fifth chapter of the *Copia Rerum* is rhetorical depiction, which the Greeks call *enargeia* . . . from especially that dialectical definition that they call a description of accidents' (*Quintum caput Copia rerum, est descriptio Rhetorica, quam Greci ἐνέργιαν . . . vocant . . . ex Dialectica praesertim illa quam accidentariam descriptionem vocant*).

19. Mack, *Renaissance Argument*, 203–11.

20. *OED*, speed, v.I.1.a.

21. Robert Weimann, *Shakespeare and the Popular Tradition in the Theater*, ed. Robert Schwartz (Baltimore: Johns Hopkins University Press, 1987) 256.

22. René Girard, 'Love Delights in Praises: A Reading of *The Two Gentlemen of Verona*', *Literature and Philosophy*, 13:2 (1989) 231–47.

23. Girard, 'Love Delights in Praises', 235.

24. Girard, 'Love Delights in Praises', 236.

25. Wells, 'Failure of the *Two Gentlemen*', 167; John D. Cox, 'Shakespeare and the Ethics of Friendship', *Religion and Literature*, 40:3 (2008) 1–29, 15.

26. The term 'bare word' translates the Law French '*nude parole*' and refers to an unsupported oral promise or assertion of having paid, invalid in common law. A. W. Brian Simpson, *A History of the Common Law of Contract* (Oxford: Clarendon Press, 1975) 13.

27. Kennedy, *Montemayor's* Diana, 87, ll. 11–12.

28. Mack, *Renaissance Argument*, 170.

29. This point was beautifully proved in the 2014 RSC performance of *Two Gentlemen* directed by Simon Godwin, which distinguished the quiet café society of Verona (home) with the fashionable designer shops and discos of Milan (abroad). 'Verona' and 'Milan' are thus realized as the product of an emotionally apprehended ethical distinction.

30. Bert O. States, *Great Reckonings in Little Rooms: On the Phenomenology of Theater* (Berkeley and Los Angeles: University of California Press, 1985) 34.

31. Erasmus, *De copia, ASD*, I:6:104, l. 933; 265, l. 733; 268, l. 830.

32. Erasmus, *De copia, ASD*, I:6:269, ll. 835–9.

33. John Kerrigan, 'Shakespeare, Oaths and Vows', *Proceedings of the British Academy* (Oxford: Oxford University Press, 2011) 61–89, 65.

34. Kerrigan, 'Shakespeare, Oaths and Vows', 81.

35. Kier Elam, *Shakespeare's Universe of Discourse: Language Games in the Comedies* (Cambridge: Cambridge University Press, 1984) 245–7.

36. Weimann, *Shakespeare and the Popular Tradition*, 118–19.

37. Sarah Beckwith, *Shakespeare and the Grammar of Forgiveness* (Ithaca, NY: Cornell University Press, 2011).

38. Lynn Enterline, *Shakespeare's Schoolroom: Rhetoric, Discipline, Emotion* (Philadelphia: University of Pennsylvania Press, 2012) 122.

39. Scott McMillin and Sally-Beth MacLean, *The Queen's Men and Their Plays* (Cambridge: Cambridge University Press, 1998) 155–60; Bart Van Es, *Shakespeare in Company* (Oxford: Oxford University Press, 2013) 21–36.

40. McMillin and MacLean, *Queen's Men*, 155–60.

41. *Tamburlaine the Great . . . Devided into Two Tragicall Discourses* (London: Richard Jones, 1590) sigs B5^r, B1^{r-v}.

42. Christopher Marlowe, *The Massacre at Paris* (London: 1594) sig. B7^v.

43. Marlowe, *Tamburlaine*, sig. A4^r.

44. William Shakespeare, *A Midsommer nights dreame* (London, 1600) sig. A2^r.

45. Shakespeare, *Midsommer nights dreame*, sig. B1^r, sig. C2^r.

46. David M. Bevington, *Mankind to Marlowe: Growth of Structure in the Popular Drama of Tudor England* (Cambridge, Mass.: Harvard University Press, 1962).

47. Lorna Hutson, *The Invention of Suspicion: Law and Mimesis in Shakespeare and Renaissance Drama* (Oxford: Oxford University Press, 2007) 165–72.

48. Richard Bernard, *Terence in English: Fabulae . . . Terentii omnes Anglicae factae* (London: 1629) 286.

49. *Gammer Gurton's Needle*, ed. Charles Whitworth (London: A & C Black, 1997) 5.2.28.

50. George Gascoigne, *The Complete Works*, ed. John W. Cunliffe (Cambridge: Cambridge University Press, 1910), ii. 79. See Hutson, *Invention of Suspicion*, 208–13.

51. John Lyly, *Mother Bombie*, in *The Plays of John Lyly*, ed. Carter A. Daniel (Lewisburg, Pa: Bucknell University Press, 1988) 250. See Hutson, *Invention of Suspicion*, 294–6.

52. Ben Jonson, *Every Man in his Humour*, quarto version (1598), ed. David Bevington, *The Cambridge Complete Works of Ben Jonson*, ed. David Bevington, Martin Butler, and Ian Donaldson, 7 vols (Cambridge: Cambridge University Press, 2012) i. 193, iii. 6.12–13. References to Jonson's plays in this edition are indicated by act, scene, and line number in the text.

53. *M. Fabii Quintiliani Institutionum Oratorium libri XII. Et Declamationes. XIX* (Paris: Jodocus Badius Ascensius, 1528), fol. LII^v. My thanks to Dr H. Carron, Librarian at Emmanuel, for letting me consult this book. David McPherson, 'Ben Jonson's Library and Marginalia: An Annotated Catalogue', *Studies in Philology*, 71:5 (1974) 3–106, thinks the note 'probably not by Jonson', 81, but does not say why.

54. Tiffany Stern, *Documents of Performance in Early Modern England* (Cambridge: Cambridge University Press, 2009).

55. Stern, *Documents*, 9, 15, 23.

56. Stern, *Documents of Performance*, 17–18.

57. *Literary Criticism: Plato to Dryden*, ed. Alan H. Gilbert (Detroit: Wayne State University Press, 1940) 632.

58. Bodleian Library Special Collections, MS Sancroft 53, 50.

59. Stern, *Documents of Performance*, 18.

60. Alan Watson, *Rome of the XII Tables: Persons and Property* (Princeton: Princeton University Press, 1976) 36–7.

61. Quintilian, '*ut si dicam: "bona mente factum, ideo palam", "mala, ideo ex insidiis, nocte, in solitudine", Inst.*, 5.10.52.

62. Francis Beaumont and John Fletcher, *The Maid's Tragedy* (3.2.192–3), in *The Dramatic Works in the Beaumont and Fletcher Canon*, ed. Fredson Bowers (Cambridge: Cambridge University Press, 1966–96) vol. ii. Further references to this edition will appear by act, scene, and line number in the text.

63. Robert D. Hume, '*The Maid's Tragedy* and Censorship in the Restoration Theatre', *Philological Quarterly*, 61:4 (1982) 484–90.

64. Eugene M. Waith, *The Pattern of Tragicomedy in Beaumont and Fletcher* (New Haven: Yale University Press, 1952) 86–98, 203–7.

65. Russell's introd. to Quintilian, iii. 145–9; Seneca the Elder, *Declamations*, tr. M. Winterbottom, 2 vols (Cambridge, Mass.: Harvard University Press, 1974) 1.1.13–14.

4

'The Innocent Sleepe'

Motive in Macbeth

4.1. Inwardness and Politics

I have been arguing against the tendency to speak of the spatial and temporal fluidity of Shakespeare's stage in terms of permissiveness—a mere freedom from the constraining neoclassical 'rules' of time and space. In place of this account, I have proposed that Shakespeare exploited a rhetorical tradition in which the circumstances of time, place, manner, and so forth were both shaped as arguments in disputes about motive and intention, and were, at the same time, metonymic details, or 'accidents' through which whole scenarios could be vividly and economically depicted in order to arouse emotion. Shakespeare's major dramaturgical innovation, I have suggested, involved the adaptation of this rhetorical and dialectical practice of circumstantial invention to the disposition of stage action and dialogue in such a way as to ensure that the information we receive as to its imagined timing, location, and conditions seems both objective and external and at the same time subliminally suggestive of an inward landscape of unspoken desires, anxieties, and emotional investments. Shakespeare was able to do this, I suggested, because of the way in which the rhetorical tradition of thinking about circumstances encouraged the imagining of details of timing, location, mode, means, and opportunity as always already animated by human purpose and forethought and so always already imbued with human desires and dreams.

What I have not done so far, however, is to move beyond these questions of form, technique, and effect to questions of their cultural and political consequences. I will attempt to do so in this

final chapter by linking the topics of circumstance to the production of tragic feeling as part of a political discourse of nationhood. Tragic feeling and the politics of nationhood go together, of
course. 'Classical tragedies were always national', as Stanley Cavell
has written.[1] The connection, for example, between Greek tragedy and Athenian self-definition is well known.[2] When it comes to
Shakespeare, however, discussions of English national identity are
usually linked to the history plays rather than the tragedies, and the
focus of discussion is usually the charisma of monarchy. Richard
Helgerson wrote that Shakespeare's 'theatrical representations of
England are . . . the most exclusively monarchic that his generation has passed on to us'.[3] With respect to the major tragedies, by
contrast, topical and political interpretations are usually felt to be
somewhat reductive. Though *King Lear* derives its central action
from Geoffrey of Monmouth's myth of a Britain united under the
sovereignty of England, John Kerrigan observes that it would 'be
fatuous to claim that the irregular, speculative world of this tragedy
[*Lear*] can be reduced to topicality'.[4]

Developing my concern with the imaginative uses of a forensic
rhetoric of circumstance, this chapter argues that both Shakespeare's
histories and tragedies can be seen as contributing to the forging of
an English-Britishness or an Anglo-dominated British identity. Yet the
identity in question depends less on the charisma of monarchy per se,
than on the arousal of more complex emotions that implicitly identify monarchical charisma with English *constitutionality*, or with English
popular custom as a source of law and justice. This identification works
perversely in *Macbeth* by presenting Scotland as a country cursed and
undone by its lack of constitutionality, its failure to identify a passion
for justice in its people. And in representing Scotland thus, I propose,
Shakespeare powerfully distorts and eclipses the constitutional foundations of Scottish national consciousness. For if Edward I had turned
to Geoffrey of Monmouth's history to argue England's sovereignty
over Scotland, the 'community of Scotland supported the construction of a Scottish national "counter-mythology"', as Colin Kidd has
written, responding to Edward I's Galfridian evidence with 'their own
pseudo-history of national independence, making use of royal gene-
alogies and origin myths'.[5] Moreover, Scotland's national consciousness had had, at least since the election of Robert the Bruce in 1306

and the Declaration of Arbroath in 1320, a distinct and unmistakably constitutional foundation, emphasizing the priority of the national community over the authority of the king.[6] The lectures on which this book is based were delivered in Oxford, but they were written not in England, but in Scotland, in the Fife of the historical Macduff, and at a time of intense political debate over the question of whether or not Scotland should return to its former status as an independent country and neighbour of England.

4.2. Revisionist Readings of *Macbeth*: A Tale Told by an Idiot

In older readings of *Macbeth*, the identification of monarchy as the embodiment of cosmic, spiritual, and political harmony was taken for granted as the source of the play's tragic feeling. *Macbeth* was read as a compliment to James VI and I, the descendant of Banquo and forger of a new Anglo-Scots unity. Such a reading required the idealization of social, political, and natural orders as familial: King Duncan, whom Macbeth murdered, was an ideal nurturer, a father-king. The haunting of Macbeth by the guilt and horror of having murdered Duncan was thus explicable and appropriately powerful. More recent critical work, however, has decisively undermined the uncomplicated idealizations of absolute monarchy at work in these readings. Some critics have pointed to the troubled and competitive dependencies exhibited in the opening scenes, in which acts of loyalty and disloyalty alike are expressed in murderous violence.[7] David Norbrook has drawn our attention to the controversial nature of the Scottish historical materials from which Shakespeare composed the play. He and others have noted the provocative presence, registered even in strenuous efforts to contain and contradict it, of the republicanism associated with the writings of the Scottish humanist George Buchanan, who interpreted the frequent occurrence of regicide in the annals of Scottish history as evidence of the location of sovereignty in the people.[8] In effect, then, readings which naturalize the sovereignty of the monarch are no longer possible: *Macbeth*, Rebecca Lemon writes, stresses the interdependent 'relationship of treason and sovereignty', while John Kerrigan observes that Scotland, in Shakespeare's play, 'is never shown as a properly functioning state. It seems to be waiting for English intervention to stabilize it.'[9]

But if readings which naturalize the legitimacy of inherited monarchy are no longer possible (and I agree that they're not) then the emotion at the heart of the play—the horror, the guilt, the sense of the creeping contamination of unfeelingness, of becoming numb and inured to ghastly atrocities—becomes oddly difficult to account for. A play about the proximity of treason and sovereignty or about the endemic instability and disfunctionality of the Scottish kingdom hardly needs to offer the killing of a not particularly good king as the source of such an extraordinary sense of looking into a moral abyss. So something must be missing in the newer accounts that focus on the play's disturbing collapse of traitor and sovereign, as it was missing in the older accounts that understood the source of tragic emotion to be the play's simple royalism. Developing the arguments of earlier chapters, I suggest that Shakespeare's dramaturgy was, by the time he wrote *Macbeth*, highly sensitized to the use of the forensic topics of circumstance both to arouse emotion and to produce the kind of motivated uncertainty that prompts us to conjecture unconscious motives and produce 'character'. In addition to this, however, I want to show that the forensic topics of circumstance that contribute, in Shakespeare's tragedies, to a profound sense of psychological realism are also implicated in the participatory judicial processes that imbue theatrical representations of English monarchy with an ethical charisma that it would not otherwise have.

So I will show how circumstantial topics in the plotting of *Macbeth* connect the play to earlier transformative uses of Roman forensic rhetoric in the development of English history plays. These plays, as I will show, connect topics of circumstance and arguments of proof with a developing political discourse of the commonwealth as defined by the administration of justice. By contrast, Shakespeare's striking innovation in *Macbeth* is to divorce forensic rhetoric from questions of law and justice, associating it instead with the depiction of a profound subjectivity, and with feelings of guilt, which become, as it were, nationally diffused through the language of domestic deprivation—sleeplessness, lack of nourishment, maternal failure—associated with witchcraft.

4.3. *Actus Secundus, Scena Secunda*: 'Alacke, I am afraid they haue awak'd'

Scene 2 of Act 2 is a good place to start. This is a scene the emotional realism of which has been lavishly praised while, at the same time, complex editorial commentaries have borne witness to its skilful illusion of objective circumstantial reality. Careful reconstructions of the architecture of the castle as imagined by the scene appear in editorial footnotes and appendices. Until this point, of course, we have been given several indicators of the passing of evening into night. Continuing these, Lady Macbeth likens the owl's cry to the 'Bell-man' who calls the hours through the night (2.2.651). She imagines, in a state of excitement, that Macbeth 'is about it', for 'the Doores are open: | And the surfeted Groomes doe mock their charge | With snores' (2.2.652–4). This excitement quickly gives way to anxiety that they 'haue awak'd, | And 'tis not done; th'attempt and not the deed | Confounds vs' (2.2.659–61). Macbeth assures her, entering with the daggers, that he has 'done the deed' and an extraordinarily tense and clipped exchange follows, evoking the hypersensitivity of each to any sound that might suggest the interruption of their excited solitude by a witness of their dark deeds. De Quincey famously enthused over the artistry of emotions at work here, proposing that the sound of knocking at the end of this scene works so powerfully because it constitutes, by interruption, the previous moments as a sequestration from the world of consequence and morality, a 'deep recess' away from ordinary life.[10]

Yet, of course, this potent and eerie sense of insulation from others' consciousness is actually brought about by a continual fretting about interruption, a continual anxious apprehension of having been overseen or overheard: 'Alack, *I am afraid they haue awak'd*'; 'My Husband?', 'Didst thou not heare a noyse?', 'I heard the Owle schreame, and the Crickets cry. | Did not you speake?', 'Who lyes i'th' second Chamber?', 'There's one did laugh in's sleepe, and one cry'd Murther, | That they did wake each other', 'Whence is that knocking? | How is't with me, when euery noyse appalls me?' (2.2.659–719). The topic of sleep here functions first as precarious safety from witness but then mutates into a sign of moral innocence, releasing a much more profound emotion. 'Me thought I heard a voyce cry, Sleep no more: | *Macbeth* does murder Sleepe, the innocent Sleepe' (2.2.691–2).

The scene has been shaped to stress the pragmatic need to deflect suspicion, that is, the anticipation of some kind of enquiry into the justice of what had been done. Yet this emphasis derives neither from Shakespeare's reading of Holinshed nor from Buchanan's *History of Scotland*, In Holinshed—who is, of course, following Hector Boece, as translated by John Bellenden—there is no suggestion of the secret, nervous, and terrible complicity of Lady Macbeth and her husband. Macbeth goes about the killing of Duncan by 'communicating his purposed intent with his trustie friends, amongst whome Banquho was the chiefest', and 'upon confidence of their promised aid, he slue the king at Enuerns [Inverness]' and then, 'hauing a companie about him such as he had made priuie to his enterprise, he caused himself to be proclaimed king, and forthwith went vnto Scone, where (by common consent) he receiued the inuestiture of the kingdome according to the accustomed manner'.[11] There's no call here for planting evidence, remembering to put on one's nightgown, washing one's hands: an openness of the intent among 'trustie friends' who promise to help is the precondition of the killing. It is true, as many editors and critics have pointed out, that Shakespeare had plenty to choose from among royal murders in the Scottish chronicles, and that he adapted, for example, the idea of the sleeping chamberlains, made drunk by the lady of the castle's hospitality, from Donwald's slaying of King Duff in 967, while the idea of a disembodied voice denying sleep to the guilty conscience comes from a 'common fame' Boece and Buchanan report about King Kenneth's murder of his nephew Malcolm Duff, from which we learn that, 'The king with this voice being striken into great dread and terror passed that night without anie sleepe comming in his eies.'[12]

But the conception of sleep in Shakespeare's scene is not limited to that of remorse of conscience. It is a more flexible, polyvalent, forensic argument involving, among other things, the argument of innocence and the possibility of witness. All the standard treatments of forensic rhetoric (in the pseudo-Ciceronian *Ad Herennium*, for example) ask students to imagine time, place, and opportunity in relation to the likelihood or otherwise of being witnessed. So the standard antitheses are *celebris an desertus, publicus an privatus, noctu an interdiu* (frequented or

deserted, public or private, night or day), and the student is also asked
to consider, for example, *cuiusmodi loci adtingant*, 'what sort of places are
adjacent?'[13] So, in *Macbeth*, sleep is an aspect of the opportunity of
night, but with spatial implications, as questions arise of who is sleeping in which room, and how the rooms are interconnected. As Lady
Macbeth says, doors are open, but the snores of the grooms are assur-
ance that the act will go unwitnessed; at the same time, the glimpse of
the victim resembling Lady Macbeth's 'Father, as he slept' evokes all
the horror of parricide as a reversal of roles, the unconscious father
suddenly as vulnerable and as a child. Someone lies—sleeps—in a
second chamber; two are 'lodg'd together'; one laughed and one
cried murder. These details are not in themselves coherent. Yet their
ekphrastic power, their *enargeia* is evident. The use of circumstantial
questions and deictic indicators as answers ('Did not you speake?';
'When?' | 'Now', | 'As I descended?', 669–70) blends immediacy with
the illusion of architectural space: a staircase is conjured to query the
moment in which a sound might have been heard. The metonymic
effect of these questions works in the manner outlined by Quintilian
in book 6 when he described how to create '*phantasiai*', 'visions', and
how to produce *enargeia* from imagining the peripheral details of a
scene. It is worth quoting Donald Russell's translation once more:

> Suppose I am complaining that someone has been murdered. Am I not
> to have before my eyes all the circumstances which one can believe to
> have happened during the event? Will not the assassin burst out on
> the sudden, and the victim tremble, cry for help, and either plead for
> mercy or try to escape? Shall I not see one man striking the blow and
> the other man falling? Will not the blood, the pallor, the groans, the last
> gasp of the dying be imprinted on my mind? The result will be *enargeia*,
> what Cicero calls *illustratio* and *evidentia*, a quality which makes us seem
> not so much to be talking about something as exhibiting it. Emotions
> will ensue just as if we were present at the event itself. (*Inst.*, 6.2.31–2)

In Quintilian's example, the 'circumstances' (which in Latin are
'accidents', or rather 'all that in the event might credibly happen',
'*omnia quae in re praesenti accidisse credibile est*') may seem more coherent
than those in Act 2, scene 2 of *Macbeth*, but the point to grasp here
is that in each case the imagined 'scene' is the effect of the mind's
determination to make the details cohere, stimulated by their vivid
suggestiveness. So Quintilian's dying gasp, the blood, pallor, and

groans find their equivalent in the grooms' snores, the crickets' cry, the staircase implied in 'as I descended', the question of who lies in the second chamber, from which seem to emanate laughter, cries of murder, and prayers. Testimony to the power of these details to suggest an imaginative architecture is found, for example, in John Dover Wilson's 'Headnote' to Act 1, scene 7, in which he explains the layout of the castle:

> The stair at the back is a private one leading direct to Duncan's bedroom. Beyond that lies the 'second chamber' in which his sons sleep, and to which we must imagine an outer door leading to passages and a main staircase, since both Lady M. and the sons find their way down without using the visible stair at the back.[14]

Nor is this powerful reality effect in any way dependent on the details being coherent among themselves. I will comment later on the significance of critical puzzlement over the question of who is sleeping next to Duncan, and who 'lyes in the second Chamber', but for the moment it is sufficient to note that Lady Macbeth's answer— '*Donalbaine*'—poses more questions than it answers.

To sum up, then: Shakespeare has structured the scene of Duncan's murder around a preoccupation with the possibility of being witnessed, and with the anticipation of suspicions being aroused. Such preoccupations are not present in this form in any of these source murders (though Donwald does go to the lengths of ensuring that King Duff's corpse is hidden beneath a river bed). The circumstantial topics that inform such a scene were, as well as being thoroughly treated in humanist rhetoric and dialectic, prominent elements in the Latin intrigue comedy widely practised at grammar school. In Latin intrigue comedy, characters are generally alert to the importance of amassing proof, gathering witnesses, and inventing topics of circumstance in order either to interrogate one another's motives and deeds or forestall similar suspicious interrogations of their own.[15] So, Shakespeare, in *Macbeth*, thinks of including what might seem in other contexts a bit of comic stage business, a bungling of the falsified evidence, when Macbeth inadvertently bringing the daggers with him from the scene, so that Lady Macbeth rebuke him: 'Why did you bring these Daggers from the place? | They must lye there: goe carry them, and smeare | The sleepie Groomes with blood' (2.2.705–7). Similarly she reminds him not to be caught wearing his daytime clothes—he must seem as if he's been sleeping ('Get on your Night-Gowne, least occasion call vs | And shew us to be Watchers' (2.2.734–6)).

4.4. Comedy, Justice, and the Commonwealth

It might seem odd that I'm suggesting that so powerful a tragic scene has structural affinities with a comic dramatic tradition, but the genealogy seems less surprising when we recall that the imitation of Latin intrigue comedy was closely bound up, in England, with what we might call the 'legal imaginary'—with the fall-out of the Reformation, and all its consequences for monarchical legitimacy, legal administration, and the fate of sacramental theatre after the abolition of the sacrament of penance. Fifteenth-century penitential drama presented the perpetual immanence of divine judgement in the debate between the four daughters of God—Truth, Justice, Mercy, and Peace—over the fate of the sinful human soul.[16] Adapting this penitential tradition, sixteenth-century humanist authors increasingly treated the allegorical personification of 'Justice' as a civic and political, rather than theological virtue.[17] In order to be represented as a civic virtue, essential to the prosperity of the public weal, justice could not continue to be represented as a divine mystery. Questions of how judgements come to be arrived at, of how facts are weighed, how mitigating circumstances taken into account, of what presumptions are made all become crucial to the representation of justice in the human commonwealth.

So, from quite early in the sixteenth century, English writers tended to adapt the forensic structure of Latin intrigue comedy to address the moral and political problems of uncertainty in judicial decision-making. John Foxe, who was later to try to take forward Henrician and Edwardian projects to reform the ecclesiastical law, wrote in the 1540s an imitation of a Latin intrigue comedy in which the amorous deceptions of the first two acts rapidly mutate, in the last three, into a murder trial, with a knife falsely planted on one of the sleeping heroes to 'fasten all the suspicion on him'.[18] The Cambridge play *Gammer Gurton's Needle*, attributed to the reformed clergyman William Stephenson, adapts Latin intrigue model to produce a brilliant theatrical comment on the power of evidential enquiry to generate fictions of interiority and thus to promote neighbourly understanding unmediated by priestly confession.[19]

In the late 1560s to the 1570s interest in the vernacular adaptation of the probabilistic forensic rhetoric of intrigue comedy moves into the Inns of Court, where George Gascoigne and George Whetstone produce experimental dramatic works which blend comic and tragic elements, and in which the intrigues and deceptions of Latin comedy are transmuted into the evidence detected by magistrate figures charged with administering impartial justice. These magistrates oppose judicial corruption and attempt to make use of evidence, reconstructing the narratives of all parties involved in cases so as to arrive at the most likely version of the case. Whole scenes are devoted to examining proof and reconstructing facts from narratives.[20]

Shakespeare, as we know, did not ignore these developments in Inns of Court drama but responded to them at the most profound creative level. In his version of an Inns of Court rewriting of Latin intrigue comedy, *The Comedy of Errors*, the whole of Acts 4 and 5 is given over to vociferous, impassioned conflict of testimony as to what exactly has just take place. This kind of experiment fed into Shakespeare's modification of the new genre of the history play. *The First Part of the Contention betwixt the two Famous Houses of York and Lancaster* (later *2 Henry VI*) adapts the forensic rhetoric of Latin intrigue comedy to a dramatization of the grievances of the English commonwealth. As Emrys Jones observed, the play features 'a striking large number of trial scenes, scenes which show justice being administered'.[21]

So the scene of Duncan's murder, in *Macbeth*, has structural affinities with English 'commonwealth' plays—morality plays and history plays—that adapt the forensic rhetoric of intrigue comedy in order to dramatize the administration of justice through circumstantial enquiry. But the big difference is, of course, that, as a play, *Macbeth* is pointedly not interested in questions of justice. Yet this very omission is, or should be, a feature for critics to note, since it is the lack of identification between the concerns of the polity and the processes of justice that distinguishes *Macbeth* most starkly from Shakespeare's English history plays.

4.5. English and Scottish Constitutional Discourses

Before we interrogate the neglect of justice in *Macbeth* as part of the politics of its representation of Scotland, there is another dimension of the discussion of the play's politics to consider. I began by noting that it has become more common to stress the presence of anti-absolutist or constitutionalist subtexts in *Macbeth*. Discussion of these tends to proceed, however, as if the polarization of constitutionalist and absolutist ideologies of monarchical legitimacy belongs indifferently to English and Scottish political discourse, and occupies the same institutional space in each country. But this is not the case. Broadly speaking, the theoretical polarization of constitutionalist and absolutist discourses is itself a product of *Scottish* intellectual culture, while English 'monarchical republicanism' manifests itself most prominently from within the institutional space of the practical administration of justice.

George Buchanan's *De jure regni apud Scotos* (*On the law of Kingship among the Scots*), published in 1579 and dedicated to James VI of Scotland, set out the constitutionalist argument that kings by birth are created by laws and the suffrages of the people no less than kings by election, and that if kings exceed the lawful limits of their power, the people will not lack remedy.[22] James's *Trew Lawe of Free Monarchies* (1598), likewise written when he was King of Scotland, responded by arguing that while monarchs have a duty to rule in the public interest and abide by the law, no one had the power to coerce them into doing so.[23] In sixteenth-century England, these positions are very rarely, if ever, polarized to the same extent; nor is theoretical literature the place where constitutional thought develops significantly. Rather, a developing discourse defining the limits and obligations of the monarch's power (and culminating in the constitutional crises of ship money and the *Five Knights Case*) is to be found embedded in the procedural writings of those administering justice: that is, with Inns of Court readings, with law reports, both published and unpublished (the most famous of which are by Plowden and Coke), with dialogues and discourses on specific jurisdictions (such as those by Christopher St German, Edward Hake, and William Lambarde on equity and the common law), and with the way in which all these made their way into administrative handbooks.[24] As well as constituting a more diffuse body of writing, all the examples I have mentioned were, crucially, products of the practical, institutionally specific work of administering justice.

One reason for the deeper embedding within judicial institutions and judicial administration of English theoretical writing on the monarch's power has to do with the 'bias towards law-bound government' which Alan Cromartie has identified as prevailing during the regimes of Henry's Protestant heirs.[25] Without claiming that Elizabeth's government saw itself as completely constrained by legal procedures, Cromartie shows that its use of extralegal power was increasingly coming under scrutiny as the independence of the judiciary was increasingly respected, and that the interest in extraordinary power, or in a 'discretion' reserved for extraordinary cases, was encouraged by administrative routinization, by 'the tightening grip of ordinary procedures'.[26] In discourses such as the *Reports* of Edmund Plowden, or in conversations among lawyers recorded by William Fleetwood, Plowden's friend at the Middle Temple, it is possible to discern a developing sense of 'limitations on the crown as things that had developed over time' as well as a developing confidence in the competence of common law to decide political questions.[27] In developing this discourse, the lawyers argued that the law of the land originated in popular custom, and that this, in turn, limited the monarch's prerogative. Robert Snagg of the Middle Temple (also a friend of William Fleetwood) gave a reading on Magna Carta in 1581 in which he declared, 'our Law is the antient Custom of the Country or Land, and of that Antiquity, that there is no Record nor Matter that can shew the Commencement thereof'.[28] Snagg went on to argue that when this was lost by conquest, it was restored again by common consent of the people:

> So as the Custom of the Realm revived by Parliament, is the Law of the Land, which is *Genus* to all; And the Parliament and the Acts thereof, and the Prerogative of the Prince, and the particular Customs of several Counties, Cities, Boroughs, & Manors, be all but *Species* of it: For that General Custom of the Realm, which is the Law of the Land, authorizeth the Parliament, limiteth the Prerogative, alloweth and disalloweth of Private Customs, and whatsoever in *England* is to be allowed, and not to be allowed, as they are consonant or dissonant thereof.[29]

Thus, in England, the development of republican thought is law centred. This explains why it is at once oppositional to and subversive of absolute monarchical power, and, at the same time, deeply invested in the idea of monarchy. Cromartie comments that Patrick Collinson's 'useful phrase, "monarchical republic" has had a certain tendency to misdirect attention'. '[W]hat really needs to be explained', Cromartie goes on, 'is less the intermittent prevalence of a republicanising way of talking than its relation to another trend: the steadily growing imaginative purchase of the idea of English monarchy.'[30] But the imaginative purchase of this idea of English monarchy, as it emerges first from Plowden's *Reports* and then, in James's reign, from the *Reports* of Sir Edward Coke, was that of an ideal played out in the drama of decision-making for the common good, an ideal of the monarch as the product, as well as the enactor of such decision-making, or of 'royal power as just an instrument, a means to, not a part of, the nation's collective well-being'.[31] Administering the law and deciding exceptions in early modern England, then, was modelled less on the notion of vicarious representation (the King as God's vicar, the Chancellor as the King's, etc.) than on a notion of equitable fiction-making, in which legislators were imagined as always-already-absent, and those in the position of decision-making (from the highest ranks of the judiciary, right down to Justices of Peace and juries) were required to proceed with a 'discretion' that was explicitly defined as 'by the right line of Law and not by private opinion'.[32] So, for example, the Justice of Peace Michael Dalton popularized Edward Coke's important conclusions with respect to the discretionary powers of Sewers (who had the power to levy rates for sea defences). Coke had said that these discretionary powers ought to be limited and bound by law, and that *salus populi est suprema lex* and that 'a true emergency could justify the levying of a rate'.[33] Dalton promulgated the view that Justices of Peace acted with a similar law-bound discretion, which he defined as 'a knowledge or understanding to discerne betweene truth and falshood, betweene right and wrong, betweene shadowes and substance, betweene equity and colourable glosses and pretences, and not to doe according to our wills and private affections' but, '*secundum legem et consuetudinem Anglia*' ('according to the laws and customs of England').[34] And, of course, the most significant and creative exercise of this discretion occurred when the Justice of Peace used the forensic topics of circumstance to take examination of felony suspects. Dalton thus concluded his remarks on the law-bound discretion of the Justice of Peace, remarking that he was, like the King, *lex loquens*:

> And (as Master *Lambert* well said) no way better shall the discretion of a Justice of Peace appeare, than if hee (remembering he is *lex loquens*) shall containe himself within the limits of the Law, and shall not use his discretion, but onely where the Law permitteth, and the present case requireth.
>
> In all cases therefore where the Statutes do referre the triall of offenders, (or the hearing and determining of offences) to the discretion of the Justice or Justices of the Peace, out of Sessions; it is very requisite, that upon such triall or hearing, the said Justices take due examination (of the offenders themselves, and also of credible witnesses) *as well concerning the facte it selfe, as the circumstances thereof*, and upon confession, or other due proofe of the offence, then to proceed according to Law and Justice.[35]

What we have in this model is a law-bound discretion, exercised in the name of the King who is himself understood to speak for the law of *salus populi*. In effect then, as the development of a vernacular political drama in the second half of the sixteenth century clearly shows, this model both invited audiences to identify monarchs with the ideal of justice as definitive of commonwealth, and equipped them to critique monarchical decision-making accordingly. This means that scenes in which monarchs and governors are held to legal account or subject to critique in the name of the common law are often those that simultaneously express the greatest reverence for monarchy as an ideal embodiment of justice and commonwealth.[36] *Richard II* opens with a legal cause—the 'boistrous late appeale' of Hereford against Mowbray (1.1.7), which, of course, opens up the King to suspicion of involvement in murder. Richard's subsequent aborting of the trial proceedings in favour of arbitrary sentences of banishment is subject to acerbic critique as a tyrannous act by Gaunt and Hereford, and, in the highly emotive scene of John of Gaunt's deathbed attempts to recall him to his monarchical obligations, seems to lead directly to his violation of Gaunt's and Hereford's hereditary rights. The Duke of York is a reluctant opponent of the King, but he links popular consent, law, and custom when he warns Richard that in barring Hereford from his inheritance, he will 'loose a thousand well-disposed hearts' (2.1.854).

In view of dramatic antecedents like these, what comes to seem distinctly odd about *Macbeth*, considered as a history play, is its absence of any identification of monarchy with the laws and customs of the country, and so, consequently, with the conception of sceptical, probabilistic enquiry made in the name and interests of justice and the commonwealth.

4.6. 'The enquirie of the kingis slaughter was quite omittit'

It is this absence, I would argue, that crucially transforms the political meaning of tragic emotion in *Macbeth*. The instructive contrast, as Emrys Jones has written, is with an earlier tragic sequence, the murder of Duke Humphrey in Shakespeare's *Henry VI, Part Two*. Jones compares the 'relief' felt by an audience at Macbeth's 'simulated (but also real) horror' on Macduff's discovery of Duncan's body to the relief felt when Warwick, in the earlier play, exposes the signs that prove Duke Humphrey to have been murdered. But the political meaning of the emotion in the scenes is quite different. In *2 Henry VI*, the two noblemen who collude in and attempt to cover up Duke Humphrey's murder are oppressors of the common people. When Warwick enters to enquire into Humphrey's death, he enters onstage with '*many Commons*', as the Folio stage direction has it, to voice a popular demand to know how the Duke died. When Warwick deduces from forensic signs that it was, as he puts it, 'probable' that Humphrey had been murdered (3.2.1882), the scene's arousal of emotion seems inseparable from the passion for justice in the commonwealth that Humphrey himself embodied.

By contrast, the discovery of Duncan's murdered body in *Macbeth*, 2.3, has quite different political implications. For Warwick's speech fulfils the people's demand for justice by performing a forensic enquiry that symbolically attributes to the people the right to pronounce a verdict, and take political action. Macbeth's account of Duncan's murdered body, by contrast—'His Siluer skinne, lac'd with his Golden Blood'—is *part* of the criminal cover-up, part of his attempt to rationalize his killing of the grooms by representing it as a kind of pious outrage in the presence of sacrilege (2.3.876). If this gives us 'relief' by expressing emotion at the revelation of a murder, it does so in the curiously duplicitous and hysterical way of making us experience the speech as a cynical abuse of the expression of love and, at the same time, the expression of heightened, tumultuous feeling ('who could refraine | That had a heart to loue?' (2.3.880–1)).

So, to come back to Act 2, scene 2, what comes to seem distinctive about the sequence of the murder scenes in *Macbeth*, then, is that the intrigue-like action of the scene—the repositioning of the daggers, remembering to change into a nightgown, the washing of hands—is, on one level, deliberately, cynically redundant. That is, it is redundant to the extent that no figure or group embodying a popular desire for justice in the King's name ever appears. No one comes on to pronounce, as Warwick does in *2 Henry VI*, that 'this Tragedie' is 'suspitious' (3.2.1898). Banquo proposes they meet to 'question this most bloody piece of worke, | To know it further' (2.4.897–8), but the following scene deflects us from the expected questioning, offering only dark hints of Duncan's sons' probable guilt, given the context of incredible portents. When, in Act 3, scene 4, we are told by Macduff that Malcolm and Donalbain are now the chief suspects because they have fled, the deadpan improbability of the report has the whiff, not of sceptical enquiry, but of the most politically cynical, or fearful collusion. We might, of course, simply refer this to Holinshed's account of Donwald's murder of Duff, when, once Donwald has accused and tried the chamberlains for the murder, we are told that the lords 'began to mislike the matter, and to smell forth shrewd tokens' of Donwald's guilt, but 'for so much as they were in that country, where hee had the whole rule, what by reason of his friends and authoritie togither, they doubted to utter what they thought, till time and place should better serve thereunto, and hereupon got them awaie every man to his home'.[37] It will also have reminded many of that notorious account of the lack of judicial enquiry into a more recent royal murder in Scotland, the murder of James's own father, Darnley, where the chief suspect, the Earl of Bothwell, himself led the judicial enquiry, suborning judges, threatening witnesses, and censoring the press. For English readers, news of this sensational royal murder came framed, in an apparently authentically Scottish account authored by Buchanan himself, as proof of the abject failure of justice north of the border. The sixteenth-century whodunit *Ane Detectioun of the duinges of Marie Quene of Scottes, touchand the murder of hir husband* (1571) was in fact 'an assemblage of multiple documents' composed by Thomas Wilson as part of Lord Burghley's propaganda against Mary, but what it offered English readers was an unforgettable account of what it feels like to inhabit a country in which the violent death of the King is silently passed over, without any serious judicial investigation. '[A]ll men', readers of *Ane Detectioun* were told,

> saw that the enquirie of the kingis slaughter was quite omittit, and other enquirie seuerely pursuit concerning bukes accusing the slaughter. What maner of iugement it was quhairby Bothwell was aquitit, you haue heard. Forsothe by hym selfe procurit, the iudges by hym selfe chosen, the accusers by him self subornit, lawfull accusers forbidden to be present unless thay wald yeld their throtes to their enemies weapons: the assise apointit nouther to a day accordyng to the law of the land, nor after the maner of the contrey, nor to enquire of the murder of the kyng, but of sic a murder as was allegit to be committit the day befoir that the king was slayne.[38]

The 'enquirie of the kingis slaughter was quite omittit': here, in Thomas Wilson's authentic sounding pseudo-Scots, English readers were invited to identify the failure of judicial procedure 'accordyng to the law of the land' and 'after the maner of the contrey' both with the horrific neglect of outrage to the royal person and with the sense of unutterable popular shock and dismay. At the Queen's 'going after the kingis slaughter to the castell through the chiefe and maist populous street of the towne, there was all the way a sad glumming silence'.[39]

On another level, however, the intrigue elements of Act 2, scene 2 are not redundant at all, because, while Scotland is shown to be abjectly collusive, that is, to lack the possibility of resistance in the name of common custom and legal procedure, it gradually comes to seem to share, as a nation, in the symptoms of vexed and horrified self-division that emerge, in this scene, as the signs of Macbeth's conscious and unconscious resistance to what he is about. If it is possible to understand Macbeth's speeches of 2.3 as expressing a 'simulated (but also real) horror', then the achievement of 2.2 is to have produced so convincingly the sense of Macbeth's unconscious, of the emotions he suppresses. As A. C. Bradley notes, actual dangers leave him unmoved, but '[w]hat appals him is always the image of his own guilty heart . . . the first "horrid image" of Duncan's murder—of himself murdering Duncan—rises from his unconscious and terrifies him.'[40] And if the play's achievement is the enduring power of its depiction of the torments of Macbeth's guilt, its politics involve the way this guilt becomes diffused and shared at a national level. The lords' failure to question or resist, their collusion, causes us to attribute to them a similar self-unknowing; as William Empson put it, 'we feel any of them may be playing their own game during this period of confusion, though we never quite get it clear. "Cruel are the times, when we are traitors, and do not know ourselves" . . . The witches say it is "fog" in the first scene, and fog it remains.'[41] The witches, as David Norbrook has said, 'function as the unconscious of the play', and as such they diffuse the sense of guilty complicity until it feels like a national pathology, a national longing for what has never been.[42]

So it begins to be clear that elements of forensic rhetoric—the rhetoric of sceptical enquiry, of the topical 'invention' of arguments of circumstance – are not merely cynical signs of the redundancy of intrigue in a land without law. Rather, they contribute primarily to the national diffusion of guilt not as a legal verdict but as a *feeling* of the most profound self-alienation: 'Alas, poore Countrey', as Rosse says, Scotland is 'Almost affraid to know it selfe' (4.3.2000–1). Earlier chapters have shown that the motivated uncertainty produced by parodic and inverted forms of circumstantial questioning can prompt us to conjecture an inner world of motive and feeling. In *Macbeth*, in particular, there is a peculiarly strong identification of the perversion of forensic enquiry with perversions of familial love. So Malcolm asks Macduff in 4.3, 'Why in that rawenesse left you Wife, and Childe? | Those precious Motiues, those strong knots of Loue, | Without leaue-taking' (4.3.1845–7). Malcolm has reason, of course, to be suspicious of Macduff's flight to England, but the very designation of family love as 'motive' is an index of how closely the languages of forensic enquiry and *familiaritas*, or family-feeling or intimacy, are identified in this play.

One particularly significant manifestation of the link between a lack, or perversion, of forensic enquiry and the perversion of family or filial love exists in the scenes that develop the argument that Malcolm and Donalbain were guilty of parricide. So at the beginning of Act 3, Macbeth cynically suggests to Banquo that they will soon be discussing 'cause of State' together, including, no doubt, deciding the fates of 'our bloody Cozens', Malcolm and Donalbain, who,

having fled to England and Ireland, are apparently 'not confessing |
Their cruell Parricide', but rather 'filling their hearers | With strange
inuention' (3.1.1016–19). Macbeth's account of the sons' 'strange
inuention' is Shakespeare's invention. In Holinshed, as in Bellenden's
Boece, Duncan's sons merely flee 'for feare of their liues', not because
they are officially under suspicion of parricide.[43] Yet the concept that
they might be accused of having murdered their father, though apparently a slight addition to the plot, is tied, in powerfully imaginative
ways, to the national diffusion of Macbeth's guilt.

The source of the argument of suspicion against Malcolm and
Donalbain, I suggest, lies at the heart of one of Cicero's famous
orations, his defence of Sextus Roscius of Ameria, a man accused of
parricide. Set texts at university, Cicero's orations were also studied
in the upper forms of many grammar schools.[44] Shakespeare may
have even reacquainted himself with the orations in the influential
edition with notes by Giovanni Michele Brutus (1517–92) and published first by Thomas Vautrollier and latterly by the Stratfordian
Richard Field.[45] Although they have not been explored in this way,
Cicero's orations would have been an important source for any
thinking about the productivity of the circumstance of *causa*, or
motive, as an argument of proof. It is often asked, said Quintilian,
whether orators should deal with 'character' (*persona*) or 'motive'
(*causa*) first: *Cicero*, he says, *frequently puts the motives first* (*Inst.*, 7.2.39,
my italics). And putting motive first was, as it happens, the key to
Cicero's early and astonishing success against all the odds in the trial
of Sextus Roscius of Ameria, not because the prosecution thought
there was no motive, but because they thought the motive so obvious
that it did not need any explicit oratorical invention or elaboration
as a proof.

It is hard, even now, not to think that the prosecution had a case
and that Sextus Roscius was indeed a neglected son with a grudge,
who, tired of being stuck on the farm, murdered his pleasure-loving
father for his patrimony. This was certainly a prevalent view in the sixteenth century, prevalent enough for Thomas Nashe to joke about the
way in which Cicero's rhetorical tour de force was deemed the more
admirable by the great Erasmus for not only acquitting but deifying
a manifestly guilty defendant. When the magician Cornelius Agrippa

offers to conjure for scholars assembled at Wittenberg, 'Erasmus', says Nashe,

> requested to see *Tully* in that same grace and maiestie he pleaded his oration *pro Roscio Amerino*, affirming, that til in person he beheld his importunitie of pleading, he woulde in no wise bee perswaded that anie man coulde carrie awaie a manifest case with rethorike so strangely.[46]

Agrippa agrees to conjure Cicero and

> at the time prefixed in entered *Tullie*, ascended his pleading place, and declaimed verbatim the fornamed oration, but with such aston-ishing amazement, with such feruent exaltation of spirite, with such soule-stirring iestures, that all his auditours were readie to install his guiltie client for a God.[47]

With dazzling irony, Nashe's narrator conveys the double-edged quality of the admiration Cicero's forensic rhetoric arouses: so brilliantly unfounded, so purely rhetorical was his defence of this man suspected of parricide that the audience was ready not only to acquit the suspect, but to celebrate him as a god. Classicists today are inclined to agree: the case against Roscius looks pretty bad.[48] For the prosecution the lawyer Erucius seems to have based his argument on Roscius' character and history, alleging that he was a disgrun-tled, uncultivated (*ferus*), and boorish (*agrestis*) rustic, disliked by his urbane, cultivated father and relegated, at the age of 40, to a servile, unmarried life managing his father's country estate. This may not, of course, have been true, though it certainly seems odd that there was no local or family support for Roscius in court and the only relative present sat on the prosecution side.[49] Cicero, however, obscured these and other inconvenient facts and instead began to pour scorn on the prosecutor's simple readiness to assume that the unsociable picture he had painted of Roscius would itself be proof enough that the lat-ter could murder his father, the man who had given him the breath of life. Key to Cicero's refutation of Erucius was his mockery of the prosecutor's failure to enquire into motive: 'In the case of the most trifling offences the object of the first and fullest inquiry is to find out the motive (*causa*) of the offence', Cicero observed, drily, 'but in a case of parricide Erucius does not think such an inquiry necessary' (§62).

Then Cicero went on, in what became a famous and anthologized passage, to expand on the particular need of careful inquiry into motive in the case of a crime so utterly unnatural as parricide: 'In the case of such a crime', he wrote,

> even when many motives (*causae*) appear to coincide and to be consistent with one another, it is not to be believed without due consideration . . . and unless the proofs are many and evident, assuredly an act so criminal, so atrocious, and so wicked cannot be believed. For the power of human feeling is very great; the ties of human blood are very strong; nature herself cries out against such suspicions; it is undoubtedly an unnatural and monstrous phenomenon that a being of human form and figure should exist so far surpassing the beasts as to have most shamefully defrauded of the light of day those to whom he is indebted for that sweetest of sights.[50]

Cicero's powerful climactically utterance moves from human feeling, to blood ties, to 'nature herself' contradicting suspicions of parricide. The brilliantly conceived Act 2, scene 4 of *Macbeth*, standing in for the pointedly omitted judicial enquiry into Duncan's murder, neatly turns Cicero's words inside out. Ross enters with an 'Old man'. The Old man cues Ross by dismissing all the strange and dreadful occurrences of former days by comparison with what has just taken place. Ross invokes the unnatural darkness of the day—'by th'Clock 'tis Day | And yet darke Night strangles the trauailing Lampe' (2.4.930–2). ''Tis vnnaturall', the Old Man concedes, capping the weird strangulation of daylight with last Tuesday's report of a falcon being killed by an owl. Ross, says Empson, has waited 'to see how much Old Man will swallow' before pushing his own outrageous claim—he says he has witnessed, with his own eyes, the cannibalism of Duncan's horses. ''Tis said, they eate each other,' hazards the Old Man. 'They did so: | To th'amazement of mine eyes that look'd vpon it,' Ross replies, preposterously (2.4.946–7). These apparent signs of cosmic unnaturalness then preclude even the most perfunctory enquiry into the motives that Malcolm and Donalbain might have had for performing the most unlikely, because *unnatural*, of crimes. Macduff enters and, in response to Rosse's question, tells him that those who did this bloody deed are 'known' to be those whom Macbeth has slain, the chamberlains. At this point Rosse takes a stab at asking the obvious question: 'Alas the day | What good they pretend?' (2.4. 956). But when Macduff replies,

> They were subborned,
> *Malcolme*, and *Donalbaine* the Kings two Sonnes
> Are stolne away and fled, which puts vpon them
> Suspition of the deed,

Ross's reply is breathtaking for its lack of resistance, its readiness to fall in with the official account: 'Gainst Nature still', he chimes (2.4.953–61). The argument that should counter the suspicion of parricide, the argument that it is against nature—'nature herself contradicts (*reclamitat*) such suspicions'—becomes its foundation. Night unnaturally strangled the travelling lamp; Duncan's horses turned wild in nature and ate each other; *ergo*, Malcolm and Donalbain killed Duncan.

4.7. Hearke, who lyes i'th' second Chamber?

I want to come back now, at last, to the question of the innocence of sleep, and to that of who laughed in his sleep, and who cried 'murder', and who it was that lay in the second chamber. Editors and critics have long been confused about exactly who or where these two disturbed sleepers were. Bradley thought they were the grooms, sleeping drunkenly in the same chamber as Duncan, but Dover Wilson thought this a ludicrous mistake: apparently it was obvious to him that the two who woke suddenly, and slept again were the two princes, sleeping in the second chamber.[51] Nicholas Brooke, however, glosses 'two' in Lady Macbeth's words thus: 'It is not clear which two—it tends to suggest the grooms, but that should not be so; the usual suggestion is Donalbain and someone else (not Malcolm, or she should have mentioned him in l. 18). The reference may be careless, and in any case is not important.'[52]

I propose that in conflating the suggestion of sleeping princes with the two asleep in Duncan's room Shakespeare was remembering the powerful ambivalence of the story Cicero tells of the presumed innocence of sleep, and of the hyperbolic unlikelihood of parricide. Even if Shakespeare did not read Cicero's oration at school, he would have come across Cicero's famous passage on parricide as Lambinus' gloss on Plautus' line 'Nothing is worse than a guilty conscience' as spoken by Tranio in *Mostellaria* ('The Haunted House'), a very funny play that Shakespeare evidently knew well.[53]

The passage comes just after the lines I have already quoted, in which Cicero insists that a case of parricide requires an especially careful enquiry into motive, because it is both portentous and monstrous. Having explained that parricide is so unnatural as to warrant those who commit it exhibiting the most evident signs of mental and emotional disturbance, Cicero goes on to tell a fascinating story of two sons who were acquitted of parricide, when all other signs pointed suspiciously at them, simply because they were able to sleep:

> Not many years ago, it is said, a certain Titus Caelius, a well-known citizen of Tarracina, went to bed after supper in the same room as his two grown-up sons and was found dead in the morning with his throat cut. And as no slave nor free man could be found, on whom suspicion might have fallen, while the two grown-up sons who slept near their father declared they had not noticed anything, they were indicted for parricide. What could be more suspicious? (*Quid poterat tam esse suspiciosem?*) that neither of them had observed anything? that someone had dared to venture into the room, at the very time when the two sons were there, who could easily have seen the crime and offered resistance? Moreover, there was no one who might have been reasonably suspected. However, the judges having been convinced that the young men had been found asleep when the door was opened [Or, 'sleeping with the door open'], they were acquitted and cleared of all suspicion. In fact, there was no-one who thought that a man could have existed capable of going to sleep immediately after he had violated all the laws of human and divine nature by an impious crime, because those who have committed such a deed are not only unable to rest peacefully, but cannot even breathe without fear. (§§64–5)[54]

Not much seems to be known about Titus Caelius or Titus Cloelius (as Valerius Maximus has the name). Yet surely this story of a father whose throat was cut while lying in bed in the same room as his peacefully slumbering sons worked its way into *Macbeth* as part of the ambiguous sleeping arrangements of the castle ('There are two lodged together') and as part of the tense drama of Macbeth's interruption and the capture of his imagination by the innocence of sleep:

> There's one did laugh in's sleepe
> And one cry'd Murther, that they did wake each other:
> I stood, and heard them: But they did say their Prayers,
> And addrest them again to sleepe. (2.2.677–80)

At least one other sixteenth-century reader singled out this whole passage, from its assertion that nature cries out against suspicion of parricide, to the hauntingly ambiguous image of the two sons 'sleeping with the door open' by their blood soaked father. In volume i of the *Orations* of Cicero edited by Giovanni Michele Brutus (1517–92) held in the University of St Andrews Special Collections, the passage from '*Magna est enim vis humanitatis; multum valet communio sanguinis*' ('For the power of human feeling is very great, the ties of blood are very strong') to '*et suspicione omni liberati sunt*' ('and cleared of all suspicion') has been picked out for special note by a marginal wedge-shaped mark in brown ink, made at either end of the passage, with a quill pen.

In this Ciceronian passage, sleep is an ambiguously hyperbolic proof of innocence but it is also, in particular, the argument Cicero makes for the ethical importance of giving serious consideration to the probability of *motive* when accusing someone of parricide. Shakespeare transforms this proof, both in the circumstantial confusion of the murder scene—where was Malcolm? Who were lodged together? Where was the second chamber?—and in the subsequent pervasive refusal of the nobles to enquire into the probabilities of Duncan's sons' motives, into an unutterable knowledge, the murdering of innocence itself, which spreads and contaminates Scotland. The horror expressed by Macbeth acknowledging his excommunication from the blessings of the domestic—of nourishment, rest, and healing—condenses the indiscriminate curses of the weird sisters and the general curse of Scotland under tyranny into something credibly inward, something which seems so real to us that it has become more powerful than history.

Recent political interpretations of *Macbeth* since the 1980s have displaced the earlier understanding of Macbeth's profound feeling as the appropriate response to a violation of the natural order of monarchy. They have not, however, been able to account for the sources of that profound emotion. I have tried to show that monarchy in the Scotland of *Macbeth* lacks a crucial identification with popular redress, with legal custom and procedure, that is part of its imaginative purchase in English history plays. But I have also tried to show that the shared ground between drama and law as discourses invested in probability and in the invention of circumstance can work, in *Macbeth*, by being turned inside out. In the passage from *Pro Roscio Amerino* which follows the story of the sleeping sons acquitted of parricide, Cicero speaks, in a suggestive phrase, about the way in which the blood of a mother and father has such great power that it produces a stain which not only can't be washed out, but which permeates the soul, bringing frenzy and madness. This, he says, is the true meaning of the Furies that poets bring on stage in tragedies. They are the evil thoughts and guilty consciences of those who have committed parricide: these are (he says) the Furies which never leave the wicked, which live with them (*hae sunt impiis assiduae domesticae Furiae*), which, night and day, exact expiation for parents from sons stained with guilt.[55] By '*domesticae Furiae*', Cicero means psychic phenomena, such as the Furies described so vividly by Euripides' Orestes ('the women with the blood in their eyes and the snakes') and praised by Longinus as an instance of the power of circumstances in 'rhetorical visualisation'.[56] But '*domesticus*' also, of course, means 'belonging to one's family; domestic, familiar, of the household'. This collapsing of the familial and the political enables Shakespeare to employ the psychologically compelling inversions of fantasies of witchcraft: Scotland has no identification of the people or the 'public good' (*res publica*) with custom as law and the procedures of legal enquiry, but it has the witches, *domesticae Furiae*, who express this lack in the form of an internal malaise, a disease of the soul. Thus Shakespeare characterizes Scotland's radical political instability as stemming from the inadequacy of mere kin-obligation or 'kindness' as the constitution of the *res publica*, and in doing so produces both an enduring tragic hero and a powerfully enduring myth of Scotland's bewitched abjection and political longing for union with England.

Notes

1. Stanley Cavell, 'The Avoidance of Love: A Reading of *King Lear*', in *Must We Mean What We Say?* (Cambridge: Cambridge University Press, 1987) 267–356, 344.

2. Edith Hall, *Inventing the Barbarian: Greek Self-Definition through Tragedy* (Oxford: Oxford University Press, 1989).

3. For example, Richard Helgerson, *Forms of Nationhood: The Elizabethan Writing of England* (Chicago: University of Chicago Press, 1992) 195–245, 245.

4. John Kerrigan, *Archipelagic English: Literature, History, and Politics 1603–1707* (Oxford: Oxford University Press, 2008) 14–15.

5. Colin Kidd, *Subverting Scotland's Past: Scottish Whig Historians and the Creation of an Anglo-British Identity, 1689–1830* (Cambridge: Cambridge University Press, 1993) 16–17.

6. Kidd, *Subverting Scotland's Past*, 17; see William Matthews, 'The Egyptians in Scotland: The Political History of a Myth', *Viator*, 1 (1970) 289–306.

7. Harry Berger, Jr., 'The Early Scenes of *Macbeth*: A New Interpretation', *ELH* 47 (1980) 1–31; Kerrigan, *Archipelagic English*, 99; Keith Brown, *Bloodfeud in Scotland 1573–1625: Violence, Justice and Politics in an Early Modern Society* (Edinburgh: John Donald Publishers, 1986) 80.

8. Alan Sinfield, '*Macbeth*: History, Ideology and Intellectuals', in *Faultlines: Cultural Materialism and the Politics of Dissident Reading* (Oxford: Clarendon Press, 1992) 95–108, 102–5; David Norbrook, '*Macbeth* and the Politics of Historiography', in Kevin Sharpe and Steven N. Zwicker (eds), *Politics of Discourse: The Literature and History of Seventeenth-Century England* (Berkeley and Los Angeles: University of California Press, 1987) 78–116, 82.

9. Kerrigan, *Archipelagic English*, 102.

10. Thomas De Quincey, 'On the Knocking at the Gate in *Macbeth*', in *De Quincey as Critic*, ed. John E. Jordan (London: Routledge and Kegan Paul, 1973) 240–4, 243.

11. Raphael Holinshed, *The Description of Scotland written at the first by Hector Boetius in Latine, and afterward translated into the Scottish speech by John Bellenden, and now in English by R.H.* (London, 1585) 171 (hereafter 'Holinshed').

12. Geoffrey Bullough, *Narrative and Dramatic Sources of Shakespeare* vii: *Major Tragedies* (London: Routledge and Kegan Paul, 1973) 482, 486; George Buchanan, *The History of Scotland*, tr. James Aikman, 6 vols (Glasgow: Blackie and Son, 1845) vi. 314–16.

13. [Cicero] *Rhetorica ad Herennium*, tr. Harry Caplan (Cambridge, Mass.: Harvard University Press, 1954) II.3.7–8.

14. *Macbeth*, ed. John Dover Wilson (Cambridge: Cambridge University Press, 1947) 112.

15. See Adele C. Scafuro, *The Forensic Stage: Settling Disputes in Graeco-Roman New Comedy* (Cambridge: Cambridge University Press, 1997).

16. Jodi Enders, *Rhetoric and the Origins of Medieval Drama* (Ithaca, NY: Cornell University Press, 1992) 169–92.

17. J. Wilson McCutcheon, 'Justice and Equity in the English Morality Play', *Journal of the History of Ideas*, 19:3 (1958) 405–10; see also Pat McCune,

'Order and Justice in Early Tudor Drama', *Renaissance Drama*, 25 (1994) 171–96.

18. John Hazel Smith (ed.), *Two Latin Comedies by John Foxe the Martyrologist* (Ithaca, NY: Cornell University Press, 1978) 146–7.

19. On *Gammer Gurton* see L. Hutson, 'Theatre and Jurisdiction', in James Simpson and Brian Cummings (eds), *Cultural Reformations: Medieval and Renaissance in Literary History* (Oxford: Oxford University Press, 2010) 227–46.

20. See L. Hutson, *The Invention of Suspicion: Law and Mimesis in Shakespeare and Renaissance Drama* (Oxford: Oxford University Press, 2007) 215.

21. Emrys Jones, *The Origins of Shakespeare* (Oxford: Clarendon Press, 1977) 162, 172. Jones refers here to the folio version, but his words are equally applicable to the quarto; see Hutson, *Invention of Suspicion*, 241–58.

22. George Buchanan, *A Dialogue on the Law of Kingship among the Scots*, ed. Roger A. Mason and Martin S. Smith (Aldershot: Ashgate, 2004) 104–5.

23. See *King James VI and I: Political Writings*, ed. Johann P. Sommerville (Cambridge: Cambridge University Press, 1994) 62–84.

24. See, for example, Margaret McGlynn, *The Royal Prerogative and the Learning of the Inns of Court* (Cambridge: Cambridge University Press, 2003); Christopher St German, *Doctor and Student*, ed. T. F. T. Plucknett and J. L. Barton (London: Selden Society, 1974); *The Reports of Sir Edward Coke, Knt.*, 6 vols (Princeton: Lawbook Exchange, 2002); Edward Hake, *Epieikeia: A Dialogue on Equity in Three Parts*, ed. D. E. C. Yale (New Haven: Yale University Press, 1953); William Lambarde, *Archeion or, a Discourse upon the High Courts of Justice in England*, ed. Charles H. McIlwain and Paul L. Ward (Cambridge, Mass.: Harvard University Press, 1957).

25. Alan Cromartie, *The Constitutionalist Revolution: An Essay on the History of England, 1450–1642* (Cambridge: Cambridge University Press, 2006) 80; see also Christopher W. Brooks, *Law, Politics and Society in Early Modern England* (Cambridge: Cambridge University Press, 2008).

26. Cromartie, *Constitutionalist Revolution*, 93–5, 93.

27. Cromartie, *Constitutionalist Revolution*, 104. See also L. Hutson, 'Not the King's Two Bodies: Reading the "Body Politic" in Shakespeare's *Henry VI*, Parts 1 and 2', in Victoria Kahn and Lorna Hutson (eds), *Rhetoric and Law in Early Modern Europe* (New Haven: Yale University Press, 2001) 166–98.

28. Robert Snagg, *The antiquity and original of the Court of Chancery and authority of the Lord Chancellor of England. Being a branch of Sergeant Snagg's Reading, upon the 28 Chapter of* Magna Charta (London, 1654) 17; for Snagg's friendship with William Fleetwood, see Thomas Wright (ed.), *Queen Elizabeth and Her Times*, 2 vols (London, 1838) ii. 20. For the 1581 date, see J. H. Baker, *Readers and Readings in the Inns of Court and Chancery* (London: Selden Society, 2000) 116.

29. Snagg, *Reading*, 19.

30. Cromartie, *Constitutionalist Revolution*, 89.

31. Alan Cromartie, 'The Constitutionalist Revolution: The Transformation of Political Culture in Early Stuart England', *Past and Present*, 163 (1999) 76–120, 100.

32. Michael Dalton, *The Countrey Justice* (London, 1635) 22.

33. Cromartie, 'Transformation of Political Culture', 91.

34. Dalton, *Countrey Justice*, 22.

35. Dalton, *Countrey Justice*, 22, my italics.

36. *The Famous Victories of Henry the Fifth*, in Geoffrey Bullough (ed.), *Narrative and Dramatic Sources of Shakespeare*, vol. iv (London: Routledge and Kegan Paul, 1962) 299–343, l. 155.

37. Bullough, *Narrative and Dramatic Sources of Shakespeare*, vii. 483.

38. [George Buchanan], *Ane Detectioun of the duinges of Marie Quene of Scottes* (London, 1571) sig. N1ʳ.

39. On the provenance and authorship of *Ane Detectioun*, see James Emerson Phillips, *Images of a Queen: Mary Stuart in Sixteenth-Century Literature* (Berkeley and Los Angeles: University of California Press, 1964) 62–3.

40. A. C. Bradley, *Shakespearean Tragedy* (Harmondsworth: Penguin, 1991) 325.

41. William Empson, *Essays on Shakespeare*, ed. David M. Pirie (Cambridge: Cambridge University Press, 1986) 145.

42. Norbrook, '*Macbeth* and the Politics of Historiography', 108.

43. Holinshed, 171.

44. Peter Mack, *Elizabethan Rhetoric: Theory and Practice* (Cambridge: Cambridge University Press, 2002) 13; T. W. Baldwin, *William Shakspere's Small Latine & Lesse Greeke*, 2 vols (Urbana: University of Illinois Press, 1944) ii. 372–3.

45. *M. Tullius Ciceronis orationum a Ioan. Michaele Bruto emendatum* (London: Thomas Vautrollier, 1579). On Vautrollier and Field, See Quentin Skinner, *Forensic Shakespeare* (Oxford: Clarendon Press, 2014), 30–3.

46. Thomas Nashe, *The Unfortunate Traveller* (1592), in *The Works of Thomas Nashe*, ed. R. B. McKerrow, rev. F. P. Wilson, 5 vols (Oxford: Basil Blackwell, 1966) ii. 252, ll. 17–22.

47. Nashe, *Works*, ii. 252, ll. 26–30.

48. Andrew R. Dyck, 'Evidence and Rhetoric in Cicero's "*Pro Roscio Amerino*": The Case against Sextus Roscius', *Classical Quarterly*, NS 53 (May 2003) 235–46; Ann Vasaly, 'The Masks of Rhetoric: Cicero's *Pro Roscio Amerino*', *Rhetorica*, 3:1 (1985) 1–20; T. E. Kinsey, 'The Case against Sextus Roscius of Ameria', *L'Antiquité Classique* 54 (1985) 188–96. But see, conversely, D. H. Berry, 'The prosecution's case against Roscius was (as far as we can judge) extremely weak.', in *Cicero: Defence Speeches*, ed. Berry (Oxford: Oxford University Press, 2000) 5. Berry accepts Cicero's own account of his defence of Roscius as a political act against the dictatorship of Lucius Cornelius Sulla. Cicero's case for Roscius' innocence rested mainly on the fact that Roscius' wealthy father had been proscribed, and his extensive properties were sold for a paltry sum to one of the prosecutors, Titus Roscius Capito, and to Lucius Cornelius Chrysogonus, Sulla's freedman.

49. Dyck, 'Case against Sextus Roscius of Ameria', 236.

50. Cicero, *'Pro Sexto Roscio Amerino'* in *Orations*, tr. John Henry Freese (Cambridge, Mass.: Harvard University Press, 1930) §62. References to this translation henceforward in the text.

51. Bradley, *Shakespearean Tragedy*, 326: 'He has brought away the daggers he should have left on the pillows of the grooms, but what does he care for that? What *he* thinks of is that, when he heard one of the men awaked from sleep say, "God bless us", he could not say "Amen", for his imagination presents to him the parching of his throat as an immediate judgement from heaven.' See also *Macbeth*, ed. Dover Wilson, 112, 123.

52. *Macbeth*, ed. Nicholas Brooke (Oxford: Clarendon Press, 1990) 127.

53. On the increasing popularity of Cicero's orations in the sixteenth century, see John O. Ward, 'Renaissance Commentaries on Ciceronian Rhetoric', in James J. Murphy (ed.), *Renaissance Eloquence* (Berkeley and Los Angeles: University of California Press, 1983) 146. Tranio's speech in *Mostellaria* is glossed thus:

> NIHIL EST MISERIUS, QVAM ANIM. H. C.] Sic . . . pro Sext. Rosc. Amer. *Sua quemq. fraus, & suus terror maximè vexat, suum quemque scelus, amentiáque afficit: suae malae cogitationes, conscientiaeque animi terrent, hae sunt impiis assiduae, domesticaeque furiae.* &c.

> [NOTHING IS WORSE THAN A GUILTY CONSCIENCE] See, 'In Defence of Sextus Roscius of Ameria': 'Their own evil deed and their own terror torments them more than anything else; each of them is driven to madness by his own crime; his own bad thoughts and conscience terrify him. These are the Furies who are the constant domestic companions of the wicked'),

in *M. Accius Plautus . . . opera Dionys. Lambini . . . emendatus*, 2 vols (Paris, 1577) i. 552.

54. 'T. Cloelius' or 'T. Caelius' of Tarracina seems to have been a money-lender and his acquitted son a general, see T. Wiseman, 'T. Cloelius of Tarracina', *Classical Review*, ns 17:3 (1967) 263–4. Valerius Maximus refers to the incident under the heading of 'Reasons for which ill-famed defendants were acquitted or condemned', suggesting the dubiousness of the verdict. See Valerius Maximus, *Memorable Doings and Sayings*, ed. and tr. D. R. Shackleton Bailey, 2 vols (Cambridge, Mass.: Harvard, 2000) ii. 198–201.

55. Cicero, *'Pro Sexto Roscio Amerino'*, §§64–7.

56. *'Longinus' on Sublimity*, tr. D. A. Russell (Oxford: Clarendon Press, 1965) 15.1; 15.8.

Conclusion

The reader who has stayed the course all the way to the end of this book may have noticed a transition, in the final chapter, from an argument about the imaginative uses of circumstantial topics in Shakespeare's drama generally to a reading, in *Macbeth*, of such a powerful and enduring imaginative achievement as serving a historically and politically specific design. I began, in the first chapters of the book, by making some fairly technical points. Whereas the language of performance and of the 'actor-character' currently dominant in Shakespeare studies tends to emphasize important continuities between the English stagecraft of the fifteenth and sixteenth centuries, we need, I have argued, to recognize that the *imagined dramatic world* is itself an achievement distinctive to the English drama of the second half of the sixteenth century. It is an achievement, moreover, not of innovations in theatrical mimesis—of staging or of bodies in performance—but of the compositional techniques of inventing arguments out of topics of circumstance. It makes a difference, I have contended, to think of rhetorical figures and tropes as part of the repertoire of dialectical arguments of proof. When such 'proofs'—whether epithets, analogies, antitheses, or the like—are discovered in answer to questions of time, place, instrument, manner, or motive, they stimulate us to imagine an extramimetic world which is both vividly concrete and specific and, at the same time, charged with emotion and ethical significance. Nor need these figures and tropes, these arguments of proof, be confined to serious representational discourse: parodic inversions of circumstantial questions, voiced by Vice figures such as the Nurse in *Romeo and Juliet*, or Lance and Speed in *Two Gentlemen of Verona*, contribute as powerfully to the 'imagined world' of the play and to our sense of the unacknowledged or unspoken feelings and desires of its inhabitants as any other discourse in the plays.

In the last chapter, however, I have taken these propositions in a new direction. If circumstantial arguments encourage us to imagine both an implied dramatic world and the inwardness of 'character', is it possible to show how, in one of Shakespeare's great tragedies, the apparent transcendence of character and imagined world over political topicality is, in fact, part of a brilliantly intricate deployment of circumstantial arguments? I used the example of 'sleep' as a proof of innocence that, in the tradition of forensic oratory, is usually linked to arguments of place and notions of proximity as proof of guilt (the sons lay next to their murdered father, but peacefully sleeping). In *Macbeth*, I suggested, the topic of sleep-as-innocence was displaced from its expected role as part of the rhetoric of forensic enquiry and became, rather, the expression of Macbeth's tormented recognition of his deed's dehumanizing effects. The combination of this displacement with the absence of any scene of public judicial enquiry into the King's death helps to produce in our minds a very powerful image of Scotland as a people vexed and haunted by memories of violence and complicity, rather than as a politically viable state.

What the final chapter has in common with the rest of the book, however, is a commitment to the argument that we need to see the Shakespearean achievements of the 'imagined dramatic world' and of 'character' as interdependent and as the products of brilliant poetic emplotments of the image-forming and emotive power of circumstantial arguments. Recent work on Shakespearean characters as 'theatrical persons' proceeds as if the emotive power of performance were somehow independent of and separable from the poetic script: 'engagement with character in the playhouse is more moving than lines of poetry, however well-crafted.'[1] If this book has succeeded, it will have shown that such a statement is meaningless. There is no 'engagement with character' that is antecedent or alternative to the play's lines of poetry, for it is Shakespeare's poetic invention of circumstantial arguments that has enabled us to imagine both play's world and its characters, whether we are actors, directors, spectators, or readers.

Note

1. Paul Yachnin and Jessica Slights (eds), *Shakespeare and Character: Theory, History, Performance and Theatrical Persons* (Houndmills: Palgrave Macmillan, 2009) 5.

Bibliography

Primary Sources

Agricola, Rodolphus, *De inventione dialecticae lucubrationes* (facsimile of the Edition Cologne, 1539) (Nieuwkoop: B. de Graaf, 1968).

Alciato, Andrea, *Emblemata* [Lyons, 1550], tr. Betty I. Knott (Aldershot: Scolar Press, 1996).

Anon., *The Lamentable and True Tragedie of M. Arden of Feversham in Kent* (London, 1592).

Anon., *Sir Clyomon and Sir Clamydes* (1599), ed. W. W. Greg (London: Malone Society Reprints, 1913).

Aphthonius, *Aphthonius Sophistae Progymnasmata, partim a Rodolpho Agricola partim a Ioanne Maria Cataneo Latinitate donate, cum . . . Scholijs Reinhardi Lorichii* (London, 1575).

Aphthonius in *Progymnasmata*, tr. George Kennedy (Atlanta: Society of Biblical Literature, 2003).

Ariosto, Ludovico, *The Comedies of Ariosto translated and edited by Edmond Beame and Leonard G. Sbrocchi* (Chicago: University of Chicago Press, 1975).

Ariosto, Ludovico, *Tutte le opere di Ludovico Ariosto* a cura di Cesare Segre (Segrate: Mondadori, 1974).

Bacon, Nathaniel, *The Papers of Nathaniel Bacon of Stiffkey*, i: *1556–1577*, ed. A. Hassell Smith (Norwich: Norfolk Record Society, vol. XLVI, 1978 and 1979).

Beaumont, Francis and Fletcher, John, *The Dramatic Works in the Beaumont and Fletcher Canon*, ed. Fredson Bowers, 10 vols (Cambridge: Cambridge University Press, 1966–96).

Boaistuau, Pierre, *Histoires tragiques extraictes de œuvres italiennes de Bandel, & mises en nostre langue françoise* (Paris, 1559).

Brinsley, John, *Ludus literarius: or, The Grammar Schoole* (London, 1612).

[Buchanan, George], *Ane Detectioun of the duinges of Marie Quene of Scottes* (London, 1571).

Buchanan, George, *A Dialogue on the Law of Kingship among the Scots*, ed. Roger A. Mason and Martin S. Smith (Aldershot: Ashgate, 2004).

Buchanan, George, *The History of Scotland*, tr. James Aikman, 6 vols (Glasgow: Blackie and Son, 1845).

Bullough, Geoffrey (ed.), *Narrative and Dramatic Sources of Shakespeare*, 6 vols (London: Routledge and Kegan Paul, 1957–75).

Castelvetro, Lodovico, *Poetica d'Aristotele vulgarizzata e sposta*, ed. Werner Romani, 2 vols (Rome: Laterza, 1978).

Castelvetro, Lodovico, *Castelvetro on the Art of Poetry*, tr. Andrew Bongiorno (New York: Binghamton, 1984).

Cicero, Marcus Tullius, *M. Tullius Ciceronis orationum a Ioan. Michaele Bruto emendatum* (London, 1579).

Cicero, Marcus Tullius, *Orations: Pro Publio Quinctio, Pro Sexto Roscio Amerino, Pro Quinto Roscio comoedio, De lege agra*, tr. John Henry Freese (Cambridge, Mass.: Harvard University Press, 1930).

Cicero, Marcus Tullius, *De inventione*, tr. H. M. Hubbell (Cambridge, Mass.: Harvard University Press, 1949).

[Cicero], *Rhetorica ad Herrenium*, tr. Harry Caplan (Cambridge, Mass.: Harvard University Press, 1954).

Cicero, Marcus Tullius, *Cicero: Defence Speeches*, tr. D. H. Berry (Oxford: Oxford University Press, 2000).

Cicero, Marcus Tullius, *Topica*, ed. and tr. Tobias Reinhardt (Oxford: Oxford University Press, 2003).

Coke, Sir Edward, *The Reports of Sir Edward Coke, Knt.*, 6 vols (Princeton: Lawbook Exchange, 2002).

Coleridge, Samuel Taylor, *Coleridge's Criticism of Shakespeare*, ed. R. A. Foakes (Detroit: Wayne State University Press, 1989).

Coras, Jean de, *Arrest memorable, du Parlement de Tolose* (Lyon, 1561).

Dalton, Michael, *The Countrey Justice* (London, 1635).

Erasmus, Desiderius, *D. Erasmi Roterodami de duplici copia verborum ac rerum commentarii duo* (London: Henry Middleton, 1573).

Erasmus, Desiderius, *Collected Works of Erasmus* (Toronto: University of Toronto Press, 1974–).

Erasmus, Desiderius, *Opera omnia* (Amsterdam: North Holland, 1969–).

Erasmus, Desiderius, *The Adages of Erasmus*, ed. William Barker (Toronto: University of Toronto Press, 2000).

Foxe, John, *Two Latin Comedies by John Foxe the Martyrologist*, ed. John Hazel Smith (Ithaca, NY: Cornell University Press, 1978).

Gammer Gurton's Needle, ed. Charles Whitworth (London: A & C Black, 1997).

Gascoigne, George, *The Complete Works*, ed. John W. Cunliffe, 2 vols (Cambridge: Cambridge University Press, 1910).

Greene, Robert, *Pandosto. The Triumph of Time* (1588), in *The Winter's Tale*, ed. Stephen Orgel (Oxford: Oxford University Press, 1996).

Grimalde, Nicholas, *Marcus Tullius Ciceroes thre bokes of duties*, ed. Gerald O'Gorman (Washington: Folger Shakespeare Library, 1990).

Hake, Edward, *Epieikeia: A Dialogue on Equity in Three Parts*, ed. D. E. C. Yale (New Haven: Yale University Press, 1953).

Holinshed, Raphael, *The Description of Scotland written at the first by Hector Boetius in Latine, and afterward translated into the Scottish speech by John Bellenden, and now in English by R.H.* (London, 1585).

James VI and I, *King James VI and I: Political Writings*, ed. Johann P. Sommerville (Cambridge: Cambridge University Press, 1994).

Johnson, Samuel, *Johnson on Shakespeare*, ed. Arthur Sherbo (New Haven: Yale University Press, 1968).

Lambarde, William, *Archeion or, a Discourse upon the High Courts of Justice in England*, ed. Charles H. McIlwain and Paul L. Ward (Cambridge, Mass.: Harvard University Press, 1957).

Lennox, Charlotte, *Shakespear Illustrated: or the Novels and Histories On which the Plays of Shakespear Are Founded, Collected and Transcribed from the Original Authors* (London, 1753).

[Longinus] *'Longinus' on Sublimity*, tr. D. A. Russell (Oxford: Clarendon Press, 1965).

Lyly, John, *The Plays of John Lyly*, ed. Carter A. Daniel (Lewisburg, Pa: Bucknell University Press, 1988).

Lyndsay, David, *Ane Satyre of the Thrie Estatis*, ed. Roderick Lyall (Edinburgh: Canongate Classics, 1989).

Montemayor, George de, *A Critical Edition of Yong's Translation of George de Montemayor's* Diana *and Gil Polo's* Enamoured Diana, ed. Judith M. Kennedy (Oxford: Clarendon Press, 1968).

Nashe, Thomas, *The Works of Thomas Nashe*, ed. R. B. McKerrow, rev. F. P. Wilson, 5 vols (Oxford: Basil Blackwell, 1966).

The Norton Facsimile: The First Folio of Shakespeare, ed. Charlton Hinman, 2nd edn with an introduction by Peter W. M. Blayney (New York: W. W. Norton, 1996).

Painter, William, *The Palace of Pleasure*, ed. Joseph Jacobs, 3 vols (New York: Dover, 1966).

Philostratus, *Imagines*, tr. Arthur Fairbanks (Cambridge, Mass.: Harvard, 1931).

Plautus, Titus Maccius, *M. Accius Plautus . . . opera Dionys. Lambini . . . emendatus*, 2 vols (Paris, 1577).

Quintilianus, Fabius, *Institutio oratoria (The Orator's Education)*, ed. and tr. Donald A. Russell, 5 vols (Cambridge, Mass.: Harvard University Press, 2001).

Quintilianus, Fabius, *M. Fabii Quintiliani Institutionum oratorium libri XII. Et Declamationes.XIX* (Paris: Jodocus Badius Ascensius, 1528).

Riche, Barnabe, *The Adventures of Brusanus, Prince of Hungaria*, ed. Joseph Khoury (Toronto: CRRS, 2013).

Rowe, Nicholas, 'Some Account of the Life, &c. of William Shakespeare', in *The Plays of William Shakespeare, accurately printed from the text of Mr Malone's Edition*, 7 vols (London: J. Rivington, 1790), vii. xiii–iv.

Sackville, Thomas and Norton, Thomas, *Gorboduc, or Ferrex and Porrex, Drama of the English Renaissance*, i: *The Tudor Period*, ed. Russell A. Fraser and Norman Rabkin (Upper Saddle River, NJ: Prentice Hall, 1976).

St German, Christopher, *Doctor and Student*, ed. T. F. T. Plucknett and J. L. Barton (London: Selden Society, 1974).

Seneca, *Tragedies*, ed. and tr. John G. Fitch, 2 vols (Cambridge, Mass.: Harvard, 2002).

Shakespeare, William, *Lucrece* (London: Richard Field, 1594).

Shakespeare, William, *An Excellent conceited Tragedie of Romeo and Iuliet* (London: John Danter, 1597).

Shakespeare, William, *The Most Excellent and lamentable Tragedie, of Romeo and Iuliet* (London: Thomas Creede, 1599).

Shakespeare, William, *M. William Shak-speare his True Chronicle Historie of the life and death of King LEAR and his three daughters* (London, 1608).

Shakespeare, William, *The Works of Shakespeare in Six Volumes Collated and Corrected by the former editions, by Mr Pope* (London: Jacob Tonson, 1725).

Shakespeare, William, *The Plays and Poems of William Shakespeare with the Corrections and Illustrations of Various Commentators . . . by the late Edmund Malone* (London: J. Rivington, 1821).

Shakespeare, William, *The Two Gentlemen of Verona*, ed. Sir Arthur Quiller Couch and John Dover Wilson (Cambridge: Cambridge University Press, 1921).

Shakespeare, William, *Macbeth*, ed. John Dover Wilson (Cambridge: Cambridge University Press, 1947).

Shakespeare, William, *The Poems*, ed. F. T. Prince (London: Methuen, 1960).

Shakespeare, William, *Two Gentlemen of Verona*, ed. Clifford Leech (London: Arden, 1969).

Shakespeare, William, *The Complete King Lear 1608–1623*, ed. Michael Warren (Berkeley and Los Angeles: University of California Press, 1989).

Shakespeare, William, *Macbeth*, ed. Nicholas Brooke (Oxford: Clarendon Press, 1990).

Shakespeare, William, *King Lear*, ed. R. A. Foakes (London: Arden, 1997).

Shakespeare, William, *Henry VI part 1*, ed. Edward Burns (London: Arden, 2000).

Shakespeare, William, *Romeo and Juliet*, ed. Jill L. Levenson (Oxford: Oxford University Press, 2000).

Shakespeare, William, *Complete Sonnets and Poems*, ed. Colin Burrow (Oxford: Oxford University Press, 2002).

Shakespeare, William, *Two Gentlemen of Verona*, ed. William C. Carroll (London: Arden, 2004).

Sidney, Philip, *An Apology for Poetry (or The Defence of Poesy)*, ed. Geoffrey Shepherd, rev. R. W. Maslen (Manchester: Manchester University Press, 2002).

Snagg, Robert, *The antiquity and original of the Court of Chancery and authority of the Lord Chancellor of England. Being a branch of Sergeant Snagg's Reading, upon the 28 Chapter of Magna Charta, at the Middle Temple, in Lent, 13 Eliz.* (London, 1654).

Valerius Maximus, *Memorable Doings and Sayings*, ed. and tr. D. R. Shackleton Bailey, 2 vols (Cambridge, Mass.: Harvard, 2000).

Wilson, Thomas, *Arte of Rhetorique* (London, 1585).

Wordsworth, William, *Lyrical Ballads* (London: Longman and Rees, 1802).

Wordsworth, William, *The Borderers*, ed. Robert Osborn (Ithaca, NY, and London: Cornell University Press, 1982).

Wright, T. (ed.), *Queen Elizabeth and Her Times*, 2 vols (London, 1838).

Secondary Sources

Allen, Mozelle Scaff, 'Broke's *Romeus and Juliet* as a Source for the Valentine–Silvia Plot in *The Two Gentlemen of Verona*', *Studies in English*, 18 (1938) 25–46.

Altman, Joel, *The Improbability of Othello: Rhetorical Anthropology and Shakespearean Selfhood* (Chicago: Chicago University Press, 2010).

Baker, J. H., *Readers and Readings in the Inns of Court and Chancery* (London: Selden Society, 2000).

Baldwin, T. W., *William Shakspere's Small Latine & Lesse Greeke*, 2 vols (Urbana: University of Illinois Press, 1944).

Baldwin, T. W., *Shakespeare's Five-Act Structure* (Urbana: University of Illinois Press, 1947).

Bartlett Giamatti, A., 'Proteus Unbound: Some Versions of the Sea God in the Renaissance', in Peter Demetz, Thomas Greene, and Lowry Nelson, Jr (eds), *The Disciplines of Criticism* (New Haven: Yale, 1968) 437–75.

Bate, Jonathan, *Shakespeare and Ovid* (Oxford: Clarendon Press, 1993).

Beckwith, Sarah, *Shakespeare and the Grammar of Forgiveness* (Ithaca, NY: Cornell University Press, 2011).

Bell, David F., *Circumstances: Chance in the Literary Text* (Lincoln: University of Nebraska, 1993).

Belsey, Catherine, *The Subject of Tragedy: Identity and Difference in Renaissance Drama* (London: Methuen, 1985).

Berger Jr, Harry, 'The Early Scenes of *Macbeth*: A New Interpretation', *ELH* 47 (1980) 1–31.

Berger Jr, Harry, 'What Did the King Know and When Did He Know It? Shakespearean Discourses and Psychoanalysis', *South Atlantic Quarterly*, 88:4 (1989) 811–62.

Booth, Stephen, *King Lear, Macbeth, Indefinition and Tragedy* (New Haven: Yale University Press, 1983).

Bradley, A. C., *Shakespearean Tragedy: Lectures on Hamlet, Othello, King Lear and Macbeth* (Harmondsworth: Penguin, 1991).

Bradshaw, Graham, *Misrepresentations: Shakespeare and the Materialists* (Ithaca, NY: Cornell University Press, 1993).

Brooks, Christopher W., *Law, Politics and Society in Early Modern England* (Cambridge: Cambridge University Press, 2008).

Brown, Keith, *Bloodfeud in Scotland 1573–1625: Violence, Justice and Politics in an Early Modern Society* (Edinburgh: John Donald Publishers, 1986).

Butler, Katherine, 'Giacomo Castelvetro, 1546–1616', *Italian Studies*, 5 (1950) 1–36.

Cavell, Stanley, *Must We Mean What We Say?* (Cambridge: Cambridge University Press, 1987).

Cogan, Marc, 'Rodolphus Agricola and the Semantic Revolutions of the History of Invention', *Rhetorica*, 2:2 (1984) 163–94.

Cooper, Helen, *Shakespeare and the Medieval World* (London: Methuen, 2010).

Copeland, Rita, *Rhetoric, Hermeneutics, and Translation in the Middle Ages* (Cambridge: Cambridge University Press, 1991).

Cox, John D., 'Shakespeare and the Ethics of Friendship', *Religion and Literature*, 40:3 (2008) 1–29.

Cox, Marjorie, 'Adolescent Process in *Romeo and Juliet*', *Psychoanalytic Review*, 63:3 (1976) 379–92.

Cromartie, Alan, 'The Constitutionalist Revolution: The Transformation of Political Culture in Early Stuart England', *Past and Present*, 163 (1999) 76–120.

Cromartie, Alan, *The Constitutionalist Revolution: An Essay on the History of England, 1450–1642* (Cambridge: Cambridge University Press, 2006).

Culler, Jonathan, *The Pursuit of Signs: Semiotics, Literature, Deconstruction* (London: Routledge and Kegan Paul, 1981).

Davis, Natalie Zemon, *The Return of Martin Guerre* (Cambridge, Mass.: Harvard University Press, 1983).

De Grazia, Margreta, *Shakespeare Verbatim: The Reproduction of Authority and the 1790 Apparatus* (Oxford: Clarendon Press, 1991).

De Grazia, Margreta and Stallybrass, Peter, 'The Materiality of the Shakespearean Text', *Shakespeare Quarterly*, 44:3 (1993) 255–83.

De Quincey, Thomas, *De Quincey as Critic*, ed. John E. Jordan (London: Routledge and Kegan Paul, 1973) 240–4.

Donaldson, Ian, *The Rapes of Lucretia: A Myth and Its Transformations* (Oxford: Clarendon Press, 1982).

Duncan-Jones, Katherine, 'Ravished and Revised: The 1616 *Lucrece*', *Review of English Studies*, NS 52:208 (2001) 516–23.

Dyck, Andrew R., 'Evidence and Rhetoric in Cicero's "*Pro Roscio Amerino*": The Case against Sextus Roscius', *Classical Quarterly*, NS 53 (May 2003) 235–46.

Eden, Kathy, *Poetic and Legal Fiction in the Aristotelian Tradition* (Princeton: Princeton University Press, 1986).

Eden, Kathy, *Hermeneutics and the Rhetorical Tradition: Chapters in the Ancient Legacy and its Humanist Reception* (New Haven: Yale University Press, 1997).

Eden, Kathy, *Friends Hold All Things in Common: Tradition, Intellectual Property and the Adages of Erasmus* (New Haven: Yale University Press, 2001).

Elam, Keir, *Shakespeare's Universe of Discourse: Language Games in the Comedies* (Cambridge: Cambridge University Press, 1984).

Elam, Keir, *The Semiotics of Theatre and Drama* (London: Routledge, 1994).

Empson, William, *Essays on Shakespeare*, ed. David M. Pirie (Cambridge: Cambridge University Press, 1986).

Enders, Jodi, *Rhetoric and the Origins of Medieval Drama* (Ithaca, NY: Cornell University Press, 1992).

Enterline, Lynn, *Shakespeare's Schoolroom: Rhetoric, Discipline, Emotion* (Philadelphia: University of Pennsylvania Press, 2012).

Everett, Barbara, '*Romeo and Juliet*: The Nurse's Story', *Critical Quarterly*, 14:2 (1972) 129–39.

Garber, Marjorie, ' "The Rest is Silence": Ineffability and the "Unscene" in Shakespeare's Plays', in Peter S. Hawkins and Anne Howland Schotter (eds), *Ineffability: Naming the Unnameable from Dante to Beckett* (New York: AMS Press, 1984), 35–50.

Girard, René, 'Love Delights in Praises: A Reading of *The Two Gentlemen of Verona*', *Literature and Philosophy*, 13:2 (1989) 231–47.

Goldberg, Jonathan, 'Dover Cliff and the Conditions of Representation: King Lear 4:6 in Perspective', *Poetics Today*, 5:3 (1984) 537–47.

Goldberg, Jonathan, 'Shakespeare Writing Matter Again: Objects and Their Detachments', *Shakespeare Studies*, 28 (2000) 248–51.

Goldhill, Simon, 'What is Ekphrasis for?', *Classical Philology*, 102 (2007) 1–19.

Greenblatt, Stephen, *Renaissance Self-Fashioning from More to Shakespeare* (Chicago: University of Chicago Press, 1980).

Greenblatt, Stephen, 'Psychoanalysis and Renaissance Culture', in Patricia Parker and David Quint (eds), *Literary Theory/Renaissance Texts* (Baltimore: Johns Hopkins University Press, 1986) 210–24.

Greg, W. W., 'Time, Place and Politics in "King Lear"', *Modern Language Review*, 35:4 (1940) 431–46.

Gruber, William, *Offstage Space, Narrative and the Theatre of the Imagination* (New York: Palgrave Macmillan, 2010).

Hacking, Ian, *The Emergence of Probability: A Philosophical Study of Early Ideas about Probability, Induction and Statistical Inference* (Cambridge: Cambridge University Press, 1975).

Hacking, Ian, *The Taming of Chance* (Cambridge: Cambridge University Press, 1990).

Hall, Edith, *Inventing the Barbarian: Greek Self-Definition through Tragedy* (Oxford: Oxford University Press, 1989).

Helgerson, Richard, *Forms of Nationhood: The Elizabethan Writing of England* (Chicago: University of Chicago Press, 1992).

Hume, Robert D., '*The Maid's Tragedy* and Censorship in the Restoration Theatre', *Philological Quarterly*, 61:4 (1982) 484–90.

Hutson, L., 'Not the King's Two Bodies: Reading the "Body Politic" in Shakespeare's *Henry VI*, Parts 1 and 2', in Victoria Kahn and Lorna Hutson (eds), *Rhetoric and Law in Early Modern Europe* (New Haven: Yale University Press, 2001) 166–98.

Hutson, L., *The Invention of Suspicion: Law and Mimesis in Shakespeare and Renaissance Drama* (Oxford: Oxford University Press, 2007).

Hutson, L., '"Che indizio, che prova . . .? Ariosto's Legal Conjectures and the English Renaissance Stage', *Renaissance Drama*, 36:37 (2010) 179–205.

Hutson, L., 'Theatre and Jurisdiction', in James Simpson and Brian Cummings (eds), *Cultural Reformations: Medieval and Renaissance in Literary History* (Oxford: Oxford University Press, 2010) 227–46.

Ioppolo, Grace, 'A Jointure More or Less: Re-measuring *The True Chronicle History of King Leir and his three daughters*', *Medieval and Renaissance Drama in England*, 17 (2005) 165–79.

Jardine, Lisa, 'The Place of Dialectic Teaching in Sixteenth-Century Cambridge', *Studies in the Renaissance*, 21 (1974) 31–62.

Johnson, Monte, *Aristotle on Teleology* (Oxford: Clarendon Press, 2005).

Jones, Emrys, *The Origins of Shakespeare* (Oxford: Clarendon Press, 1977).

Kahn, Victoria, *Rhetoric, Prudence and Skepticism* (Ithaca, NY: Cornell University Press, 1985).

Kerrigan, John, *Archipelagic English: Literature, History, and Politics 1603–1707* (Oxford: Oxford University Press, 2008).

Kerrigan, John, 'Shakespeare, Oaths and Vows', *Proceedings of the British Academy* (Oxford: Oxford University Press, 2011) 61–89.

Kidd, Colin, *Subverting Scotland's Past: Scottish Whig Historians and the Creation of an Anglo-British Identity, 1689–1830* (Cambridge: Cambridge University Press, 1993).

Kiernander, Adrian, '*The Two* (?) *Gentlemen* (?) *of Verona* (?): Binarism, Patriarchy and Non-Consensual Sex Somewhere in the Vicinity of Milan', *Social Semiotics*, 4:1–2 (1994) 31–46.

Kinsey, T. E., 'The Case against Sextus Roscius of Ameria', *L'Antiquité Classique* 54 (1985) 188–96.

Knights, L. C., 'How Many Children had Lady Macbeth? An Essay in the Theory and Practice of Shakespeare Criticism', *Explorations* (New York: George W. Stewart, 1947) 15–54.

Krammick, Jonathan Brody, 'Reading Shakespeare's Novels: Literary History and Cultural Poetics in the Lennox–Johnson Debate', *Modern Language Quarterly*, 55:4 (1994) 429–53.

Lausberg, Heinrich, *Handbook of Literary Rhetoric: A Foundation for Literary Study*, tr. Matthew T. Bliss, Annemiek Jansen, and David E. Orton (Leiden: Brill, 1998).

Leff, Michael C., 'The Topics of Argumentative Invention in Latin Rhetorical Theory from Cicero to Boethius', *Rhetorica*, 1:1 (1983) 23–44.

Lynch, Dierdre, *The Economy of Character: Novels, Market Culture and the Business of Inner Meaning* (Chicago: University of Chicago Press, 1998).

McCune, Pat, 'Order and Justice in Early Tudor Drama', *Renaissance Drama*, 25 (1994) 171–96.

McCutcheon, J. Wilson, 'Justice and Equity in the English Morality Play', *Journal of the History of Ideas*, 19:3 (1958) 405–10.

McGlynn, Margaret, *The Royal Prerogative and the Learning of the Inns of Court* (Cambridge: Cambridge University Press, 2003).

Mack, Peter, 'Rudolph Agricola's Reading of Literature', *Journal of the Warburg and Courtauld Institutes*, 48 (1985) 23–41.

Mack, Peter, *Renaissance Argument: Valla and Agricola in the Traditions of Rhetoric and Dialectic* (Leiden: Brill, 1993).

Mack, Peter, *Elizabethan Rhetoric* (Cambridge: Cambridge University Press, 2002).

McLeod, Randall, 'Un "Editing" Shak-speare', *SubStance*, 10:11 (1981/2) 26–55.

McLeod, Randall (Random Cloud), ' "The very names of the Persons": Editing and the Invention of Dramatick Character', in David Scott Kastan and

Peter Stallybrass (eds), *Staging the Renaissance: Reinterpretations of Elizabethan and Jacobean Drama* (London: Routledge, 1991) 88–96.

McMillin, Scott and MacLean, Sally-Beth, *The Queen's Men and Their Plays* (Cambridge: Cambridge University Press, 1998).

McPherson, David, 'Ben Jonson's Library and Marginalia: An Annotated Catalogue', *Studies in Philology*, 71:5 (1974) 3–106.

Maguire, Laurie, 'Audience–Actor Boundaries in *Othello*', *Proceedings of the British Academy*, 181 (2011) 123–42.

Matthews, William, 'The Egyptians in Scotland: The Political History of a Myth', *Viator*, 1 (1970) 289–306.

Meek, Richard, *Narrating the Visual in Shakespeare* (Aldershot: Ashgate, 2009).

Mulready, Cyrus, ' "Asia of the One Side, and Afric of the Other": Sidney's Unities and the Staging of Romance', in *Staging Early Modern Romance: Prose Fiction, Dramatic Romance and Shakespeare* (New York: Routledge, 2009) 47–71.

Mulryan, John, 'A Parochial Twist on a Secular Proverb: Occasio's Bald Pate and the "Opportunity" to be Good in Joannes David's *Typus Occasionis* and *Occasio Arrepta*', *Emblemata*, 16 (2008) 133–50.

Muslin, Hyman L., 'Romeo and Juliet: The Tragic Self in Adolescence', *Adolescent Psychiatry* (1982) 106–17.

Myers, Kelly A., 'Metanoia and the Transformation of Opportunity', *Rhetoric Society Quarterly*, 41:1 (2011) 1–18.

Nelson, Alan H., 'The Universities: Early Staging in Cambridge', in John D. Cox and David Scott Kastan (eds), *A New History of English Drama* (New York: Columbia University Press, 1997).

Norbrook, David, '*Macbeth* and the Politics of Historiography', in Kevin Sharpe and Steven N. Zwicker (eds), *Politics of Discourse: The Literature and History of Seventeenth-Century England* (Berkeley and Los Angeles: University of California Press, 1987) 78–116.

Oliveira e Silva, J de, 'Structures and Restructures in Montemayor's *Diana*, Books I–III', *Bulletin of Hispanic Studies*, 72:2 (April 1995) 165–73.

Patey, Douglas Lane, *Probability and Literary Form: Philosophic Theory and Literary Practice in the Augustan Age* (Cambridge: Cambridge University Press, 1984).

Phillips, James Emerson, *Images of a Queen: Mary Stuart in Sixteenth-Century Literature* (Berkeley and Los Angeles: University of California Press, 1964).

Riggs, David, 'The Artificial Day and the Infinite Universe', *Journal of Medieval and Renaissance Studies*, 5 (1975) 155–85.

Roberts, R. J., 'New Light on the Career of Giacomo Castelvetro', *Bodleian Library Record*, 13:5 (1990) 365–9.

Robertson, D. W., 'A Note on the Classical Origin of "Circumstances" in the Medieval Confessional', *Studies in Philology*, 43 (1946) 6–14.

Rossignoli, Claudia, ' "Dar Materia di ragionamento": strategie interpretative della *Sposizione*', in Roberto Giliucci (ed.), *Lodovico Castelvetro, Filologia e acesi* (Rome: Bulzoni Editore, 2007) 91–113.

Rossignoli, Claudia, 'Castelvetro on Dante: Tradition, Innovation and Mockery in the *Sposizione*', in Paola Nasti and Claudia Rossignoli (eds), *Interpreting Dante: Essays on the Tradition of Dante Commentary* (Notre Dame, Ind.: University of Notre Dame Press, 2013) 359–88.

Scafuro, Adele C., *The Forensic Stage: Settling Disputes in Graeco-Roman New Comedy* (Cambridge: Cambridge University Press, 1997).

Schrijvers, P. H., 'Invention, imagination et théorie des émotions chez Cicéron et Quintilien', in J. den Boeft and A. H. M. Kessels (eds), *Actus: Studies in Honour of H. L. W. Nelson* (Utrecht: Instituut voor Klassieke Talen, 1982).

Schwaber, Paul. 'For Better and for Worst: *Romeo and Juliet*', *Psychoanalytic Study of the Child*, 61 (2006) 294–307.

Silva, J. Oliveira e, 'Structures and Restructures in Montemayor's *Diana*, Books I–III', *Bulletin of Hispanic Studies*, 72:2 (April 1995) 165–73.

Simpson, A. W. Brian, *A History of the Common Law of Contract* (Oxford: Clarendon Press, 1975).

Sinfield, Alan, *Faultlines: Cultural Materialism and the Politics of Dissident Reading* (Oxford: Clarendon Press, 1992) 52–79.

Skinner, Quentin, *Forensic Shakespeare* (Oxford: Clarendon Press, 2014).

Sloan, Michael C., 'Aristotle's *Nicomachean Ethics* as the Original Locus for the *Septem Circumstantiae*', *Classical Philology*, 105:3 (2010) 236–51.

Snow, Edward, 'Language and Sexual Difference in *Romeo and Juliet*', in John F. Andrews (ed.), *Romeo and Juliet: Critical Essays* (London and New York: Garland, 1993) 371–401.

Snuggs, Henry L., *Shakespeare and the Five Acts: Studies in a Dramatic Convention* (Washington: Vantage Press, 1960).

States, Bert O., *Great Reckonings in Little Rooms: On the Phenomenology of Theater* (Berkeley and Los Angeles: University of California Press, 1985).

Stern, Tiffany, *Documents of Performance in Early Modern England* (Cambridge: Cambridge University Press, 2009).

Stern, Tiffany and Palfrey, Simon, *Shakespeare in Parts* (Oxford: Oxford University Press, 2007).

Stewart, Alan, *Shakespeare's Letters* (Oxford: Oxford University Press, 2008).

Tanselle, G. Thomas, 'Time in *Romeo and Juliet*', *Shakespeare Quarterly*, 15:4 (1964) 349–61, 355.

Taylor, Gary and Warren, Michael (eds), *The Division of the Kingdoms: Shakespeare's Two Versions of King Lear* (Oxford: Clarendon Press, 1983).

Tucker, Patrick, *Secrets of Acting Shakespeare: The Original Approach* (London: Routledge, 2002).

Turner, Robert Y., 'Pathos and the "Gorboduc" Tradition', *Huntington Library Quarterly*, 25 (1962) 97–120, 113.

Van Es, Bart, *Shakespeare in Company* (Oxford: Oxford University Press, 2013).

Vasaly, Ann, 'The Masks of Rhetoric: Cicero's *Pro Roscio Amerino*', *Rhetorica*, 3:1 (1985) 1–20.

Watson, Alan, *Rome of the XII Tables: Persons and Property* (Princeton: Princeton University Press, 1976).

Watson, Gerard, *Phantasia in Classical Thought* (Galway: Galway University Press, 1988).

Watson, Robert, 'Dialogue and Invention in the "Book of the Duchess"', *Modern Philology*, 98:4 (2001) 543–76.

Weaver, William, ' "O teach me how to make mine own excuse": Forensic Performance in *Lucrece*', *Shakespeare Quarterly*, 59 (2008) 424–30.

Weaver, William, *Untutored Lines: The Making of the English Epyllion* (Edinburgh: Edinburgh University Press, 2012).

Webb, Ruth, 'The *Progymnasmata* as Practice', in Yun Lee Too (ed.), *Education in Greek and Roman Antiquity* (Leiden: Brill, 2001) 289–316.

Webb, Ruth, *Ekphrasis, Imagination and Persuasion in Ancient Rhetorical Theory and Practice* (Farnham: Ashgate, 2009).

Weimann, Robert, *Shakespeare and the Popular Tradition in the Theater*, ed. Robert Schwartz (Baltimore: Johns Hopkins University Press, 1987).

Wells, Stanley, 'The Failure of the *Two Gentlemen of Verona*', *Shakespeare Jahrbuch*, 99 (1963) 161–73.

Welsh, Alexander, *Strong Circumstances: Narrative and Circumstantial Evidence in England* (Baltimore and London: Johns Hopkins University Press, 1992) 18–31.

Whitworth, Charles, 'Reporting Offstage Events in Early Tudor Drama', in Andre Lascombes (ed.), *Tudor Theatre: 'Let There be Covenants'* (Berne: Peter Lang, 1977) 45–66.

Wilder, Lina Perkins, 'Toward a Shakespearean "Memory Theater": Romeo, the Apothecary, and the Performance of Memory', *Shakespeare Quarterly*, 56:2 (2005) 156–75.

Wiseman, T., 'T. Cloelius of Tarracina', *Classical Review*, ns 17:3 (1967).

Womack, Peter, 'Nobody, Somebody and *King Lear*', *New Theatre Quarterly*, 23:3 (2007) 195–207, 205.

Womack, Peter, 'The Comical Scene: Perspective and Civility on the Renaissance Stage', *Representations*, 101 (Winter 2008).

Yachnin, Paul and Slights, Jessica (eds), *Shakespeare and Character: Theory, History, Performance and Theatrical Persons* (New York: Palgrave Macmillan, 2009).

Index